Oscar Wilde and the Radical Politics of the Fin de Siècle

Edinburgh Critical Studies in Victorian Culture
Series Editor: Julian Wolfreys

Recent books in the series:

Rudyard Kipling's Fiction: Mapping Psychic Spaces
Lizzy Welby

The Decadent Image: The Poetry of Wilde, Symons and Dowson
Kostas Boyiopoulos

British India and Victorian Literary Culture
Máire ní Fhlathúin

Anthony Trollope's Late Style: Victorian Liberalism and Literary Form
Frederik Van Dam

Dark Paradise: Pacific Islands in the Nineteenth-Century British Imagination
Jenn Fuller

Twentieth-Century Victorian: Arthur Conan Doyle and the Strand Magazine, 1891–1930
Jonathan Cranfield

The Lyric Poem and Aestheticism: Forms of Modernity
Marion Thain

Gender, Technology and the New Woman
Lena Wånggren

Self-Harm in New Woman Writing
Alexandra Gray

Suffragist Artists in Partnership: Gender, Word and Image
Lucy Ella Rose

Victorian Liberalism and Material Culture: Synergies of Thought and Place
Kevin A. Morrison

The Victorian Male Body
Joanne-Ella Parsons and Ruth Heholt

Nineteenth-Century Settler Emigration in British Literature and Art
Fariha Shaikh

The Pre-Raphaelites and Orientalism
Eleonora Sasso

The Late-Victorian Little Magazine
Koenraad Claes

Coastal Cultures of the Long Nineteenth Century
Matthew Ingleby and Matt P. M. Kerr

Dickens and Demolition: Literary Afterlives and Mid-Nineteenth-Century Urban Development
Joanna Hofer-Robinson

Artful Experiments: Ways of Knowing in Victorian Literature and Science
Philipp Erchinger

Victorian Poetry and the Poetics of the Literary Periodical
Caley Ehnes

The Victorian Actress in the Novel and on the Stage
Renata Kobetts Miller

Dickens's Clowns: Charles Dickens, Joseph Grimaldi and the Pantomime of Life
Jonathan Buckmaster

Italian Politics and Nineteenth-Century British Literature and Culture
Patricia Cove

Cultural Encounters with the Arabian Nights in Nineteenth-Century Britain
Melissa Dickson

Novel Institutions: Anachronism, Irish Novels and Nineteenth-Century Realism
Mary L. Mullen

The Fin-de-Siècle Scottish Revival: Romance, Decadence and Celtic Identity
Michael Shaw

Contested Liberalisms: Martineau, Dickens and the Victorian Press
Iain Crawford

Plotting Disability in the Nineteenth-Century Novel
Clare Walker Gore

The Aesthetics of Space in Nineteenth-Century British Literature, 1843–mc1907
Giles Whiteley

The Persian Presence in Victorian Poetry
Reza Taher-Kermani

Rereading Orphanhood: Texts, Inheritance, Kin
Diane Warren and Laura Peters

Plotting the News in the Victorian Novel
Jessica R. Valdez

Reading Ideas in Victorian Literature: Literary Content as Artistic Experience
Patrick Fessenbecker

Home and Identity in Nineteenth-Century Literary London
Lisa Robertson

Writing the Sphinx: Literature, Culture and Egyptology
Eleanor Dobson

Oscar Wilde and the Radical Politics of the Fin de Siècle
Deaglán Ó Donghaile

The Sculptural Body in Victorian Literature: Encrypted Sexualities
Patricia Pulham

Forthcoming volumes:

Her Father's Name: Gender, Theatricality and Spiritualism in Florence Marryat's Fiction
Tatiana Kontou

Olive Schreiner and the Politics of Print Culture, 1883–1920
Clare Gill

Victorian Auto/Biography: Problems in Genre and Subject
Amber Regis

Gissing, Shakespeare and the Life of Writing
Thomas Ue

Women's Mobility in Henry James
Anna Despotopoulou

Michael Field's Revisionary Poetics
Jill Ehnenn

The Americanisation of W.T. Stead
Helena Goodwyn

Literary Illusions: Performance Magic and Victorian Literature
Christopher Pittard

Pastoral in Early-Victorian Fiction: Environment and Modernity
Mark Frost

Edmund Yates and Victorian Periodicals: Gossip, Celebrity, and Gendered Spaces
Kathryn Ledbetter

Literature, Architecture and Perversion: Building Sexual Culture in Europe, 1850–1930
Aina Marti

Manufacturing Female Beauty in British Literature and Periodicals, 1850–1914
Michelle Smith

New Media and the Rise of the Popular Woman Writer, 1820–60
Alexis Easley

For a complete list of titles published visit the Edinburgh Critical Studies in Victorian Culture web page at www.edinburghuniversitypress.com/series/ECVC

Also available:
Victoriographies – A Journal of Nineteenth-Century Writing, 1790–1914, edited by Diane Piccitto and Patricia Pulham
ISSN: 2044-2416
www.eupjournals.com/vic

Oscar Wilde and the Radical Politics of the Fin de Siècle

Deaglán Ó Donghaile

EDINBURGH
University Press

Edinburgh University Press is one of the leading university presses in the UK. We publish academic books and journals in our selected subject areas across the humanities and social sciences, combining cutting-edge scholarship with high editorial and production values to produce academic works of lasting importance. For more information visit our website: edinburghuniversitypress.com

© Deaglán Ó Donghaile, 2020, 2022

Edinburgh University Press Ltd
The Tun – Holyrood Road, 12(2f) Jackson's Entry, Edinburgh EH8 8PJ

First published in hardback by Edinburgh University Press 2020

Typeset in 11/13 Adobe Sabon by
IDSUK (DataConnection) Ltd

A CIP record for this book is available from the British Library

ISBN 978 1 4744 5943 3 (hardback)
ISBN 978 1 4744 5944 0 (paperback)
ISBN 978 1 4744 5945 7 (webready PDF)
ISBN 978 1 4744 5946 4 (epub)

The right of Deaglán Ó Donghaile to be identified as the author of this work has been asserted in accordance with the Copyright, Designs and Patents Act 1988, and the Copyright and Related Rights Regulations 2003 (SI No. 2498).

Contents

Series Editor's Preface	vi
Acknowledgements	viii
Introduction: Wilde and Politics	1
1. Anticolonial Wilde	29
2. Coercion and Resistance: *Vera . . . or the Land War*	57
3. Class, Criticism and Culture: 'The Soul of Man Under Socialism'	88
4. Fairy Tales for Revolutionaries	120
5. The Politics of Art and *The Picture of Dorian Gray*	150
6. Civil Disobedience and *The Importance of Being Earnest*	174
7. 'De Profundis', 'The Ballad of Reading Gaol' and the Politics of Imprisonment	200
8. Conclusion: Oscar Wilde – The Lost Revolutionary?	226
Bibliography	233
Index	246

Series Editor's Preface

'Victorian' is a term, at once indicative of a strongly determined concept and an often notoriously vague notion, emptied of all meaningful content by the many journalistic misconceptions that persist about the inhabitants and cultures of the British Isles and Victoria's Empire in the nineteenth century. As such, it has become a by-word for the assumption of various, often contradictory habits of thought, belief, behaviour and perceptions. Victorian studies and studies in nineteenth-century literature and culture have, from their institutional inception, questioned narrowness of presumption, pushed at the limits of the nominal definition, and have sought to question the very grounds on which the unreflective perception of the so-called Victorian has been built; and so they continue to do. Victorian and nineteenth-century studies of literature and culture maintain a breadth and diversity of interest, of focus and inquiry, in an interrogative and intellectually open-minded and challenging manner, which are equal to the exploration and inquisitiveness of its subjects. Many of the questions asked by scholars and researchers of the innumerable productions of nineteenth-century society actively put into suspension the clichés and stereotypes of 'Victorianism', whether the approach has been sustained by historical, scientific, philosophical, empirical, ideological or theoretical concerns; indeed, it would be incorrect to assume that each of these approaches to the idea of the Victorian has been, or has remained, in the main exclusive, sealed off from the interests and engagements of other approaches. A vital interdisciplinarity has been pursued and embraced, for the most part, even as there has been contest and debate amongst Victorianists, pursued with as much fervour as the affirmative exploration between different disciplines and differing epistemologies put to work in the service of reading the nineteenth century.

Edinburgh Critical Studies in Victorian Culture aims to take up both the debates and the inventive approaches and departures from convention that studies in the nineteenth century have witnessed for the last half century at least. Aiming to maintain a 'Victorian' (in the most positive sense of that motif) spirit of inquiry, the series' purpose is to continue and augment the cross-fertilisation of interdisciplinary approaches, and to offer, in addition, a number of timely and untimely revisions of Victorian literature, culture, history and identity. At the same time, the series will ask questions concerning what has been missed or improperly received, misread, or not read at all, in order to present a multi-faceted and heterogeneous kaleidoscope of representations. Drawing on the most provocative, thoughtful and original research, the series will seek to prod at the notion of the 'Victorian', and in so doing, principally through theoretically and epistemologically sophisticated close readings of the historicity of literature and culture in the nineteenth century, to offer the reader provocative insights into a world that is at once overly familiar, and irreducibly different, other and strange. Working from original sources, primary documents and recent interdisciplinary theoretical models, Edinburgh Critical Studies in Victorian Culture seeks not simply to push at the boundaries of research in the nineteenth century, but also to inaugurate the persistent erasure and provisional, strategic redrawing of those borders.

Julian Wolfreys

Acknowledgements

Since embarking on this project I have enjoyed the friendship of countless people who have helped my research in many ways. I have also had considerable support from libraries, research institutes and universities, which is where my thanks must begin. My research on Wilde found a very warm welcome at the William Andrews Clark Memorial Library at the University of California, Los Angeles, where I spent two months as a Visiting Fellow in 2009. I was awarded another Clark Library Fellowship in 2013, and returned again to conduct more research there in 2016. My thanks go to the Clark Library and to its administering body, the UCLA Center for Seventeenth- and Eighteenth-Century Studies, which awarded both Visiting Fellowships and facilitated my research in every way possible. During each of these stays the hospitality and expertise offered by the Clark Library's staff and Directors guided this project from its inception to its closing stages. Scott Jacobs, Rebecca Fenning Marschall, Nina Schneider, Carole Sommer, Bruce Whitman and Gerald Cloud were always on hand with their extensive knowledge of and insights into the collection, *Oscar Wilde and His Circle*. Staff at the Bancroft Library, the University of California, Berkeley, and at the San Francisco Public Library helped me to locate rare newspapers and periodicals. I have also been helped by staff at the National Library of Ireland, the Trinity College Dublin Library, the Aldham Roberts Library at Liverpool John Moores University, the Sydney Jones Library at the University of Liverpool, the Working Class Movement Library, Salford and the British Library.

The award of a Huntington Library Mayers Fellowship in 2013 allowed me to consult the library's important holdings on Irish and British political periodicals of the 1880s and 1890s and to participate in the library's esteemed community of scholarship. My research at the Clark and Huntington libraries was also supported in 2013 with a British Academy Small Research Grant. I received a University of Salford Vice Chancellor's Research Fellowship in 2012, and Liverpool John Moores University supported my research with grants awarded from 2016 to 2018 and a research sabbatical in 2016. All of this provided vital help at a time when university research budgets have been so badly cut in England.

Many of the ideas in this book were raised during lectures, seminars and symposia held in venues in Ireland, Scotland, England, France, Belgium and the United States. These include the Huntington Library, Sorbonne University, KU Leuven, the San Francisco Irish Literary and Historical Society, the San Francisco Mechanics' Institute and Library, the Open University, the USAC Irish Studies Summer School at the National University of Ireland, Galway, Arizona State University, Drew University, the Foyle Pride Festival, Derry, the North-West Long Nineteenth-Century Studies Seminar in Manchester, the Liverpool 1916 Commemoration Committee, the Liverpool John Moores University Research Institute for Literature and Cultural History, Edinburgh Napier University, and the University of Portsmouth. Questions and responses from audiences at each of these events have helped me to reflect upon and further shape my research on Wilde.

Friends and fellow academics freely offered advice and insights that guided this project in many ways. These include: Lynda Dryden, Laurence Davies, Darryl Jones, Willie McLaughlin, Kryss MacLeod, Alex Tickell, Sarah Crabtree, Anthony Galluzzo, Daniel Lewis, Sasha Hoffmann, Sarah Wood, Michael Calabrese, Jennifer Coleby, Joan O'Neill, Tina O'Toole, John L. Murphy, Niall Carson, Edward Molloy, Mark Quigley, David Lloyd, Patrick Bixby, Caoilfhionn Ní Bheacháin, Angus Mitchell, Tim Keane, Scott Brewster and Lucie Armitt. Ever since my undergraduate days, Nicholas Daly has been an advocate and inspirer of my research on fin de siècle literature, culture and politics, and his help and advice with this project have been immeasurable. I have also benefited from the wisdom and advice offered by Professor Joseph Bristow of UCLA, who guides Wilde scholarship with immense intellectual generosity.

Tony Bucher and Taryn Edwards also helped over the years by hosting public events and facilitating networking and outreach activity in the San Francisco Bay Area, as did Robert and Rebecca Tracy. Jim Doherty of the Foyle Pride Festival has time and again helped me to bring Wilde's ideas directly to audiences in my home town of Derry, from whom I have learned much. Joe Yates and Alex Miles, in their roles as Dean of Arts and Director of Humanities and Social Sciences at Liverpool John Moores University, provided my work with all of the institutional support at their disposal. Glenda Norquay, Director of the LJMU Research Institute for English Literature and Cultural History has also always been on hand to offer wisdom and practical support. So too have Colin Harrison, Filippo Menozzi,

Sondeep Kandola, Ross Dawson, Gerry Smyth, Joe Moran, Alice Ferrebe, Rebecca Bailey, Brian Maidment and Christinna Hazzard. Go raibh míle maith agaibh go léir!

Edinburgh University Press has been greatly supportive of this project. The anonymous readers who read early draft material offered valuable insights on how to improve its tone and content. Their suggestions were enormously helpful with the overall shaping of my arguments and encouraged me to define my key points more clearly. As Commissioning Editor at EUP, Michelle Houston has shown much kindness and patience while carefully guiding this monograph through the writing and publishing process, as has Ersev Ersoy as Assistant Commissioning Editor. Julian Wolfreys, Series Editor for Edinburgh Critical Studies in Victorian Culture, also provided much valued practical support and critical encouragement.

The greatest debts incurred by writing and researching this monograph are owed to my family. I have been discussing Wilde and his radical beliefs for some time now with my mother- and father-in law, Barbara and Alan Jones, and I hope that they will enjoy the finished product as much as I value their insights into nineteenth-century political history. My brother, Ruairí and my sisters, Úna, Niamh and Caoimhe, have followed my work on Wilde with deep interest and I hope that this book will continue to answer their questions on this great man. Another great man, my father, Michael, inspired my research and still helps me to better understand the historical continuities that make Wilde's radicalism so relevant to our present moment. My mother, Martina, died before this book was completed but her love, influence and compassion live on in every one of its pages. It was upon her knee that I first heard the name of Oscar Wilde and it was from her that I first learned about the Selfish Giant and the Happy Prince. She told me why these stories are concerned with real people whose dignity and humanity will always outlive the violence of empires and capitalism. Like Wilde, my mother loved the poor and oppressed in every land, and this book is proudly dedicated to her memory.

It is also dedicated to three other brilliant women. My wife, Sam, has guided my thinking at every turn and each day helps me to better understand why art, culture, collectivity and community are as vital to us now as they were to Oscar Wilde. My daughters, Niamh and Bláithín, both budding Wildeans in their own right, never cease to inspire and amaze me with their own compassion, wisdom and insight.

Introduction: Wilde and Politics

How radical was Oscar Wilde, and how were his beliefs regarded, portrayed, mediated and distorted by contemporary conservatives? These questions are answered in an unsigned article that appeared in the ironically entitled British periodical, *Truth*, which, in 1883, berated Wilde for his rebellious nature. Over a decade before Max Nordau depicted him as a conceited megalomaniac in his famously hyperbolic tome, *Degeneration*,[1] *Truth* described Aestheticism as an expression of deep-seated mental illness and social decay. The magazine amplified this personal attack on Wilde by complaining about the nefariously 'Celtic origin of Oscar' and drew its readers' attentions to his curious history at Oxford, all the better to queer him with: from his earliest days at university, it complained, he showed 'no inclination to do for himself what others were only too ready to do for him'. This unmanly selfishness isolated Wilde from his peers as he was 'held in abhorrence by masculine athletes', all of whom had no time for him, or any other 'feminine undergraduates'. Linking Wilde to the university's subcultural scene of effete, 'epicene youth, who first began to talk art jargon, to worship blue china, and to adore the wall-papers of Mr. William Morris', the journal claimed that his characteristic unpleasantness had distinctively political origins:

> Of this cult Oscar was admitted as the head [. . .] he preferred Radical aestheticism to Tory ritualism, and, once elected high priest, he allowed his locks to grow, and tucked them behind his ears. With the applause bestowed on 'Ravenna' ringing in his ears, he complacently waited for something to turn up, and in the meantime called upon all to observe that a new light had risen on the horizon. His success in London society was not at first very marked. He condescended to tea-parties in Kensington and Bayswater, and hunted up the Irish brigade that had attended the Wilde receptions in the old Dublin days.[2]

Oscar Wilde, *Truth* complained, was both radical and oppositional. At once queer, alternative and politically suspect, he was, it warned, an opponent of the standards that had been established and carefully maintained through the cultural routines and general machismo of British conservatism. Most seriously of all, this rogue and upstart Celt had proceeded to dupe the unsuspecting public immediately after graduating from university and, upon his arrival in London, in another act of subversive trickery, he renewed the dissident intellectual network that his separatist parents had established in Ireland decades before. Circulating among anticolonial writers, dissident literary types and countercultural artists, he had no difficulty infiltrating society soirées and insinuating himself among the influential. Sneakily promoting Aestheticism by disguising its revolutionary position on politics and culture, Wilde's true objective, *Truth* declared, was the destruction of the stabilising influence of tradition, thereby bringing about the ultimate, clammy nightmare of every British conservative since the days of Edmund Burke. His infiltration of the metropolis and its cultural spheres had already succeeded because, now, every 'Irishman of a certain type possesses a very amiable art of insinuation, particularly if he has a striking individuality and can talk fluently'.

Wilde's true, subversive genius, then, lay in his capacity to speak, charm and deceive – gifts that drew their power from the fusion of his novel public personality with an especially Celtic type of mendacity that secured his celebrity status in late Victorian England. To be Irish *and* articulate, *Truth* protested, was particularly dangerous:

> Every Johnson must have a Boswell, and the Irish Oscar, being an agreeable companion, soon found a dozen Boswells ready to do for him what the photographers do for professional beauties. They got him talked about. When people, week after week, kept hearing about what Oscar Wilde did and said, they became anxious to know who Oscar Wilde was. Such in our days is the manufacture of notoriety [. . .] It was his Irish persistency, his unruffled good-nature, and his calm indifference to the sneers of his own sex, that made Oscar for the moment the jester and joke of a certain section of society.[3]

Framing Aestheticism as a dangerously progressive movement that countered the conservatism of existing high cultural practice, *Truth* portrayed Wilde as a hazardously radical figure who operated on multiple levels. The incarnations at work in this representation include the subversive Irish genius, the queer upstart and the radical aesthete. In combination they produced a politically-conscious artist, something that was later acknowledged by anarchists upon Wilde's imprisonment in 1895, when they praised his radical literary and political beliefs and practices.[4]

What distinguishes *Truth*'s representation of Wilde as a dangerously innovative and uniquely rebellious individual is its attempt to portray him as a public figure whose utterances, writings and beliefs ultimately counted for nothing. This reassuring denial of the value of Oscar Wilde's words, actions and agency was part of a broader and very consistent effort whereby his opponents tried to dismiss him as a meaningless curiosity. The magazine represented him as a strange and alien, if sometimes entertaining presence within the metropolitan scene whose deceptive use of language, combined with an unusual degree of personality and charm, had allowed him to manipulate the public and secure his place at the heart of British imperial society. This attempt to reduce Wilde to a sexually ambiguous cipher, or 'joke', and depict him as a foppishly intellectual (though still-threatening) countercultural figure appeared elsewhere in 1883, when other hostile publications also portrayed him as an impostor. He was identified as an 'Irishman by birth' in one regional newspaper, which noted that Wilde's 'tongue hardly ever reveals the fact, although, according to Mr. Punch, he speaks with a strong Irish brogue!'[5]

Wilde was frequently accused of dullness and unoriginality by his critics in the British press[6] but the popular satirical magazine, *Punch*, went further than portraying him as a 'played-out Charlatan'[7] when it directly associated him with revolutionary politics. Upon the cancellation of the London premiere of his first and most explicitly political play, *Vera; or, The Nihilists*, in the winter of 1881, *Punch* accused Wilde of being an evasive 'Veerer' for refusing to explain the reasons behind the play's abandonment.[8] One month later, and shortly after his arrival in the United States, the magazine equated his literary writing with anarchist and Fenian violence in the parodical poem, 'Murder Made Easy: A Ballad à la Mode'. Attributed to '"Brother Jonathan" Wilde', the poem compared him to the Fenian leader, Jeremiah O'Donovan Rossa, and to nihilists, anarchists and other 'Poisoning Worms' of the militant Left. Still furious with the political content of *Vera; or, The Nihilists*, *Punch* accused him of inspiring attacks carried out with 'Gunpowder, Shots and Stabs!'. It also likened the political content of Wilde's dramatic writing to the deadly *matériel* of 'Nitroglycerine, Potions, and Pills [. . .] Bombs and Gun-Cotton, Dagger and Bowl!'. In the magazine's opinion, Wilde's fusion of Aestheticism and anticolonialism posed a clear threat to British imperialism and the domestic class system that upheld it. Equating his literary avant-gardism with the militancy of Fenian dynamiters, its message was clear: the insurgent Irish, including Wilde, had 'shaken off babyhood's bands' and were now at large in the metropolis, equipped with a dangerous arsenal of 'Knives, Nux Vomica, Bullets, and Brains!'. The well-documented racist Victorian stereotype of the Irish as infantile, unevolved and degenerate subhumans was updated by *Punch* to include the unique contribution that it charged Wilde with adding to the revolutionists' armoury: his subversive intellect and disarming wit.[9] Included among the revolutionaries bucking against the 'checks and restrains' of constitutional politics, Wilde is portrayed here as an instigator of revolutionary violence and his literary writings are condemned for expressing radical beliefs.[10] Comparing the cultural work of Aestheticism to the activities of Russian revolutionaries and militant Irish nationalists, *Punch* depicted Wilde as a seditious writer whose message was heard and understood across the political spectrum of the international Left, and whose works also appealed to the anticolonial imagination.

This equation of radical politics with the subversive cultural practice of the Aesthete reveals much about the late Victorian conservative imagination. This projection of the spectre of revolt onto the contemporary cultural scene by *Punch* depicts Wilde as the representative of a particularly modern and articulate type of insurgency.[11] In case the poet's pseudonym was not suitably accusatory ('Brother Jonathan' was a contemporary moniker for the United States, where Wilde had just begun his lecture tour when the poem was published), the piece is immediately followed by another attack. Hoping to prolong the critical battering to which *Punch* had subjected Wilde's *Poems* in 1881 (it described his verse as a diluted mixture of 'Swinburne and Water'),[12] its next skit was addressed 'To an Æsthetic Poet' who deserved to be tied to the stocks for inflicting 'sick'ning maudlin gush' on the British public.[13]

Sensitive to the threat posed to imperial hegemony by the combined menace of political and artistic radicalism, the Tory press remained consistently hostile towards Aestheticism and what it perceived as its links to the 'dirty politics' of Irish nationalism.[14] By adopting this position, *Punch* excused and normalised the repressive legislation with which Ireland was being governed from Westminster, and stressed the imperialist orthodoxy that the Irish, like every other colonial subject population, had to be violently disciplined. The magazine popularised colonial discourse within the literary and cultural fields at this key point in Wilde's early career, and these attempts to isolate and ridicule him had as their objective the elimination of his reputation as a public intellectual. The coercion Acts that sanctioned police and military violence across late-nineteenth-century Ireland were accompanied by newspaper propaganda which, like these examples, validated imperial power while also justifying the force with which it was imposed. This comparison of Wilde, who was by 1881 already known as a socialist and Irish republican, with assassins, agitators and revolutionaries, represents an important node in the ideological network that included parliament, the press, the police and the repressive legislation that, as we shall see, the young Oscar Wilde publicly condemned.

This monograph offers a necessarily selective analysis of Oscar Wilde's radical politics. The limitations of space have prevented my study from including the full range of radicalism as expressed across all of his work and I hope that more will be written about these matters in future projects. I explore here Wilde's engagement with politics in relation to the crises generated by late Victorian imperialism and capitalism, issues that were at the forefront of his literary, cultural and political thought. Chapter 1 examines Wilde's expression of radical anticolonial beliefs through the speeches, lectures and statements that he delivered during his 1882 tour of the United States. Chapter 2 explores how his first play, *Vera; or, The Nihilists*, which was abandoned before it was even performed in London in 1881 and then staged briefly in New York in 1883, used its dramatic setting of Csarist Russia to criticise British imperial policy in Ireland. Chapter 3 discusses Wilde's treatment of class as a cultural issue in his 1891 essay, 'The Soul of Man Under Socialism'. Chapter 4 concentrates on the critiques of imperialism and capitalism offered in his short stories, particularly his fairy tales and fables; and Chapter 5 considers his discussion of the relationship between art and politics in his novel, *The Picture of Dorian Gray*. Chapter 6 proposes that the matters of civil disobedience and rebellion are key concerns of Wilde's 1895 social comedy, *The Importance of Being Earnest*; and Chapter 7 interprets Wilde's critique of the politics of imprisonment, as expressed in *De Profundis* and 'The Ballad of Reading Gaol'.

While I have discussed these issues at length, more can be said about Wilde's wider engagements with politics. These include his progressive analyses of the cultural and political conservatism in the essays collected in *Intentions*, his expressions of support for feminism in his journalism and plays, his confrontation with homophobia in *The Picture of Dorian Gray*, and his challenge to religious dogma in 'The Soul of Man Under Socialism', to cite just several of his broader concerns. The sheer volume of Wilde's literary output and the consistency of his radical expression throughout his entire *oeuvre* testify to his progressive perspectives on all of these matters, and it is hoped that this study will encourage further scholarship in these areas.

Coercion and Culture

Oscar Wilde criticised imperialist violence in Ireland, where, he complained, 'the English conquest destroyed art';[15] his 1889 review of Wilfrid Scawen Blunt's collection of poems, *In Vinculis*, also described coercive legislation as 'ungodly'. Blunt, who had been imprisoned for chairing an anti-eviction meeting in County Galway a year earlier, had been prosecuted, in Wilde's opinion, for supporting 'a noble cause'.[16] Michael Davitt, the former Fenian prisoner and leader of the Irish Land League, with whom Wilde corresponded on the issue of prison reform, described the 'permanent ring' of repressive legislation with which successive British administrations governed Ireland. This 'rule-by-state-of-siege principles' was modernised with the passage of fifty-two separate coercion Acts between 1830 and 1885.[17] Wilde's claim in 'The Soul of Man Under Socialism' that human progress had only ever been achieved 'through disobedience and through rebellion' echoes Davitt's claim that Irish nationalists had only ever wrested concessions from the British as a result of their centuries-long anticolonial struggle.[18]

During the 1840s Wilde's mother, Jane Francesca Elgee Wilde, who wrote under the pseudonym, Speranza, criticised the repression and surveillance through which Ireland was ruled by the British. Privately, she complained: 'What an incubus this English government is on our country [. . .] It strangles all life.'[19] Publicly, she called for an armed rebellion in her 1848 essay, 'Jacta Alea Est',[20] and her son inherited these anticolonial sentiments. During his tour of the United States, when he was also being ridiculed in the British press as an 'Ass-thete',[21] Wilde referred an audience in Minnesota to his mother's writings and argued that an understanding of the long tradition of anticolonial resistance that she had participated in during the 1840s was essential for anyone who wanted to comprehend Irish history. He insisted that his country's past was marked by its prolonged exposure to imperialist violence, dispossession and the profound cultural losses that resulted from these intense and destructive cycles of colonial conquest: '[W]ith the coming of the English, art in Ireland came to an end, and it has had no existence for over seven hundred years [. . .] for art could not live and flourish under a tyrant.'[22]

Wilde's anger at the 'squalid' treatment of the Irish by their British occupiers, gaolers and landlords resurfaced in an 1887 review of his mother's book, *Ancient Legends, Mystic Charms and Superstitions of Ireland*, in which he described Irish mythology as 'the genius of the race' that Britain 'essayed in vain to assimilate or subdue'. He also described the subjugation of Ireland as Britain's 'perpetual difficulty and disgrace'.[23] Later, in 1888, Wilde described himself 'a most recalcitrant patriot',[24] but as John Stokes and Mark Turner have argued in their analysis of his journalism in their 'Introduction' to the Oxford *Complete Works of Oscar Wilde*, his commitment to anticolonial politics was broader than this self-effacing disclaimer indicates: 'to see Wilde as merely "recalcitrant" may be to define the sphere of the political far too narrowly and to misunderstand his own sense of political engagement'.[25] Wilde was keenly aware of the political and cultural potential of the book review, both as an influential form and medium. Along with his public lectures in San Francisco and Minnesota, he repeatedly used reviewing to criticise British policy in Ireland. Wilde was also opposed to the stage Irishness that dominated much literary writing about the country. 'The Celtic element in literature is extremely valuable,' he wrote, 'but there is absolutely no excuse for shrieking "Shillelagh!" and "O'Gorrah!"'[26]

Socialism and Radical Aestheticism

Wilde's anticolonial beliefs were accompanied by a thoughtful and sustained belief in the socially-committed individual. Throughout his career, he addressed the profound tension that distanced capitalism and imperialism from Aestheticism's oppositional 'ideal of self-culture and self-development'. He insisted that this progressive doctrine should motivate the artistic and political imagination of the aesthete.[27] Wilde's own political views aligned very clearly with his aesthetic beliefs, and he argued for unrestricted artistic expression during a time when culture was being rigorously policed. As Gilbert complains in 'The Critic as Artist': 'Anything approaching to the free play of the mind is practically unknown.'[28] Wilde also believed that the era's restrictive moral and political values ensured that literary practice was undertaken in an atmosphere of 'sordid terror'. Writers, readers and audiences, he insisted, were compelled to adhere to 'sterile' middle-class and imperialist strictures. Ernest's response to Gilbert that 'all Art is immoral, and all thought dangerous'[29] subtly conveys how the British metropolis had assimilated the coercive atmosphere of the colonies.

Wilde warned his readers that, in this repressive climate, the artist should be an insurgent figure dedicated to the decolonisation of art. He believed that modern imperialism represented the private aggrandisement of the bourgeoisie writ large and on a global scale, and he was convinced that capitalist modernity was inherently violent. Writing in *The Nineteenth Century* almost a decade after his tour of the United States, he revisited this idea by proposing that the democratic evaluation of art and culture would encourage identification with the Other. In this piece, which was republished as 'The Critic as Artist', Wilde predicted that conflict between states could be discredited by developing and expanding popular awareness of art. Doing so would highlight the contrast between the grandeur of culture and the baseness of state violence:

> Criticism will annihilate race-prejudices, by insisting upon the unity of the human mind in the variety of its forms. If we are tempted to make war upon another nation, we shall remember that we are seeking to destroy an element of our own culture, and possibly its most important element. As long as war is regarded as wicked, it will always have its fascination. When it is looked upon as vulgar, it will cease to be popular. The change will of course be slow, and people will not be conscious of it. They will not say 'We will not war against France because her prose is perfect,' but because the prose of France is perfect, they will not hate the land. Intellectual criticism will bind Europe together in bonds far closer than those that can be forged by shopman or sentimentalist. It will give us the peace that springs from understanding.[30]

For Wilde, Aestheticism was a social project that had explicitly political objectives as well as artistic ambitions, and 'criticism' – by which he meant meaningful and deeply reflective immersion in culture – involved the individual in the practice of a decidedly humanist form of internationalism. Wilde believed that the late nineteenth century was a characteristically 'selfish age' but he was also convinced that empire and capital, with their 'vulgar and discordant' drives, could be subverted by the artist. This idealism, along with his proposal for the development of a reflective and progressive 'self-culture', was clearly informed by his anticolonial beliefs, as he argued that autonomy had political as well as personal consequences: 'England will never be civilised till she has added Utopia to her dominions. There is more than one of her colonies that she might with advantage surrender for so fair a land.' This cultural, political and social transformation would counter the influence of fanatical critics and politicians by encouraging mutual sympathy and solidarity across classes and national borders. It would sustain what Wilde termed 'the peace that springs from understanding.'[31]

Wilde's declaration that 'Criticism [. . .] makes us cosmopolitan'[32] was also critical of the violence through which capitalism and imperialism functioned. He proposed art as a serious counter-strategy to the state's apparatus of coercion and its continual provocation of conflict. Whereas for Matthew Arnold culture suggested the need for government and 'the idea of the State',[33] Wilde believed that culture could be deployed to dismantle it. He was recognised by his contemporaries as a member of what Leela Gandhi has described as the dissident 'affective communities' that confronted imperialism from within the British metropolis. These progressive circles provided the ideological and aesthetic spaces from which a wide range of radical writers, artists and thinkers could mount symbolic and material acts of resistance. Circulating within these broader networks of 'association, alliance, relationality, community',[34] Wilde's work, like Blunt's anti-imperialist poetry and the experimental socialist writings of Edward Carpenter, contributed to a significant current of radical discourse that opposed the dangerously live circuits of imperial power and coercion.[35]

Resistance against the hegemonising forces of empire and capital was a central theme in Wilde's fiction, drama, poetry and essays, and it remained an important theme in many of his book reviews and public lectures. In all of these works, Wilde addressed the historical realities of poverty, suffering, hunger and colonisation. For example, social inequality provided the material backdrop to his 1887 story, 'The Sphinx Without a Secret', which opens with its narrator observing 'the strange panorama of pride and poverty' that Wilde associated with late Victorian London.[36] Here and in his more explicitly political writings, he repeatedly identified with what he termed 'the community of suffering'.[37] This allowed him to develop a radical position as an aesthete: by drawing on the experiences of the marginalised, the dispossessed and the colonised, his writings connected radical class politics with anti-imperialism; his work also associated queerness with creativity and aligned anarchism with Aestheticism. All the while, he constantly depicted authority as being harmful to the creative spirit.[38]

Radical Politics and Wilde's Literary Practice

Radical political thought was central to Wilde's creative consciousness as an aesthete and, as Terry Eagleton has shown, the question of style is intimately linked in his work to the issues of commitment and identity.[39] The political atmosphere in late Victorian Britain was characterised by the intensification of class conflict, the deployment of increasing levels of imperialist violence in its colonies, and the domestic application of coercive laws that had been honed in Ireland. England's nearest and oldest contested colony, Ireland served as a military and political laboratory where violent strategies and practices of coercion were developed throughout the nineteenth century.[40] Wilde's fictions, plays and essays criticised imperial policy in more distant colonies while always paying close attention to the persecution of the English poor, as domestic state violence remained a persistent theme in his work.

Wilde's assumption of a bourgeois, metropolitan identity was subversive. More than a simple contrarian or a reluctant rebel, he strategically and sometimes explicitly placed radical political ideas at the centre of his literary writing.[41] His writings often reflect the experiences of British society's subaltern classes – the destitute workers, women, children, prisoners and colonised peoples with whom he identified. Whenever the privileged take centre stage in these works they often appear against the background of the '[r]eality' of labour, which, for example, interrupts a conversation on the relationship between pleasure and slavery in *The Picture of Dorian Gray* 'in the shape of a servant'.[42] Despite the imaginative settings of Wilde's fantastic stories and fairy tales, and despite the bourgeois social remove from which his plays appear to discuss class and colonialism, these works address very immediate political problems, including the concealed forms of state violence that, as he complained, in 'The Critic as Artist', always accompanied the manipulation of public opinion and popular taste.[43]

Malcontents are present throughout Wilde's plays, poems and fiction. They appear as political revolutionaries in *Vera; or, The Nihilists* and as the 'Christs that die upon the barricades', for whom he composed his 1881 'Sonnet to Liberty'.[44] Dissent is expressed by the heroically insolent butler, Lane, in *The Importance of Being Earnest* and by the starving peasants and workers who populate his short stories, along with those who attempt to rectify inequality, even if doing so will guarantee their own destruction, as happens to the Happy Prince. In them we find the expression of his own self-positioning as a radical author, theorist and critic whose work was determined by his sympathy with the oppressed. All of this underlines the subversiveness of Wilde's treatment of appearances, deception and the forgery of identity in works such as *The Picture of Dorian Gray*, 'The Portrait of Mr W.H.' and *The Importance of Being Earnest*.

As Kevin Whelan has shown, the coding of unspeakable colonial truths was not an unusual feature of nineteenth-century Irish literature. In his essay on James Joyce's short story of 1914, 'The Dead', Whelan points to the long history of repression and censorship that compelled Irish nationalist and republican authors to develop strategic forms of literary and political expression. These authors could not articulate their beliefs openly without leaving themselves open to accusations of political subversion. Instead, they subtly structured their complaints about the condition of occupied Ireland as a kind of literary and political survival technique. When read from the historically sensitive perspective that is vital for an understanding of late-nineteenth- and early-twentieth-century Irish literary culture, texts like the stories collected in *Dubliners* or Joyce's 1922 novel, *Ulysses*, assume an entirely different, even insurgent quality. Saturated with references to the historical traces of colonisation and the ongoing resonances of imperial violence, literary works by writers like James Clarence Mangan, Thomas Moore and Joyce were charged with what Whelan terms 'a spiral of connectivity, a recursive, clotted, elliptical matrix' within which politics was at once camouflaged and communicated. This was the cultural-political source from which the works composed by these writers extracted 'their power and presence, their aura'.[45] While lecturing in San Francisco in 1882, Wilde referred directly to this problem when he described Ireland's cultural destruction at the hands of its English colonisers, views that he expressed later through the encoded means that Whelan describes.

The assumption that Wilde never took political risks and instead concealed himself behind a screen of privilege overlooks his ideological beliefs and commitments. These were more complex than the narcissistic motivations described by his biographer, Richard Ellmann.[46] Conscious of the dangers posed to anticolonial writers, Wilde encoded his rebellious ideas within the broader framework of aesthetic discourse, facilitating a safer distribution of his republican and socialist thought. This was particularly the case after the commercial failure of his first, openly political play, *Vera; or, The Nihilists*, in 1883. Wilde's cautious explorations of politics occurred along what Leela Gandhi terms the necessarily 'faint battle lines' of his later writing. These works should be read against the context of the more politically explicit points made in his earlier work, including his lectures and book reviews.[47] In these texts, written throughout the 1880s and 1890s, Wilde condemned coercion in Ireland, criticised class violence and offered nuanced discussions of the distortion of history in the service of power. These radical statements appeared in a range of works, including *Vera*, book reviews published in the *Pall Mall Gazette* and public lectures delivered in Britain, Ireland and the United States. His anticolonial and socialist ideas were not diluted as his career progressed, but were conveyed to readers through more tactically conscious discourse. By the spring of 1895, this threw playgoers into subversive laughter, after having already provoked indignation among readers of his short stories.[48]

When Irish writers did directly criticise empire at home, or when they advocated complete decolonisation, as Wilde's mother did in 1848, and as her friend, Christopher Manus O'Keeffe had also done during the Fenian insurgency of the 1860s, they did so under the very immediate threat of prosecution and imprisonment. The publication of her militant essay, 'Jacta Alea Est' in the Young Ireland newspaper, *The Nation*, in July 1848, led to the publication's seizure and suppression.[49] Later, in 1865, O'Keeffe was imprisoned for writing anti-imperialist articles in the Fenian newspaper, the *Irish People*. He was sentenced along with Jeremiah O'Donovan Rossa, who after his release went on to organise the Fenian dynamite campaign of the 1880s. An Irish language scholar, antiquarian, novelist and journalist, O'Keeffe wrote to William Wilde, praising 'those beautiful children of yours' and predicted great things for them, underlining the progressive class views and anticolonial opinions of the Wildes' milieu in Dublin: 'In a few years they will be men. Full of talent & highly educated they must feel that natural pride which is inseparable from intellectual superiority. This will make it impossible for them to fawn on aristocratic patrons.'[50] More advanced than the constitutional nationalism of Charles Stewart Parnell's Irish Parliamentary Party, Wilde's Irish republicanism – the ideology that he shared with the militant Fenian movement – was concealed in his literary writing within what Whelan terms 'the language of the politically unsayable, of the impossible public sphere'. In this way, like Joyce, Wilde articulated ideas that were censored, forbidden and deemed subversive by the state.[51] This strategic concealment was not a matter of evasiveness on Wilde's part, but evidence of his consistent, radical and carefully planned strategic engagements with contemporary politics. Through these slightly encrypted expressions of radicalism his works conveyed ideological proposals and ideas that were discernible to politically-informed readers like Alexander Cohen, the anarchist who defended Wilde's literary, political and sexual reputations in *The Torch* when he was imprisoned for committing the crime of 'gross indecency' in 1895.

Wilde and the Anarchists

From the earliest stages of his career Wilde was conscious of the need to secure influential and prominent sponsors and contacts. His networking efforts included meeting the Tory peer, poet and philanthropist, Richard Monckton Milnes, on instruction from the unionist academic, John Pentland Mahaffy, who had been Wilde's tutor at Trinity College, Dublin. Weeks beforehand, he also sent his work to the former Fenian prisoner, John Boyle O'Reilly, for publication in the *Boston Pilot*. O'Reilly owned and edited the paper, through which he promoted Irish separatism in the United States.[52] A year later, Wilde wrote to the former Prime Minister, William Ewart Gladstone, hoping that his approval might secure the publication of his work in journals like *Nineteenth Century* and the *Spectator*.[53] Moving among powerful circles when at his most famous, and by appealing to these influential figures when he was younger, Wilde cultivated his reputation as a writer, celebrity and public intellectual by strategically positioning himself at those points where the political and cultural spheres overlapped. His agitational stance was central to his public identity and this was recognised by the Scottish anarchist, Thomas Hastie Bell, who believed that Wilde 'opposed [. . .] all governmentalism'. He was, in Bell's opinion, 'undoubtedly [. . .] an Anarchist of the type of Edward Carpenter or Elisee [sic] Reclus [. . .] an Anarchist philosophic and humanitarian' whose 'clean-cut and clean-spoken' radicalism attracted more people to the anarchist cause than the less polished writings of other revolutionaries.[54] Likewise, the poet and critic, Arthur Symons, urged readers to study Wilde's prose and its sophisticated 'convolutions of sentiment' so as to better understand his political genius.[55]

In 1907, Benjamin Tucker's anarchist journal, *Liberty*, reprinted the French poet, Saint-Georges de Bouhélier's article, 'The Soul of Man Under Socialism', which praised Wilde's original essay. The article first appeared in the socialist newspaper, *L'Aurore*, which in 1898 had famously published Émile Zola's defence of Alfred Dreyfus, 'J'accuse . . . !' (the paper's full title was *L'Aurore Litteraire, Artistique, Sociale*). De Bouhélier complained that contemporary politics amounted to the absorption of 'inner liberty [. . .] by the mass': in a bourgeois democracy, he warned, 'originality attracts suspicion, strips off power, annihilates'. Thus the creative and resistant individual always found himself at odds with 'the innumerable absurdity of the fanatical and illiterate multitude'.[56] Writing in 1916, John Cowper Powys also claimed that Wilde was 'the most extreme of individualists' who stood for 'an affiliation in revolt between the artist and the masses'. This radicalism, Powys believed, was practical rather than theoretical because it associated the possibility of political progress with a 'natural human craving for life and beauty'. His cultural position was revolutionary because it proved that 'life with all its emotional, intellectual and imaginative possibilities, can be endured without the gross, coarsening, dulling "anæsthetic" of money-making toil'.[57] Wilde's radical views were also clear to Robert Hichens, whose 1894 satire, *The Green Carnation*, parodied the aesthetic movement. Although the novel was critical of Wilde, who is represented by the irritatingly flamboyant and paradoxical aesthete, Esmé Amarinth, Hichens was unable to dismiss his target's political views. Instead, he cast Esmé as a figure who recognises the crises generated by capitalism and regards society as existing directly 'upon the edge of a precipice'.[58]

The concealment of outrage was a necessary strategy for Wilde as he assumed an increasingly central public role as a writer who stood in 'symbolic relation' to the wider culture of the fin de siècle.[59] His theories on the links that bound art to revolutionary politics suggested that Aestheticism could be an agitational movement capable of countering the cultural and political hegemony of capital: as he stressed in 1883 while promoting *The Duchess of Padua*, '[A]ll art must be capable of scientific analysis; it is not mere prettiness.'[60] Wilde also echoed and politicised Walter Pater's ideas about the intensity of art with his own claim that 'we burn with a hundred flames'. By making 'culture [. . .] a gem that reflects light from a myriad facets', Wilde believed that Aestheticism could define the beautiful as the product of material and historical experience.[61] From Wilde's perspective, culture engaged with every aspect of contemporary life, adding a political charge to Pater's claim that it should express the artist's 'spirit of rebellion and revolt against [. . .] moral and religious ideas'.[62] Art, he argued, was reflective of and informed by political and economic realities. It circulated among the social classes that produced and paid for it and, while their interests were embedded within the political, the artist's quest for autonomy paradoxically resisted the hegemony of capital and the state. Responding to James Abbot McNeill Whistler's claim that art should be socially disengaged, Wilde asserted that no work could function in a social or political vacuum. 'An artist is not an isolated fact,' he maintained, because 'he is resultant of a certain milieu and a certain entourage'. This was why the writer, painter or musician 'can be no more born of a nation that is devoid of any sense of beauty than a fig can grow from a thorn or a rose blossom from a thistle'.[63]

Wilde was as interested in anarchism as he was supportive of what Joe Cleary terms the 'outlaw ideology' of Irish republicanism,[64] and these sympathies were recognised by his contemporary, Thomas Hastie Bell, who drew attention to Wilde's alignment of anarchism with anticolonialism in his application of 'autonomy against empire'.[65] Anarchism was a transnational, decentralised ideology that travelled across borders, undermining contemporary bourgeois notions of citizenship, cultural identity and the legitimacy of the state.[66] For conservatives, it highlighted the problem of working-class mobility, which was equated in journalism and popular fiction with the threat of terrorism.[67] Described by its political opponents as a movement of violent transients, criminals and immigrants, anarchism articulated the oppositional, alternative consciousness of those who existed on the margins of late-nineteenth-century capitalism. Although severely critical of anarchism himself, George Bernard Shaw complained that the popular 'imaginative' association of anarchists with criminality resulted from their misrepresentation by the conservative press.[68] Like the influential anarchist theorist and historian, Peter Kropotkin, along with other anarchist contemporaries like Emma Goldman and Bell, Wilde regarded capitalist competition as a 'waste of energy', and sought to replace it with a utopian, co-operative ideal in which authority played no part.[69]

While some critics have dismissed Wilde's commitment to anarchism and have worked to depoliticise his writing, the close readings provided in this monograph show how, in his journalism and literary publications, Wilde clearly and repeatedly engaged with anarchism's radical cultural and political perspectives.[70] In response, Kropotkin, Bell and Goldman engaged enthusiastically with his work.[71] For Wilde, anarchic subjectivity and radical consciousness were timeless phenomena that resisted the implicit and explicit violence of being governed. He insisted that these crises were not irreversible because they could be countered by art and by the aesthetically conscious individual. In his essay on the ancient Chinese philosopher, Chuang Tsŭ, Wilde accepted that the aesthete's fusion of artistic and political subversion was perilous activity because late Victorian society was ultimately governed through coercion. He was not the only writer to make this connection, as anarchists regarded the cultural field as offering practical and artistic analogues to their political efforts, and many emphasised the centrality of art and literature to rebellion during this period.[72] As John Barlas, another anarchist who was also a friend of Wilde's, indicated in his 1892 review of *The Picture of Dorian Gray*, anarchism did not function in straightforwardly political terms but was instead a more comprehensive form of resistance that integrated political and cultural activity in its expressions of revolt. Consequently, it appealed quite directly to the creatively minded. During the 1890s anarchists became increasingly interested in literary expression and in the political purchase of cultural Symbolism, a process that, in turn, associated their politics with the *déclassé* consciousness of avant-garde bohemians.[73] Wilde was equally interested in the synthesis of avant-garde art with radical politics, an issue that came, increasingly, to characterise aesthetic literary and cultural production at the fin de siècle.

Anarchism was a highly mediated form of radicalism: French anarchists circulated their ideas in journals such as *La Révolte* and the edgier *Le Père Peinard*, while journals such as *Freedom*, *Anarchy* and *The Torch* were published and circulated in Britain. It applied a range of artistically-oriented images, codes and practices because its political culture was underlined by its keenly aestheticised consciousness. Trading in shocking political images, French anarchists also moved comfortably within Symbolist circles and the relationship between the literary and political avant gardes cultivated 'total rather than relative comprehension' within both circles, whose adherents valued immediate experience over critical reflection.[74] This was complicated further because the French anarchist movement practised the strategy of 'propaganda par le fait', or propaganda by deed – violent strikes that targeted politicians (including, even, the French president, Sadi Carnot, who was stabbed to death in 1894), political institutions like the national assembly, and sites of conspicuous consumption such as the Café Terminus in Paris. With these spectacular *attentats*, militant anarchists acquired a fearsome reputation for causing political shocks that countered the systematic and institutional violence of *belle époque* capitalism. Wilde publicly declared his support for anarchism and his contacts and friends within the anarchist movement included Sergius Kravchinsky, also known as Stepniak, who killed General Mezentsev, the chief of the Russian secret police, in 1878. Wilde was also close to John Barlas, admired Peter Kropotkin and mingled with the socialist writers, George Bernard Shaw and William Morris. His acquaintances in Paris numbered Félix Fénéon, the journalist, propagandist, editor and alleged bomber with whom he remained a close friend after his release from prison in 1897.[75] Another French anarchist, Adolphe Retté, corrected an early draft of Wilde's deeply politicised play, *Salome*.

Art and Empire

As an Irish republican Wilde felt the impact of imperialism very acutely, and Ireland's centuries-long history of occupation and resistance generated the dialectical tension from which his own radical avant-gardism emerged. As we have seen, his anti-imperialist views were made very apparent during his lecture tour of the United States but on his return Wilde became necessarily more circumspect in voicing these views directly.[76] His famous statement that '[a]ll art is quite useless', announced at the end of the preface to *The Picture of Dorian Gray*[77] subversively underlines how art, when not hindered or co-opted by the dead weight of capital, can oppose bourgeois-imperial values and practices. Despite Aestheticism's perceived stress on the social isolation of art and the artist, Wilde believed that art's radical potential, like the revolutionary charge carried by the self-aware individual, lay squarely within its claims to autonomy. For these reasons, he was convinced that the true 'value of beautiful surroundings'[78] had a significantly social purchase.

Wilde stressed the entanglement of imperial politics, nationalist culture and aesthetic concerns in his first published article, 'The Grosvenor Gallery', which appeared in the *Dublin University Magazine* in July 1877. Drawing attention to the works of the Irish artist, Frederick Burton, he indicated his own nationalist views, stating Burton had sympathised with the Young Ireland movement of the 1840s.[79] Later that year, he returned to the subject of Irish cultural politics by praising the artist and antiquarian, Henry O'Neill, for influencing the Celtic Revival of the 1880s. The now elderly O'Neill was enduring financial distress and Wilde called for donations from 'those who have any appreciation of an unselfish and patriotic life'. Stressing that O'Neill's monograph, *The Most Interesting of the Sculptured Crosses of Ancient Ireland*, was an important nationalist work, Wilde emphasised the hold that it exerted over the modern Irish imagination:

> Of Mr. O'Neill's practical influence we can give no better example than the great change which has taken place in our funeral art, since the publication of his book. Everywhere in our cemeteries there are now to be seen stately and graceful Irish crosses, which are suitable memorials of our dead, not merely as being Christian emblems, but as the works of native hand and brain. These beautiful crosses have quite displaced the urns and sarcophagi, formerly so common; emblems which were meaningless, since we neither burn nor embalm our dead, and inartistic, as being unsuited to the material and the climate.[80]

Regarding the Victorian fixation with neoclassical decoration as artless and redundant, Wilde proposed that the Celtic cross was a superior, indigenous form that remained uncontaminated by colonial influences. The significance of O'Neill's researches lay in their popularisation of a specifically Irish art form, the material evidence of which could be found in the fashion for elaborate and expensive reproductions of ancient Irish crosses that his scholarly work had encouraged. Wilde believed that O'Neill had placed the Celtic cross firmly within the modern Irish cultural imaginary, ending the fad for what he regarded as alien funerary decoration by proposing a more suitable style drawn from native labour and art. As a symbol of the cultural revival of the second half of the nineteenth century, the Celtic cross had enormous symbolic purchase, while it also served as a distinctive emblem of Irish political nationalism.[81] Wilde promoted it as such, along with O'Neill's scholarly efforts to preserve surviving originals.

The recycling of these artefacts and images from the past did not just have cultural and aesthetic significance: Wilde confirmed that their modern application was deeply political because O'Neill had 'benefitted his country, in rescuing her from the imputations of barbarism in early ages'. Propaganda representing the Irish as violent and bestial had been circulated by colonial propagandists since the composition of Giraldus Cambrensis' twelfth- century travelogue, *Topographica Hibernica*.[82] This continued during Wilde's lifetime in simian caricatures of the Irish published in *Punch* and in racist depictions of the Irish by authors such as the Oxford historian, James Anthony Froude, who in 1872 described the Irish peasantry as 'some animal working by instinct, some missing link'.[83] As we shall see in Chapter 1, Wilde did not just target the images of Irish savagery being circulated by Tory historians and the imperialist press: even the great liberal intellectual, John Ruskin, included the Irish in his own catalogue of backward and ultimately doomed races. When considered against the long-term history of racist caricatures, distortions and propaganda that remained influential during Wilde's own lifetime, his journalistic promotion of Celtic revivalism, along with the general significance of 'Irish genius in the field of art',[84] seems a clear public acknowledgement of Irish culture's role in the wider struggle against empire.

'Civilization', 'Barbarism' and Art for the Workers

In 1882, when a reporter from the *Philadelphia Press* asked, 'What are your politics, Liberal or Conservative, Mr. Wilde?' he answered: 'Those matters are of no importance to me. I know only two terms – civilization and barbarism; and I am on the side of civilization.' With a deliberate swipe at British parliamentarianism, he added: 'It is very strange that in the House of Commons you never hear the word "Civilization"'. Wilde believed that Westminster, with its divisive atmosphere and 'wretched party spirit' distracted the public from the threat posed by the bourgeoisie's relentless self-aggrandisement and 'vast accumulation of capital'. Wilde had witnessed capitalism operating on a vast scale in the United States, and during his 1882 trip he noted that American plutocrats were outmatching the British aristocracy:

> We have as yet nothing like it in England. We call a man rich over there when he owns a share of Scotland, or a county or so. But he doesn't have such a control of ready money as does an American capitalist.[85]

During his visit to Chicago, he described alienation as the fundamental problem of capitalist modernity and proposed that instead of being dedicated to the generation of wealth for the elite, society could be improved by harnessing technology and industry so as to 'create a civilization greater or even as great' as ancient Greece.[86] Social equality could be achieved through the sharing of economic resources and this would, in turn, facilitate the democratisation of art and culture. Their appreciation would ensure that culture would no longer remain another example of 'luxury confined to the rich'.[87]

In another interview, Wilde explained that Aestheticism could enhance the quality of life for the working classes. When asked whether he wanted to 'teach the "common people", even the abjectly poor, to find these beauties, and by them to elevate their lives?' he answered:

> The two classes we must directly work upon are the handicraftsmen and the artists. As for the class between, the idle people, rich or poor, it is useless to go to them, and tell them, 'You must do this, and you ought to do that.' There must be a great mass of handicraft produced before you can hope to affect the masses. And the handicraftsmen must be directed by the artists; and the artists must be inspired with true designs. It is only through those classes we can work.[88]

Beauty was to be found in the products of skilled labour, and if made well, these would facilitate the development of a popular and democratic Aestheticism. The growth of a broader appreciation of the value of art among the working class could be fostered by socially-engaged workers and artists. Mass culture was not the problem, Wilde explained; it was authority, with the prescriptive demands it imposed on workers, that was stifling culture. The exploitation of labour and the misdirection of the energy of skilled workers was unsettling for Wilde, and he outlined his critique of material culture under capitalism by explaining that 'it is absurd to seek to make the material include the spiritual, to make the body mean the soul'.[89] The reporter noted that Wilde appeared melancholy as he asked:

> [W]hy does not science busy itself with drainage and sanitary engineering? Why does it not clean the streets and free the rivers from pollution? Why, in England, is there scarcely a river which at some point is not polluted; and the flowers are all withering on the banks![90]

Nature, culture, art and consciousness, he believed, were all suffering under the stress of capitalism and the 'intolerable noise' that it created.[91] The misery of labour lay in this dissonance: 'All art depends upon exquisite and delicate sensibility,' Wilde told his English audiences, 'and such continual turmoil must ultimately be destructive of the musical faculty.'[92] Industrial modernity was damaging the aesthetic capacity of the individual and reducing the value attached to culture by society as a whole, and the Denver *Daily Times* elaborated on Wilde's views when it reported:

> What he comes to proclaim is, that in the rush and hurry of modern civilization we have lost that appreciation of the beautiful in nature and art which gives joy and zest to life. We do not stop to think for ourselves, but let others think for us.[93]

Following a lecture in Philadelphia, one of Wilde's admirers wrote to the local press to defend Aestheticism against its political enemies within the city's 'aristocratic' establishment. The correspondent was convinced that it was an ideology that could never be rationalised or appreciated by the capitalists whose economic interests were harming American society:

> Mr. Wilde's lecture was a very clear defense of men, who whatever their faults, are certainly poets in the best sense, and, to his aestheticism, is it not a higher and nobler thing than the mercantile spirit of our age – a spirit once confined to tradesmen – but which now invades the noble professions of the law and of medicine? We hear more of the fees men make than of their speeches or their cures.[94]

Halfway through Wilde's US tour another reporter praised 'the great and catholic purpose of aesthetic culture' and defended the accuracy of his criticisms of American society by recommending that '[t]he more closely we follow his trainings and adopt his hints and suggestions, the more nearly we shall approach the beautiful and avoid the ugly and repulsive in our civilization'.[95] After the tour ended, these public discussions of Aestheticism's political and social relevance continued during 1883 and 1884 when Wilde delivered his lecture, 'Impressions of America'. He told audiences in England and Ireland that 'poverty is not a necessary accompaniment to civilisation' and emphasised the importance of 'the beauty of the word Freedom and the value of the thing Liberty'.[96] Connecting language to liberation, he criticised the assumption that poor people and workers were culturally incapable 'unaesthetics' and stressed that they possessed an acute aesthetic consciousness that underlined their right to participate in culture.[97] This book explores Wilde's admiration for those he described as the 'best classes' in society; these were the poor, the dispossessed and the colonised. Believing that the political, economic and cultural establishments refused to comprehend or implement the lessons of Aestheticism, he remained convinced that these marginalised communities understood culture and insisted that their appetite for art and beauty was greater than both the capitalist's demands for profit and the imperialist's desire for conquest.[98]

Notes

1. Max Nordau, *Degeneration* (originally published in 1893 as *Entartung* (New York: D. Appleton and Company, 1895)), pp. 317, 497.
2. 'Exit Oscar', *Truth*, 19 July 1883 (no page no.), UCLA Clark Library, *Wildeana*, Box 10: 'Wilde in America', 10.19.
3. Ibid.
4. Alexander Cohen, untitled, *The Torch*, 2.1, 18 June 1895, p. 6.
5. 'Mr. Oscar Wilde on America', *The West Midlands Advertiser and Chelsea and Pimlico Chronicle*, 14 July 1883 (no page no.), UCLA Clark Library, *Wildeana*, Box 10: *Wilde in America*, 10.17 A.
6. See, for example, 'Mr. Oscar Wilde's "Impressions"', *The Daily Telegraph*, 12 July 1883 (no page no.), UCLA Clark Library, *Wildeana*, Box 10: *Wilde in America*, 10.17B.
7. 'Impressions of an Impressionist', *Punch*, 21 July 1883 (no page no.), UCLA Clark Library, *Wildeana*, Box 10: *Wilde in America*, 10.16.
8. *Punch*, 10 December 1881, p. 12, quoted in Stuart Mason, *Bibliography of Oscar Wilde* (London: T. Werner Laurie, 1914) p. 255.

9. For an account of this racist stereotyping, see L. Perry Curtis, *Apes and Angels: The Irishman in Victorian Caricature* (Washington, DC: Smithsonian Institution Press, 1997). Liz Curtis also examines Victorian anti-Irish caricatures in relation to later examples published during the 1970s and 1980s. Her research has shown how the frequency of their publication increases during periods of anticolonial insurgency dating from the Middle Ages until the mid-1980s. See Liz Curtis, *Nothing But the Same Old Story: The Roots of Anti-Irish Racism* (London: Information on Ireland, 1983).
10. 'Murder Made Easy: A Ballad à la Mode. By "Brother Jonathan"' Wilde', *Punch*, 14 January 1882, p. 18.
11. For a historical overview of anti-anarchist paranoia and other 'red scares' that were invented and manipulated by European governments during the fin de siècle, see Alex Butterworth, *The World That Never Was: Dreamers, Schemers and Secret Agents* (London: Bodley Head, 2010).
12. 'Swinburne and Water', *Punch*, 23 July 1881, p. 26.
13. 'To an Æsethtic Poet', *Punch*, 14 January 1882, p. 18.
14. 'Home Rule', *Punch*, 4 April, 1885, p. 162.
15. Quoted in Robert D. Pepper, 'Introduction', in Oscar Wilde, *Irish Poets and Poetry of the Nineteenth Century* (San Francisco: The Book Club of California, 1972), p. 3.
16. Oscar Wilde, 'Poetry and Prison: Mr. Wilfrid Blunt's "In Vinculis"', *Pall Mall Gazette*, 3 January 1889, p. 3, in *The Complete Works of Oscar Wilde*, vol. 7: *Journalism* 2 (Oxford: Oxford University Press, 2013), pp. 149–52, pp. 149, 151.
17. Michael Davitt, *Leaves from a Prison Diary; Or, Lectures to a 'Solitary' Audience*, vol. 2 (London: Chapman and Hall, 1885), pp. 222, 197.
18. Oscar Wilde, 'The Soul of Man', in *The Complete Works of Oscar Wilde*, vol. 4: *Criticism* (Oxford: Oxford University Press, 2007), pp. 231–68, p. 235.
19. Jane Francesca Wilde to Lotten von Kramer, undated, quoted in Joy Melville, *Mother of Oscar Wilde: The Life of Jane Francesca Wilde* (London: Allison and Busby, 1999), p. 97.
20. 'Jacta Alea Est' ('The Die is Cast'), appeared in the Young Ireland newspaper, *The Nation*, when its editor, Charles Gavin Duffy, was being tried for treason. In this piece, Speranza called for the Irish to initiate a 'war' against their British occupiers. The essay was reprinted in its entirety by Robert Harborough Sherard in his 1906 biography of Wilde. See Robert Harborough Sherard, *The Life of Oscar Wilde* (London: T. Werner Laurie, 1906, reprinted 1911), pp. 46–55, p. 50.
21. 'Oscar Wilde – Very Wild', *Moonshine*, Saturday, 18 March 1882, p. 129.
22. Undated report in the *Saint Paul Globe*, quoted in Lloyd Lewis and Henry Justin Smith, *Oscar Wilde Discovers America, 1882* (New York: Harcourt, Brace and Company, 1936), p. 225.

23. Oscar Wilde, 'Ancient Legends of Ireland', *Pall Mall Gazette*, 19 February 1887, p. 4, in *The Complete Works of Oscar Wilde*, vol. 6: *Journalism 1* (Oxford: Oxford University Press, 2013), pp. 125–8, p. 125.
24. Oscar Wilde to James Nicol Dunn, November-December 1888, *The Complete Letters of Oscar Wilde* (London: Fourth Estate, 2000), p. 371.
25. John Stokes and Mark W. Turner, 'Introduction', in *Complete Works*, vol. 6, pp. xi–li, p. xxvii.
26. See 'The Poet's Corner', *Pall Mall Gazette*, 20 January 1888, p. 3, in *Complete Works*, vol. 7, pp. 52–5, p. 53.
27. Oscar Wilde, 'A Chinese Sage', *The Speaker*, 8 February 1890, in *Complete Works*, vol. 7, pp. 237–43, p. 242.
28. Oscar Wilde, 'The Critic as Artist', in *Complete Works*, vol. 4, pp. 123–206, p. 204.
29. Ibid. p. 205.
30. Ibid. p. 203. The dialogue was originally published in two parts in *The Nineteenth Century* as 'The True Function and Value of Criticism' in July and September 1890. It appeared as a single piece in the collection, *Intentions*, published in May 1891.
31. *Complete Works*, vol. 4, pp. 181, 191, 204.
32. Ibid. p. 202.
33. Matthew Arnold, *Culture and Anarchy* (Cambridge: Cambridge University Press, 1994), p. 96.
34. Leela Gandhi, *Affective Communities: Anticolonial Thought, Fin-de-Siècle Radicalism, and the Politics of Friendship* (Durham, NC: Duke University Press, 2006), p. 36.
35. See Edward Carpenter's fusion of autobiographical writing, poetry, political and historical observation and manifesto in *Towards Democracy* (London: John Heywood, 1883), which was published in four parts between 1883 and 1902, and then issued as a single volume in 1905 (reprinted London: GMP, 1985).
36. Oscar Wilde, 'The Sphinx Without a Secret: An Etching', in *The Complete Short Stories* (Oxford: Oxford University Press, 2010), p. 205.
37. Oscar Wilde to the editor of the *Daily Chronicle*, 27 May 1897, in *Complete Letters*, pp. 847–55, p. 851.
38. Ibid.
39. Terry Eagleton, 'Foreword', in *Saint Oscar* (Derry: Field Day, 1989), pp. vii–xii, p. ix.
40. David Lloyd argues that the British imperial project in Ireland was dedicated to the 'deep penetration of civil society by surveillance techniques through which the population is reconstituted as subjects of state authority rather than as citizens'. See Lloyd's essay 'Regarding Ireland in a Postcolonial Frame' in his *Ireland after History* (Cork: Cork University Press, 1999), pp. 37–52, quotation from p. 47.
41. Wilde's political views are dismissed by Jerusha McCormack, who regards him as a contrarian. Robert Pepper, who edited his important

lecture, 'Irish Poets and Poetry of the Nineteenth Century', claimed that Wilde's defence of Irish nationalism was the circumspect articulation of 'second thoughts'. See Jerusha McCormack, 'Oscar Wilde: As Daoist Sage', in Michael Y. Bennett (ed.), *Philosophy and Oscar Wilde* (Basingstoke: Palgrave, 2017), pp. 73–104, and Robert Pepper, in Bennett (ed.), *Philosophy*, p. 20. Norbert Kohl's 1980 study, *Oscar Wilde: The Works of a Conformist Rebel*, reduces him to an 'eccentric Irish Londoner' and a conflicted, guilt-ridden and self-serving nihilist whose reputation was posthumously and artificially inflated by his admirers. Kohl believed that Wilde's literary writing could only be redeemed by focusing 'squarely upon the individuality of the work and not upon that of the author'. See Norbert Kohl, *Oscar Wilde: The Works of a Conformist Rebel* (Cambridge: Cambridge University Press, 1989), originally published as *Oscar Wilde: Das literarische Werk zwischen Provokation und Anpassung* (Heidelberg: Carl Winter Universitätsverlag, 1980), pp. 1, 13.
42. Oscar Wilde, *The Picture of Dorian Gray* (1891), in *The Complete Works of Oscar Wilde*, vol. 3: *The Picture of Dorian Gray: The 1890 and 1891 Texts* (Oxford: Oxford University Press, 2005), pp. 165–357, p. 205.
43. As Margot Gayle Backus has argued, the Irish gothic articulates ideas about violence that have been purged from official colonial culture, exposing modernity's occluded and marginalised voices and rendering official violence more visible. See Margot Gayle Backus, *The Gothic Family Romance: Heterosexuality, Child Sacrifice and the Anglo-Irish Colonial Order* (Durham, NC: Duke University Press, 1999), pp. 14–16.
44. Oscar Wilde, 'Sonnet to Liberty', in *The Complete Works of Oscar Wilde*, vol. 1: *Poems and Poems in Prose* (Oxford, Oxford University Press, 2000), p. 149, l.11.
45. Kevin Whelan, 'The Memories of "The Dead"', *The Yale Journal of Criticism*, 15.1 (2002), pp. 59–97, pp. 77, 87.
46. Richard Ellmann, *Oscar Wilde* (New York: Knopf, 1988), p. 305. The anarchist historian, George Woodcock, also dismissed Wilde as a political fraud. See George Woodcock, *The Paradox of Oscar Wilde* (London and New York: Boardman & Co., 1949).
47. Gandhi, *Affective Communities*, p. 145.
48. George Bernard Shaw noted that Wilde's drama 'plays with everything: with wit, with philosophy, with drama, with actors, and audience, with the whole theatre'. Quoted from George Bernard Shaw, *Our Theatres in the 'Nineties*, in Nicholas Freeman, *1895: Drama, Disaster and Disgrace in Late Victorian Britain* (Edinburgh: Edinburgh University Press, 2011), p. 47.
49. Melville, *Mother of Oscar*, p. 46.
50. C. M. O'Keeffe to William Wilde, 20 September 1862. Clark Library Wilde 04122L W6723 1862 Sep. 20.

51. Whelan, 'The Memories of "The Dead"', p. 71.
52. Wilde to Lord Houghton, October 1876, in *Complete Letters*, p. 33; Wilde to Lord Houghton, c. 17 May 1877, *Complete Letters*, pp. 49–50; Wilde to John Boyle O'Reilly, September 1876, in *Complete Letters*, p. 33.
53. Wilde to W. E. Gladstone, 14 May 1877, in *Complete Letters*, p. 46.
54. Bell claimed that Wilde did so in order to prevent his work from being associated with violence. Thomas Hastie Bell, *Oscar Wilde without Whitewash*, UCLA Clark Library MS. Wilde B435M3 0814 [19–]?, p. 93.
55. Arthur Symons, *A Study of Oscar Wilde* (London: Charles J. Sawyer, 1930), p. 22.
56. Saint-Georges de Bouhélier, 'The Soul of Man Under Socialism', *Liberty*, 16.4, October 1907, pp. 45–9, p. 47.
57. John Cowper Powys, 'Oscar Wilde', in *Essays on Joseph Conrad and Oscar Wilde* (Girard, KS: Haldeman-Julius, 1916), pp. 29–49, pp. 38, 39.
58. Robert Hichens, *The Green Carnation* (London: Robin Clark, 1992), p. 72.
59. Wilde to Alfred Douglas, January–March, 1897, in *Complete Letters*, pp. 683–780, p. 729.
60. Wilde to Mary Anderson, 23 March 1883, Ibid. pp. 196–203, p. 203.
61. Wilde to Rebecca Smith, July 1883, Ibid. pp. 215–16, p. 215. Pater's views on the necessary intensity of art were expressed in the conclusion to his essay collection of 1873, *The Renaissance: Studies in Art and Poetry*. He continued his discussion of the necessity of the unifying intensity of art in his 1885 novel, *Marius the Epicurean*. See Walter Pater, *The Renaissance: Studies in Art and Poetry* (Oxford: Oxford University Press, 1998) and *Marius the Epicurean* (London: Penguin, 1985).
62. Pater, *The Renaissance*, p. 16.
63. Oscar Wilde, 'Mr. Whistler's Ten O'Clock', *Pall Mall Gazette*, 21 February 1885, pp. 1–2, in *Complete Works*, vol. 6, pp. 34–6, p. 35.
64. Joe Cleary, 'Republicanism and Aristocracy in Modern Ireland', *Field Day Review*, 10 (2014), pp. 4–39, p. 15.
65. Thomas Hastie Bell, *Oscar Wilde without Whitewash*, UCLA Clark Library MS. Wilde B435M3 0814 [19–]?, p. 455.
66. For an account of how culture was used to cultivate subjectivity in relation to the nineteenth-century state, see David Lloyd and Paul Thomas, *Culture and the State* (New York: Routledge, 1998).
67. For discussions of the association of anarchism with terrorist violence in the literary imagination, see my *Blasted Literature: Victorian Political Fiction and the Shock of Modernism* (Edinburgh: Edinburgh University Press, 2011), David Mulry's *Joseph Conrad Among the Anarchists: Nineteenth-Century Terrorism and The Secret Agent* (London: Palgrave,

2016) and Sarah Cole's *At the Violet Hour: Modernism and Violence in England and Ireland* (Oxford: Oxford University Press, 2012).
68. George Bernard Shaw, *The Impossibilities of Anarchism* (London: The Fabian Society, 1895), p. 4.
69. Oscar Wilde, 'A Chinese Sage', in *Complete Works*, vol. 7, p. 238. Emma Goldman's key writings are anthologised in *Anarchism and Other Essays* (originally published 1911, reprinted New York: Dover, 1969) and a comprehensive selection of Kropotkin's work is published in *Anarchism: A Collection of Revolutionary Writings* (New York: Dover, 1970).
70. David Rose, Josephine Guy and Ian Small have dismissed Wilde's political commitment, particularly his sympathy with anarchism. For example, Guy regards 'The Soul of Man under Socialism' as an essay that is 'not serious' about its subject matter. See David Rose, 'Oscar Wilde: Socialite or Socialist', in Ewe Boker, Richard Corballis and Julie Hibbard (eds), *The Importance of Reinventing Oscar: Versions of Wilde during the Last 100 Years* (Amsterdam: Rodopi, 2002), pp. 35–56; Josephine M. Guy, '"The Soul of Man Under Socialism": A (Con)Textual History', in Joseph Bristow (ed.), *Wilde Writings: Contextual Conditions* (Toronto: Toronto University Press, 2003), pp. 59–85; Ian Small, 'Introduction', in *Complete Works*, vol. 4, pp. xix–lxxxvi, especially lxxiii–lxxvi.
71. Bell, *Wilde without Whitewash*; Emma Goldman, 'The Hypocrisy of Puritanism', in *Anarchism and Other Essays*, pp. 167–76, p. 168; Peter Kropotkin to Robert Ross, 6 May 1905, in Margery Ross (ed.), *Robert Ross, Friend of Friends: Letters to Robert Ross, Art Critic and Writer* (London: Jonathan Cape, 1952), pp. 112–14, p. 113.
72. See Charlotte Wilson (as 'An English Anarchist'), 'Justice', *The Anarchist*, 1.5, July 1885, reprinted in Charlotte Wilson, *Anarchist Essays* (London: Freedom Press, 2000), pp. 29–30.
73. Richard D. Sonn has documented French anarchism's engagement with culture at the fin de siècle, focusing on the crossover between bohemian and radical political circles and networks in Paris, including the activities of revolutionaries like Wilde's friend, Felix Fénéon and others including Thadée Nathanson and Jean Grave. See Richard D. Sonn, *Anarchism and Cultural Politics in Fin de Siècle France* (Lincoln: University of Nebraska Press, 1989). See also Joan Ungersma Halperin, *Félix Fénéon: Aesthete and Anarchist in Fin-de-Siècle Paris* (New Haven: Yale University Press, 1989).
74. For a detailed discussion of anarchism's influence over contemporary literary writing, see David Weir, *Anarchy and Culture: The Aesthetic Politics of Modernism* (Amherst: University of Massachussetts Press, 1992). Quotation from p. 117.
75. Nicholas Frankel, *Oscar Wilde: The Unrepentant Years* (Cambridge, MA: Harvard University Press, 2017), pp. 202–3.

76. In addition to attacks on Wilde that were published in *Punch* in Britain, his visit to the United States provoked a rash of attacks in Ambrose Bierce's weekly magazine, *The Wasp*, that appeared in the publication for years after his departure from the country.
77. Wilde, *The Picture of Dorian Gray*, p. 168.
78. Wilde, 'Mr. Whistler's Ten O'Clock', in *Complete Works*, vol. 6.
79. Oscar Wilde, 'The Grosvenor Gallery', *Dublin University Magazine*, 90, July 1877, pp. 118–26, in *Complete Works*, vol. 6, pp. 1–11, p. 5.
80. Oscar Wilde, 'Mr. Henry O'Neill, Artist', *Saunders's News Letter*, 29 December 1877, p. 3, in *Complete Works*, vol. 6, pp. 13–15, p. 15. Wilde repeated his call for financial support for O'Neill in January 1879 in the *World*. See John Stokes and Mark Turner, 'Mr Henry O'Neill, Artist: Publishing History', in *Complete Works*, vol. 6, p. 214.
81. For a detailed discussion of the evolution and modernisation of Irish cultural nationalism during the nineteenth century, see Joep Leerssen's *Remembrance and Imagination: Patterns in the Historical and Literary Representation of Ireland in the Nineteenth Century* (Cork: Cork University Press, 1996).
82. The text was written to justify the Anglo-Norman occupation of Ireland. Giraldus accompanied an invading force led by Henry II's youngest son, John, which landed in 1185, and reported that the Irish were murderous, ignorant, treacherous and inclined towards bestiality. See Gerald of Wales, *The History and Topography of Ireland*, trans. from the Latin by John J. O'Meara (London: Penguin, 1982).
83. James Anthony Froude, 'A Fortnight in Kerry. Part 1', in *Short Studies on Great Subjects* (New York: Charles Scribner and Company, 1872), pp. 178–210, p. 201.
84. Oscar Wilde, 'Grosvenor Gallery (First Notice)', *Irish Daily News*, 5 May 1879, p. 5, in *Complete Works*, vol. 6, pp. 16–18, p. 18.
85. *Philadelphia Press*, 17 January 1882, quoted in Lewis and Smith, *Oscar Wilde Discovers America*, p. 41.
86. Uncited, quoted in Lewis and Smith, *Oscar Wilde Discovers America*, p. 168.
87. 'Oscar Wilde's Lecture', *Denver Daily Times*, 13 April 1882, recorded in Richard Butler Glaenzer, *Oscar Wilde in America* (unpublished ms. and notes), *Wildeana*, UCLA Clark Library, Folder 11.
88. Wilde, interview with the *Philadelphia Enquirer* (undated, 1882), quoted in Lewis and Smith, *Oscar Wilde Discovers America*, p. 65.
89. Lewis and Smith, *Oscar Wilde Discovers America*, p. 64.
90. Ibid. p. 65.
91. Ibid. p. 65.
92. Oscar Wilde, 'Impressions of America' (privately published by Mildred Sherrod Bissinger, Kentfield, CA, 1975), pp. 3–4.
93. 'Editorial', *Denver Daily Times*, 13 April 1882, recorded in Glaenzer, *Wildeana*, UCLA Clark Library, Folder 11.

94. E. M. N. to the *Philadelphia Times*, undated (early 1882), quoted in Glaenzer, *Wildeana*, Folder 6, p. 20. UCLA Clark Library, Wilde G54M3 081.
95. From the *Trenton State Gazette*, September 1882, quoted in Glaenzer, *Wildeana*, Folder 6, p. 20. UCLA Clark Library, Wilde G54M3 081.
96. Oscar Wilde, 'Impressions of America', pp. 15, 16.
97. Quoted in 'Art and Aesthetics', *The Tribune* (Denver), 13 April 1882, p. 8, recorded in Glaenzer, *Wildeana*, UCLA Clark Library, Folder 11.
98. 'The Theories of a Poet', recorded in Glaenzer, *Wildeana*, Folder 6, p. 20. UCLA Clark Library, Wilde G54M3 081.

Chapter 1

Anticolonial Wilde

In 1882, during his year-long lecture tour of the United States, Oscar Wilde told audiences of the violence done by British imperialism to Irish people and their culture. On several occasions he described how, despite historical waves of conquest and colonisation and the ongoing application of coercion, the imposition of 'alien English thought' was still being resisted in Ireland. Influenced by his mother's earlier writings, Wilde complained that this violence was accompanied by a careful programme of historical erasure, aimed at cultivating a popular consciousness 'far removed from any love or knowledge of those wrongs of the people'.[1] Decades earlier, Speranza's poem, 'The Stricken Land', which was published in the Young Ireland movement's newspaper, *The Nation*, in 1847, declared that the British rulers of Ireland were deliberately starving the country into submission. Her 1879 essay, 'The American Irish', repeated her claim that Britain's key political objective was the 'extermination' of the Irish. During his US tour Wilde added to her complaint by protesting that Britain was inhibiting the imagination of an entire people.

Wilde's explicit self-identification as an Irish republican is more subversive than the emotive Celticism that has been attributed to him: throughout his career he identified with the rebellious, the violently oppressed and the economically vulnerable, particularly during the land insurgencies of the late 1870s and 1880s.[2] As David Lloyd has argued, mid nineteenth-century Irish nationalist intellectuals responded to Britain's dismissal of their political agency by turning towards the cultural sphere. *The Nation*, which was the newspaper of the Young Ireland movement and for which Wilde's mother wrote under the pseudonym, 'Speranza', was a key platform for their political and cultural expression. Wilde's own public criticism of British rule should be understood against the context of this literary and political tradition, which Lloyd refers to as a radical type of 'minor writing' that was thoroughly resistant to imperialist culture: 'a minor writing in the positive sense of one whose very "inauthenticity" registers the radical non-identity of the colonized subject'.[3] Wilde's Irish background includes the political-cultural context of his experience as an emerging Irish writer, along with his consciousness of his mother's very public and internationally recognised role. Wilde's writing was informed by his mother's work; as he told a journalist in San Francisco, her writings 'inspired him with the desire to become a poet', and he responded subversively to the British occupation of Ireland.[4]

Matthew Arnold and the Aesthetics of Empire

Nineteenth-century Ireland was a colonial police state where coercive powers were repeatedly deployed, modified and integrated into everyday political and social experience.[5] Following the unsuccessful Fenian rebellion of 1867, the militarised Royal Irish Constabulary (RIC) enforced scores of 'peace preservation' acts and other coercive laws passed by successive British governments at Westminster. These acts outlawed public gatherings, banned demonstrations, legislated for mass internment, imposed press censorship, frequently suspended *Habeas Corpus* and subjected entire districts to military authority. A decade after the formation of the RIC, one of Wilde's earliest poems, 'Italia', appeared in the former Fenian, John Boyle O'Reilly's nationalist newspaper, the Boston-published *Pilot*, in 1877.[6] A former member of the Fenian Brotherhood, O'Reilly escaped from the British penal colony in Fremantle, Western Australia, in 1869 before planning the successful escape of another six political prisoners in 1876. Named for the whaling ship on board which these men escaped from Australia, the 'Catalpa rescue' became a major propaganda coup for the Fenian movement.[7] O'Reilly had already published and promoted Speranza's work in the *Pilot* and Wilde met him at the beginning of his US tour.[8] At several points during the tour Wilde revealed his own republican beliefs. In lectures delivered in Saint Paul and San Francisco and in interviews he emphasised the relationship between Irish literary writing and anticolonialism. These talks drew on but also criticised Matthew Arnold's romanticised construction of Irishness, while they also confronted the kind of anti-Irish prejudice being circulated by John Ruskin.

Arnold's extended essay, 'On the Study of Celtic Literature', is drawn from a series of lectures delivered at Oxford from 1865 to 1866 which were published in book form in 1867, the year of the

Fenian uprising. Although it is cited as an influential precursor to the Irish Literary Revival of the late nineteenth century, Amy E. Martin stresses how state violence is central to Arnold's vision of culture and its function within British imperial modernity.[9] Key to this is his reductive construction of 'the Celt', by which term he principally meant the Irish. While depicting them as an enchanting people, Arnold also cast the Irish as violent, unpredictable, irrational and ungovernable, and as in urgent need of cultural, political and even scientific discipline. While the 'spell of Celtic genius' could provide a healthy counter to the scientific bias of Anglo-Saxon rationalism, Arnold also warned that the Irish were radically estranged from British culture and that their 'incurable' political difference posed a threat to the Union. Dismissing the Tory, Lord Lyndhurst's description of the Irish as 'aliens in blood from us', he proposed, instead, their assimilation into imperial culture. This would not be an incorporation of equals into the British mainstream, however, as Arnold's ultimate goal was the containment of this disruptive, resistant and marginal people and their ethereal culture. Colonial policy had already left Ireland in a state of open and hostile rebellion against British authority, rendering the Union 'violently disturbed'; and Victorian modernity, Arnold believed, was characterised by this crisis. The remedy that he proposed involved dispensing a cultural cure: the English could only know the Irish – and maintain some necessary distance from them – by studying their literature. This would 'break [. . .] down barriers between us', strengthen the Union and, most importantly, limit the 'political and social Celticisation' being popularised by the militants of the Irish Republican Brotherhood, or Fenian movement.[10]

Arnold's plan for the full and proper co-option of the Irish into the British Empire was based on his assumption of their inferiority, as their emotional intensity and intransigence excluded them from the rational currents of industrial and imperial modernity. Their 'energetic national life and self-consciousness' was articulated through intense 'bursts' of literary expression, particularly poetry, as political and poetic impulses were fused in the Celtic imagination. Their spontaneity could be understood via 'constructive criticism' – a rational, imperial model of cultural observation that had a markedly surveillant dynamic: '[W]hat we want is to *know* the Celt and his genius; not to exalt him or to abase him, but to know him.' Irish literature was the 'great key' with which the anticolonial imagination might be unlocked, understood and finally commanded and contained by the liberal imperialist. The knowledge acquired from this study could then be used to subdue and integrate this 'violent stormy people'.[11]

The false objectivism, or 'protocol of pretended suprapolitical' neutrality that Edward Said has associated with Orientalism's denial of its own political motivations was key to Arnold's imperial-critical project.[12] Unlike politicians, scholars with expertise on Irish literature could decode the Irish people in a 'disinterested' but 'positive' manner that would serve the political interests of the imperial state. His model of colonial criticism could be applied far more gently than the coercive policies favoured by Tories like Lord Lyndhurst but they would still be used in the service of the same objective: knowing and controlling the Irish imagination. The exclusion of the Irish from the cultural and political life of the Union prevented the necessary 'intermingling' of Irish and British interests, but with this approach Britain could tie Ireland more firmly to its imperial authority through the medium of literary and cultural criticism.[13]

The native's lack of analytical ability is a familiar trope in Victorian colonial writing: 'balance, measure, and patience are just what the Celt has never had', Arnold claimed. The 'steadiness, patience, [and] sanity' with which 'expression [can] be given to the finest perceptions and emotions' are also lacking in the Celt,[14] whose life is spent, as Arnold famously put it, 'chafing against the despotism of fact' and 'straining after mere emotion'. This explained why Irish culture had 'accomplished nothing':

> In the comparatively petty art of ornamentation, in rings, brooches, crosiers, relic-cases, and so on, he has done just enough to show his delicacy of taste, his happy temperament; but the grand difficulties of painting and sculpture, the prolonged dealings of spirit with matter, he has no patience for.[15]

Arnold's dismissal of these ancient works contrasts with Wilde's recognition of their importance as evidence against imperialist representations of the Irish as savages.[16] The Celt's 'want of sanity and steadfastness' is reflected in such inferior artwork, which Arnold considered to be as frustrating and exhilarating as the Irish themselves. Although fascinating to observe, they were a defective people incapable of success in the fields of science, art, music and literature. While their poetry was invested with a uniquely 'splendid' genius, it was badly hindered by its emotional intensity which rendered it inferior to the literary outputs of other European nations, and Arnold believed that literary works such as *Agamemnon* and *The Divine Comedy* were products of a 'steady, deep-searching survey' of which the Irish were incapable. These superior, self-reflexive examples had been made possible by 'a firm conception of the facts of human life' that the easily distracted Celt 'has not patience for': 'in the contents of his poetry you have only so much interpretation of the world as the first dash of a quick, strong perception, and then sentiment, infinite sentiment, can bring you'.[17]

Contemporary politics is always discernible in Arnold's essay, which is really a proposal on how best to contain the 'Titanism' of Irish republicanism. Irish poetry's 'power of style' is so closely connected to the Celt's uncontrollable 'passion of revolt', that Arnold cites it as providing the model for the rebellious Satan's hatred of authority in John Milton's seventeenth-century epic poem of political conflict, *Paradise Lost*. However, he explains that revolution is a costly enterprise as Ireland's permanent state of disobedience has come with dire material consequences: not only are the Irish inferior on the intellectual or 'spiritual' level, their impulsive, undisciplined, emotional, irrational, ultimately feminine and anarchic 'rebellion against fact' has also 'lamed the Celt [. . .] in the world of business and politics'. The responsibility for their cultural, political, economic and intellectual inferiority lay squarely in the hands of the Irish because 'the sensuousness of the Celt proper has made Ireland'. Passionate, undisciplined and 'cut [. . .] off from command of the world of fact', the Irish were at once unreal and wholly fascinating – perfect subjects for the colonial laboratory where Britain's cultural, political and military experiments could flourish. Arnold's essay ultimately reassures the reader that despite the Celt's unpredictability, with careful study his comprehensively inferior subjectivity could be harnessed for imperial purposes.[18]

While drawing on Arnold's arguments about the uniqueness of Irish literary and cultural expression, and repeating some of his ideas about the inherent sentimentalism of the Celt, the lectures that Wilde delivered in the US on Irish literature and history had a distinctively rebellious tone that contradicted the calls for political and cultural containment made in 'On the Study of Celtic Literature'. These talks challenged the normalisation of British violence and countered Arnold's representation of the Irish as both conquerable and commodifiable. Despite Arnold's hope that the authenticity and spiritual intensity of Celtic literature might provide Victorian modernity with a reassuring image of its colonised others, his essay conceals the political facts of occupation and coercion that are more explicitly discussed and lauded in his 1869 book, *Culture and Anarchy*. It is with this avoidance that Arnold concluded his essay, claiming that Fenianism was the result of the political and cultural philistinism of the Tories, and not the organised expression of the anticolonial agency of Irish revolutionaries. With this claim he attempted to decontextualise Irish cultural and political history by ignoring the influence exercised by colonial violence over both.

John Ruskin and Empire

Four years before Wilde arrived in Oxford, John Ruskin delivered a series of similarly reductive lectures at the university that were ostensibly focused on the subject of sculpture. In the second of these, entitled 'Idolatry', the great cultural critic and 'master' aesthetic theorist whom Wilde admired greatly before publicly rejecting his teachings,[19] connected the development of culture directly to the violent practices of imperial conquest. Discussing what he regarded as the brutality of colonised peoples, he placed China, India and Ireland among the most defective 'nations of inferior race'. Ruskin believed that their sculpture, architecture and other forms of design were significantly inferior to modern British works. Having been produced under 'conditions of vile terror', they were artistically sterile and 'destitute of thought'. Sharing Arnold's views on the inferiority of the Irish, he explained how the world's 'greatest races' had conquered its 'baser' cultures before 'rapidly naturalizing and beautifying them'. While Arnold wanted to absorb the Celt, Ruskin believed that colonisation had an aestheticising dynamic made possible by the processes of cultural exclusion: by 'admitting less of monster or brute', the British Empire would filter and improve the cultures of those under its dominion. These cultures could be modified and upgraded by the 'happy and holy imagination' of the occupier, as Ruskin's model of assimilation did not involve the study of subject cultures advocated by Arnold so much as it demanded their adaptation and obedience. While Arnold's Celt could be observed from a distance, Ruskin's defeated cultures could be forcibly fitted into more metropolitan moulds. Once modernised and civilised in this way, they could contribute to the prosperity of the British Empire and its superior conditions of national existence.[20]

In justifying the aesthetic subjugation that accompanied the political and economic violence of empire, Ruskin also conveyed his anxiety about contemporary demands for democratic reform in Britain. The colonised shared their worst characteristics and 'earthliest vices' with the English poor, whose experience and history were equally alien to the 'industrious, chaste and honest race' from which Britain's cultural élite was composed. The mass of the dispossessed posed an immediate threat by demanding that art, like political participation, was the preserve of 'the whole mob of the nation'.[21] Ruskin's fear of the social potential of the creative arts expresses lingering conservative anxiety over what Mike Sanders, in his discussion of Chartist poetry, describes as the dynamic and mobilising 'political effect of poetical affect'.[22] Chartism's cultivation of the imaginative capacity of the working class was still perceived as a danger by Ruskin, who warned that the cultural boundaries established in the laboratories of empire also required strong domestic foundations because art and culture's protective 'intellectual design can never be discerned but by the few'. Maintaining class barriers was as important as policing colonial borders because if the great minds of these 'perfect men and women' were not defended from the impulses of the domestic crowd, then their refined interests and values would be eroded by 'every form of sensual and insane sin'. Ruskin estimated that it would take only fifty years for British culture to collapse under such pressure from within and without, before terminating 'in hopeless shame the career of the nation in literature, art, and war'. This warning about imperial fragility and the possibility of Britain's sudden degeneration into a state of intellectual paralysis equated cultural decline with military inactivity: empires desperately required time as well as territory, and violence was the currency with which both could be acquired. Ruskin claimed that, as defeated nations were coerced into the British Empire, scholars, cultural theorists and Orientalists could examine the wreckage of their cultures by filtering out their lesser elements; in doing so, imperial power could control occupied peoples by narrating their histories. The useful, logical, even splendid fragments of these fractured societies could then be put to use in the service of imperial power with whatever remained being abandoned to decay.

Ruskin's ideas about the advantages of expansion and appropriation, accompanied with his acute anxiety over the possibility of hubristic decline, reveal how his theories on aesthetics owe much to the Victorian ideology of imperial expansion, as opposed to Arnold's more flexible, hegemonic model of imperial assimilation.[23] Despite these differences, culture, violence, pacification and assimilation are closely connected themes in this lecture, as they also are in Arnold's writing. Despite the variations in their competing models for imperial progress, both proposed that culture and counterinsurgency were closely linked phenomena. Art and literature, they believed, could be registered and appropriated within the violent and surveillant grids of empire and capital, and lessons learned in colonial settings could be applied very directly in domestic situations. According to Ruskin, the colonised, like the British working class, would only submit under the threat or implementation of violence as the coloniser and the capitalist appropriated and reconfigured territories, markets and goods. For Arnold, the process was a softer but no less insidious form of coercion, as his study of Celtic literature had as its objective the pacification of the insurgent Celtic imagination.

Wilde's US Tour and the Violence of Empire

In their account of Wilde's 1882 tour of the United States, *Oscar Wilde Discovers America*, Lloyd Lewis and Henry Justin Smith cited contemporary Anglomania as the reason for his popularity but much of the press coverage that he generated was characterised by sustained expressions of Hibernophobia.[24] These attacks led Robert Ross to believe that the tour permanently damaged Wilde's reputation in England, despite its commercial success.[25] His presence in the United States initiated a political debate in Boston, where a local paper, the *Sun*, defended the 'young Irish poet' and 'Bard of Erin' against claims levelled by a rival publication, the *Transcript*, that his visit and the aesthetic ideology that he represented posed a direct threat to American values.[26] Aestheticism, the *Transcript* complained, made 'the wine glass more important than the wine'.[27] As he travelled across the United States, Wilde encountered further press hostility aimed at discouraging attendance at his lectures. Intended to prevent him from reaching out to artistic and political circles in the states that he visited, these attacks were aimed at hindering his social and cultural influence. In Philadelphia, the quip, 'Oscar Wilde always dresses in mourning out of respect for his wits' was doing the rounds;[28] the *Chicago Morning News* described him as 'having nothing of the least value to say' and being 'utterly incompetent to say it'.[29] In California he was condemned as a political subversive and portrayed as a terrorist in league with the 'mad revolutionists' of the Fenian movement.[30]

At the outset of the tour, the *New York Tribune* complained about the 'disgusting' spectacle of Americans 'playing the toady' by entertaining a 'foreign adventurer' whose 'well advertised [. . .] spice of immorality' was now threatening to corrupt the nation.[31] Eleven months later, it was still berating his supporters for hosting an 'uninvited' alien 'only known to us through caricatures in

Punch'.[32] This London-based anti-Irish magazine was an important source for Wilde's conservative American opponents and its keynote caricature of the degenerate, simian Celt was recycled by the *Washington Post*, which mocked Wilde on the eve of his lecture in the US capital by comparing him to an ape in the caricature, 'Mr Wild of Borneo'.[33] Such representations were accompanied by Wilde-themed minstrel shows,[34] disruptive heckling, hate mail and even threats to commit physical violence against him. The British press also weighed in, when the former soldier and *Daily News* war correspondent, Archibald Forbes, wrote to Wilde three days after he spoke in Washington DC, promising to punish him for his 'utterly mercenary' behaviour with a beating.[35] Wilde's enemies in California were less circumspect than Forbes, whose threat was issued privately: in San Francisco, Ambrose Bierce's magazine, *The Wasp*, publicly called for his murder.[36] However, these attacks did not lessen Wilde's popularity: his next lecture in Baltimore attracted 800 people,[37] and the tour's overall commercial success prompted Elizabeth Marbury, the agent and publicist who handled performances of *Lady Windermere's Fan* and *An Ideal Husband* in the United States, to ask Wilde to return to give another series of lectures in 1894.[38]

While critics and biographers have described the tour as an extended exercise in self-branding, Wilde used it as a radical political platform from which he repeatedly criticised British domination in Ireland.[39] While in the United Sates he engaged directly with the ongoing political crisis in Ireland, where the Land League was breaking up the political hegemony of the aristocratic, landowning Anglo-Irish ruling class. From its very beginning, the tour was politicised by his publicist, Richard D'Oyly Carte. Having originally advertised Wilde's lectures on 'The Artistic Spirit of the New English Renaissance',[40] Carte decided to promote his client's republican views as well as his credentials as an aesthete. In publicity notices circulated after Wilde's arrival in New York, Carte described him as the product of his family's radical milieu:

> Lady Wilde, the poet's mother, was fully as remarkable as his father. She was a woman of splendid beauty and conspicuous talent [. . .] She gathered around her a notable company of artists, litterateurs, politicians, and especially republicans, whose imaginations teemed with visions of a millenium, [sic] almost here. She had the only literary salon in Dublin. Under the influence of his father, filled with a passionate love and reverence for the past; under the influence of his mother enthusiastic over a

future for the world which others painted for her, and which she painted for herself in all kinds of marvellous colours; among a crowd of choice spirits, who sympathized with either or both; in the midst of such surroundings young Wilde passed the earlier part of his life, and acquired his early education.[41]

Carte informed the press that, with its unique fusion of literary, artistic and republican influences, Wilde's upbringing established his radical cultural and political credentials and informed his practice as an aesthete. Wilde discussed these matters along with the topics of labour, class and colonialism, and the relationship between colonisation and culture was addressed very directly in his San Francisco lecture, 'Irish Poets and Poetry of the Nineteenth Century'. While this lecture has been interpreted as an uncharacteristically political piece, it should be read against the context of his radical views on Irish literature, history and politics, and in relation to his consistent support for Irish nationalism. As Gregory Castle has noted, the tour became a platform for a complex and historically reflective performance that projected the very complex 'nuance and difference' of Wilde's Irish identity.[42]

This came at a point when imperialist historians, cultural theorists, novelists and journalists were representing the Irish and their culture as primitive, degenerate, bestial and insane: Arnold's and Ruskin's influential lectures were more scholarly contributions to the well-established, centuries-long canon of anti-Irish racism.[43] Wilde's focus on the historical longevity of Irish resistance challenged this prejudice along with its denial of the force with which Ireland had been occupied and subdued. The British state's concealment of the material, economic, social and political violence it was inflicting in Ireland was exposed and challenged in the San Francisco lecture and in a speech that he delivered on St Patrick's Day in Saint Paul, Minnesota. In both talks Wilde also associated the art and culture of Ireland's pre-colonial past with the modern political and literary expression of nationalist writers of the Young Ireland movement. This was in character with his frequent pronouncements on Ireland: he told the press in Chicago that he had recently met a relative of Robert Emmet, the executed leader of the second United Irish rebellion of 1803; in Milwaukee, Wilde declared that he was 'strongly in sympathy with the Parnell movement' and told audiences there about his family's connections with the Young Irelanders. In Chicago, he also described Ireland as a 'Niobe among nations' that had been 'wrecked by the folly of England', and in Atlanta he told reporters that '[w]e in Ireland are fighting for the principle of autonomy against empire'.[44]

Wilde's description of Ireland as an occupied country being subjected to colonial violence mirrored Friedrich Engels' views on Ireland. These are documented in his *History of Ireland*, an ambitious but unfinished account of the country's prolonged history of imperial occupation. While Arnold and Ruskin discussed the artistic, cultural, political and economic failures of the Irish as the outcome of racial inferiority, Engels discussed British colonial practice in nineteenth-century Ireland in direct relation to imperialist violence, under the title 'The Period of Extermination'.[45] By celebrating the Young Irelanders' literary and political protests against British rule in his San Francisco lecture, Wilde continued his father's strategy of placing Irish culture within its historical context and repeated his mother's depictions of British authority in Ireland as unjust, catastrophic and dangerous.[46] Drawing directly on her explanation that the contemporary Irish crisis was the result of a long-term process of colonisation and dispossession, Wilde told audiences that the British occupation of Ireland had been thoroughly destructive. His direct identification with Irish republicanism and with the objectives of the Fenian movement was influenced by the manifestoes, essays and pamphlets that Jane Francesca Wilde wrote from the 1840s until the late 1870s, including 'Jacta Alea Est' (1848), 'Irish Leaders and Martyrs' and 'The American Irish' (1879), and her haunting poem, 'The Stricken Land' (1847).

By rejecting contemporary descriptions of Irish culture as the expression of a degenerate society well on its way to extinction, Wilde contradicted the key claims of Victorian cultural imperialists. On a number of occasions during the tour, he described the Irish experience of colonialism as a prolonged encounter with state violence that had, through shock and attrition, destroyed complex practices and artefacts of cultural and artistic expression. Ruskin's proposal that the British should sift through the ruins of Irish culture is challenged by Wilde's explanation that colonialist violence had shattered it in the first place.

Speranza, Republicanism and the Land War

While the influence of Arnold's ideas about Irish difference is evident in 'Irish Poets and Poetry of the Nineteenth Century', Wilde's lecture also drew heavily on his mother's bellicose 1879 pamphlet,

'The American Irish', which he circulated among friends in England as an illustration of her anticolonial sentiments.[47] Originally published in New York at the commencement of the first Irish Land War, and reissued in Dublin two years later, it described the outbreak of a new, resistant popular consciousness and its expression by means of 'a revolution, silent but certain', that was 'now going on in the Irish mind'. Speranza reminded her readers that while the Irish had recently been 'reduced to the level of a root-eating people' during the Great Hunger, the latest and ongoing political insurgency of the Land War was directly related to their intellectual and cultural activity: 'The English strove to crush the mind of the subject race, knowing that culture is power.' This was in contrast to the spread of Hellenic culture, which had been established through an organic development of the 'divine gifts' of 'civilization and refinement, art, science, and philosophy'. Whereas Greek culture was marked by its Arnoldian 'trail of light', the English conquest of Ireland could be discerned through the 'trail of blood' left in its historical wake. Speranza described the colonisation of Ireland as a psychological exercise as well as a military one, and argued that its enduring legacy of violence was part of a longer, centuries-long continuum of atrocity: 'No nation ever endured greater horrors, and no people but the Irish could have survived them.' Sharing Engels' anaylsis, she explained that the Irish had endured centuries of 'confiscation', 'degradation' and finally, during the 1840s, a systemic and officially-sanctioned process of 'extermination'. As a result, late Victorian Ireland was now 'a country that has been devastated, plundered'. Having been 'reduced by want and famine from eight millions to five millions during the last thirty years', the country's remaining population was facing further repression from the British, whose immediate answer to protest and dissent was the imposition of martial law: 'Complaint is answered by a coercion bill, and the only remedial act is to proclaim a district.'[48]

Irish history was an ongoing dialectic of conquest, coercion and resistance forming a living memory, or a 'tale (that) still lives in Irish hearts with enduring vitality':

> Every century has witnessed some fierce effort to throw off the foreign yoke, and every generation adds new names to the long roll of martyrs and victims doomed to suffer for the vain but beautiful dream of national independence. Exile, confiscation, the prison and the scaffold form the leading chapters of Irish history, even to our own day, – an endless martyrology written in tears and blood.[49]

Defining themselves against the imperial power that they resisted, the Irish had a highly developed national consciousness, and because of this 'some good' had 'come of the evil':

> Many holy and sacred things spring up in a nation's soul from the seed sown by persecution. Suffering purifies and refines, and a people learns the value of coherence and unity mainly through oppression. There is also something ennobling in the love of an object out of self, in the devotion to an abstraction called Country; in this dream of freedom, with all the word means, dignity, honour, self-reverence, and self-respect.[50]

Enduring conquest was, Speranza believed, aesthetically productive because it inspired idealism and pointed toward liberation. The principle of moral victory achieved by means of resistance also appears in Wilde's 1891 essay, 'The Soul of Man Under Socialism', in which he praised the Russian anarchist, Peter Kropotkin's mystic and Christ-like capacity for suffering. Like her son, Speranza regarded such selflessness as a sign of divinity: 'When they say of a man, "He died for Ireland," the voice is low and tender, as if they spoke of the passion of Christ.'[51]

Emphasising Irish nationalism's predication on the symbolic purchase of self-sacrifice, the essay stresses how an awareness of the likelihood of failure, and even the prospect of death, would not deter the committed Irish republican:

> It will be a sad day, perhaps, for the higher national life when Ireland has no more dreams, and the country no more martyrs, for then an ideal will have passed out of the life of the people, and a nation without an ideal aim on which to concentrate the passions, soon becomes hopelessly materialized, inarticulate, and dull. The subtle, spiritual fancies and the finer issues of human feeling are stifled by the sensuous, selfish enjoyment of the actual and the present, and nations, as well as individuals, become hard and cold without the divine impulse of sacrifice and self-abnegation.[52]

Culture is inextricably tied to martyrdom here and the patriot is depicted as possessing the noble, elevated state of consciousness that defined Irish separatism for Speranza. She believed that without the idealistic and romantic qualities that distinguished the Irish from the British, the very concept of nationhood would be extinguished. As articulate as they were capable of self-sacrifice, these martyrs offered an alternative model of being that was defined by their passionate investment in revolutionary change. Divine in his perfection and so idealised as to be represented as being independent of the material concerns that motivated more compromised constitutional politics, Speranza's model of the perfect Irish revolutionary drew on Matthew Arnold's construction of the Celtic sensibility as a form of counter-consciousness. Like Arnold, Speranza proposed that Victorian modernity was an age of hubris, but total investment in the struggle for national liberation animated these Irish rebels. Language itself was deployed as a weapon against the oppressor:

> To the impassioned nationality of the Irish, with its large indefiniteness of aim and instincts of resistance, may be also due much of the fervour of Irish eloquence. All oppressed nations are eloquent. When laws forbid a people to arm, they can only speak or sing. Words become their weapons, and the Irish armoury is always bright and burning.[53]

Romantic and indistinct, the political and cultural desires of the Irish were conveyed and materialised through language, which Speranza depicts as a colonised people's only defence in times of total oppression. Resistance is represented as a continual, evolving and formative process presenting itself much like Walter Pater's model of the crystallising modern aesthetic.

The idea that the Irish possessed a popular, residual cultural memory of nationhood was a key claim of the modern, romantic nationalism of the Young Ireland movement. However Speranza's writing also acknowledges the political and cultural essence of the historical chain of resistance that drove Irish nationalism and mobilised its modern, republican advocates.

While her son was planning his own career with its public interventions in what he later described in 'De Profundis' as the symbolic relations defining the art and culture of the fin de siècle, Speranza stressed the importance of combing ideological consciousness with cultural defiance in answer to questions of political difference. According to her historicised model of Irish resistance, the language of the colonised conveyed the intensity of the subaltern imagination along with the dissident speech, songs and writing that reflected its values. Nationalist politics was, she believed, essentially poetic. During prolonged periods when armed resistance was impossible, separatism assumed the primarily cultural dynamic that distinguished the Irish from their conquerors. This was animated by its subaltern origins:

> Nationality, this dream of an ideal future, illumines their poetry and oratory, their music and song with a vague splendour of passion and pathos, and preserves even the common speech and popular literature of the people from the coarseness and vulgarity so obtrusively characteristic of the English lower classes.[54]

Conscious of her friend, Christopher O'Keeffe's description of Ireland as 'a country in which the very beggars are eloquent',[55] Speranza maintained that, despite their dispossession, the Irish poor remained culturally and intellectually superior to the English working and workless classes, whose sensibilities had been eroded and vulgarised. Despite its objective of eradicating resistance, colonial violence generated resistance and by engaging with the enemy on cultural and political fronts the colonised conferred dignity upon themselves. Speranza believed that the burgeoning national culture through which they expressed their refusal to submit – itself a signal of their willingness to continue – was the most powerful weapon that the Irish people possessed. Politically eclipsed by British power, the now-submerged but developing Irish nation was drawing subtly on the 'many fine-toned chords' that composed the complex 'nature of her people'.

Believing that the aural resonances of historical resistance still sounded in the present, she argued that the Irish had been endowed through their suffering with qualities that their nemesis, 'the stolid English organization, with its plethoric prosperity and self-centered egotism', lacked. The centralised forces of empire and capital were no substitutes for the disaggregated but more flexible and poetic consciousness of the colonised, as had been revealed in the efforts of Irish republicans who had transformed political defeat into symbolically aestheticised performances of moral victory. By participating in their country's ongoing independence struggle, they had become powerful figures in their own right. Drawing on the theme of memorialisation that had been popularised in Thomas Moore's political ballad, 'Forget Not the Field', Speranza claimed that the efforts of Irish political martyrs were documented in the subaltern history of struggle and recorded in the most inconspicuous sites of memory: 'The Greeks of old wrote the names of their heroes in letters of gold upon the walls of their temples; the Irish must search for the names of their heroes on the walls of a prison.' Having inherited this legacy of often residual but continual resistance, Ireland now required a new drive towards insurgency that would achieve a 'consecration of revolt'. The literary would take its place alongside the revolutionary in this new revolt, when 'words' would again 'clang like swords' and 'keep the martyrs of freedom for ever living before the eyes of the people'.[56]

Revolution was clearly a cultural affair as much as it was a matter of politics for Jane Wilde, who regarded both types of activity and expression as inseparable. In a point repeated by her son in Saint Paul and San Francisco, she argued that separation from England was the only remedy to this crisis: 'National Independence' was 'the magic phrase' that would animate, motivate and unite the scattered Irish diaspora 'as one people all over the world'. Liberation would lead to cultural renovation as well as political independence, with the new political ideas of republicanism finding 'visible expression in perhaps a higher national life than any Ireland has yet known'. This political modernity based on independence would heal the cultural wounds that had been inflicted by England during the 'national annihilation' of the Irish people, along with the destruction of their culture and institutions:

> Naturally the object of an alien Government was to extinguish the idea of a country; to degrade and obliterate heroic memories; to brand a patriot as a traitor, and nationality as treason; and in this manner the pride, self-respect, and self-reliance of the Irish people have been slowly murdered through the centuries [. . .][57]

Ireland's slow death by colonisation could be countered by preserving the memory of 'men [. . .] who have toiled, and fought, and suffered for some great idea, or some sublime word'. Words and deeds maintained the political and historical continuum of resistance that they represented. Popular recollection of 'warriors and orators' driven by 'swift impulses' that were 'fast and fiery as electric flashes' would counter the contemporary violence inflicted on the Irish through the legal means of coercion and the British state's continued imposition of a 'position of inferiority' on its Irish subjects. Ireland required a fresh infusion of these patriots' 'passionate fanaticism' as this was the only thing capable of preserving the remnants of Irish culture and identity against 'the uprooting of a nation' and its final 'extermination'.[58]

The Saint Patrick's Day Speech

During the US tour Wilde continued to publicly explore his mother's ideas about the need for Ireland to assume a decolonised republican modernity. Before he visited San Francisco, he drew directly on her radical ideas in an uncompromising speech that he delivered in Saint Paul, Minnesota, on Saint Patrick's Day. Before speaking to a large crowd consisting largely of Irish immigrants and Irish-Americans at the city's Opera House, he was introduced to the audience as the son of 'one of Ireland's noblest daughters'. Wilde delighted the audience by addressing them as 'my countrymen' and by describing the long history of colonial conquest beginning with the Anglo-Norman invasion of 1169. Praising his listeners for their efforts in igniting 'the fire of patriotism' among the Irish diaspora and keeping it 'burning brightly in the hearts of Ireland's sons', he expressed his own pride in the literary and political efforts expended by his mother 'in Ireland's cause'. Wilde described his country's experience of imperialist aggression, warfare, political breakdown and cultural destruction, all of which had reduced the Irish, 'a race once the most aristocratic in Europe', to a condition of slavery. Drawing on his parents' claims that Ireland had been the cultural hub of Europe prior to its conquest, he drew attention to its literary, architectural and artistic achievements:

> There was a time before the time of Henry II when Ireland stood at the front of all the nations of Europe in the arts, the sciences, and genuine intellectuality. The few books saved from the general wreck are remarkable for their literary excellence and beauty of illustration. There was a time, too, when Ireland was the university of Europe – when young monks educated in Ireland went forth as educators to all other European countries, while at the same time students from these same countries flocked to Ireland to study [. . .] under the great masters of Ireland. There was a time when Ireland led all other nations in working in gold. In those times no nation built so splendidly as did Ireland. The cathedrals, monasteries, and other edifices of those days showed a higher style of architecture than that of any other nation.[59]

Informed by his father's research in antiquarianism, Wilde's revivalist vision portrayed pre-colonial Ireland as a cultural sanctuary. Ruskin's Victorian shock doctrine, with its proposals for the destruction of colonised cultures and the appropriation of their material expressions is also challenged here.[60] Like his mother and her comrades in the Young Ireland movement, Wilde emphasised how colonial violence had achieved the near-annihilation of the Irish, and he lamented the destruction of a once-coherent, aesthetically-focused and recognisably intellectual culture that was now being eroded from the historical record. While Ruskin regarded political aggression as integral to the formation and development of a centralised and ever-advancing imperial culture, Wilde emphasised its catastrophic effect on the victims of colonisation. Their dispossession and displacement had almost destroyed a society that contributed much to the development of European civilisation, and little now remained of its architectural achievements:

> Those proud monuments to the genius of intellectuality of Ireland do not exist today. When the English came they were burned. But portions of these blackened moldering walls still remain to remind visitors of the beauty of the work wrought by Ireland, for the pleasure and enjoyment of Ireland in the days of her greatness.[61]

Despite their defeat and the civilisational decay that followed it, the Irish aesthetic heritage was resistant and could not be subdued by occupation, dispossession or political repression. 'Art,' Wilde declared, was the undiluted and final expression of 'the liberty-loving sentiment of a people.'

Articulated through its very mobile cultural turn, Irish nationalism defied censorship and state oppression through alternative means, ensuring that 'the artistic sentiment of Ireland was not dead in the hearts of her sons and daughters, though allowed no expression in their native country'. Appealing to the current of popular, diasporic nationalism now prevalent among the Irish and Irish Americans in the United States, Wilde reminded his audience that his presence in Saint Paul was due to this crisis:

> It is the sentiment which has induced you to meet here tonight to commemorate our patron saint [...] It finds expression in the love you bear for every running brook of your native land. It is shown in the esteem you bear for the names of the great men whose deeds and works have shed such luster upon Irish history. And when Ireland gains her independence, its schools of art and other educational branches will be revived and Ireland will regain the proud position she once held among the nations of Europe.[62]

As Wilde would also emphasise in his San Francisco lecture, artistic, cultural and political resistance were not abstract or atomised phenomena but expressions of radical agency and difference that materialised around the actions of those who continued to oppose the occupation of Ireland. A national cultural renaissance would establish political independence: by referring to pre-colonial Ireland as a fully formed 'nation' in the modern sense, he insisted that this would end with the liberation of the country.

Two days after he gave this lecture, *The Omaha Bee* accused Wilde of exhibiting 'depravity' in front of his audiences and reacted to his political and aesthetic beliefs with some racist verse accusing him of exploiting the trip for financial gain. In doing so it attacked his political stance by portraying him as being driven by the more privatised logic of the entrepreneur:

> Oh, Oscar Wilde, Aesthetic, mild,
> With hair well iled,
> And shirt front 'biled.'
> Oh, poet and scholar,
> You charge but a dollar
> For sight of your collar
> Which we willingly pay,
> And bless the bright day
> You happened our way.
> Midst Ireland's commotion
> You seized on the notion
> To cross the wide ocean
> To teach a great nation
> Its proper relation
> And aesthetic station [. . .][63]

In contrast to this and other attacks, the southern press was more sympathetic to Wilde during his summer visit to former Confederate states, where his comparisons of the postbellum reconstruction of the South to the conquest of Ireland were well received.[64]

Art and the Question of Occupation

Wilde gave the most important lecture of his US tour in San Francisco, where he spoke on four occasions to enthusiastic audiences that appreciated his countercultural sensibility, or what the journalist, Mary Watson, admiringly described as his air of 'eccentric individuality'.[65] The lecture, 'Irish Poets and Poetry of the Nineteenth Century', was given in Platt's Hall on the evening of Wednesday,

5 April 1882.⁶⁶ Wilde gave this talk by special request during his final public appearance in the city, which he again used as an opportunity to explain that modern Irish literary and cultural expression had been formed within the violent atmosphere of colonial occupation and emphasise the connections that bound literary writing to militant Irish separatism, as his mother had already done.

By the time he arrived in the city, Michael Davitt and Charles Stewart Parnell had been imprisoned for leading the Land League insurgency, and his visit coincided with that of the nationalist MP for Galway, Thomas Power O'Connor, who was in San Francisco at the close of his West Coast lecture tour, where he was soliciting American financial support for the Land League. The Young Ireland leader, John Mitchel also visited San Francisco in October 1881.⁶⁷ Described in the city's newspapers as his 'Celtic Song' and 'Burst of Patriotism', the local press reported that Wilde had now 'blossomed out into a full-blown Land Leaguer'.⁶⁸

The bulk of the poems discussed in the lecture outlined Irish militancy. Repeating the points that he raised in Saint Paul, Wilde stressed that, despite their destruction of Gaelic society and despite the harm done by English colonisers to the native 'beauties of Irish art', such violence 'could not destroy the poetry of the Celtic people, as that was something beyond the reach of the sword, and vandal hand of the conquering Saxon'. Addressing the destructive momentum of colonial violence and Irish resistance to it, Wilde explained to his audience that 'art sickens in slavery, rows languid in luxury, but reaches its full fruition under the fostering care of liberty'. Political submission represented the death of a culture because 'when the chains of slavery rust on a people's limbs, art dies'. Art was resistant to this withering because 'The poetry of the Irish people [. . .] ever kept alive the fires of patriotism in the hearts of the Irish people.'⁶⁹

Repeating his mother's ideas on the relationship between language and resistance (he told his audience that Thomas Davis' poems had schooled his mother in 'the meaning of the word country'), Wilde described poetry as compensating for Ireland's lack of political structure.⁷⁰ In the centuries-long struggle for liberation, poetry served as the primary medium of Irish resistance because, as a mobile, subaltern form, it evaded, challenged and subverted colonial power. Wilde argued that culture was the prime locus of national resistance, and was applauded when he declared that British policy in Ireland was inhibiting cultural expression as much as it was damaging the country's political development. Building on

Speranza's depiction of Ireland as a country struggling under 'the insulting tyranny of English rule',[71] he added:

> Since the English occupation we have had no national art in Ireland at all, and there is not the slightest chance of our having it ever until we get that right of legislative independence so unjustly robbed from us; until we are really an Irish nation – a nation for whose constitutional liberty Henry Grattan lived and died [. . .] There is, however, one art which no tyranny can kill and no penal laws can stifle, the art of poetry – an art which is one of the supreme triumphs of the race to which we belong [. . .][72]

As a subversive and intersticial form of cultural expression, poetry had survived prolonged and repeated inflictions of imperialist violence because it was practised and transmitted among the dispossessed. Wilde believed that it had proven more resilient than Grattan's parliament of the late eighteenth century, which, when it was dissolved with the Act of Union in 1800, underlined the transience of political institutions in comparison to the permanence of art. The poor, disenfranchised Irish had preserved and cultivated this literary and traditionally oral art form, ensuring its survival, along with native musical forms.

The *San Francisco Chronicle* reported Wilde's thoughts on this underground repository of Irish culture:

> 'The poetry and music of Ireland,' he said, 'have been not merely the luxury of the rich, but the very bulwark of patriotism, the very seed and flower of liberty.' He spoke of the beauty and glamour of the old Celtic legends, the romance that hung over the land, her fascinating old ruins and the predominance of the poetic spirit in the country, where of every old house had two harps ready for the traveller, and the highest place at the board was given to the man who could sing best of liberty.[73]

Wilde had inherited his parents' admiration for the cultural accomplishments of the Irish poor and presented this claim in highly romanticised terms. Stored and protected within the popular imaginary of the defeated, this enormously subversive archive formed the 'primary basis of Irish politics, the keystone of Irish liberty', and gave expression to their resistant 'Celtic imagination'. Unlike Arnold, who regarded Celtic (and, specifically, Irish) consciousness as primitive and unformed, Wilde believed that this heritage provided the Irish with their unique 'sentiment of modern thought'.[74] For Wilde, the modern Irish imagination had been forged by this long history of imperial violence and resistance.

Wilde also complained that the Dublin intelligentsia, themselves the cultural representatives of the Anglo-Irish élite, were profoundly hindered by their alienation from this native consciousness. This more authentic culture did not express their anachronistic views but articulated an inherently modern and liberating ideology of self-determination.[75] He claimed that the 'pure poetry' of the colonised and dispossessed Irish influenced the key literary figures of European Romanticism, including Goethe, Byron and Keats, while also inspiring Napoleon Bonaparte, the key political antagonist of Romantic-era Britain. In Dublin, Thomas Moore's poetry had 'sounded the right national note' by amplifying these literary and political connections and tensions, drawing Victorian Ireland's present very closely to its anticolonial past. His literary writing 'did quite as much as the eloquence of Grattan or the power of O'Connell for Irish liberty', providing an ideological and aesthetic bridge between these figures and the consciously modernising radicalism of the Young Ireland movement. The work of writers who had been involved in the movement combined literary endeavour with revolutionary avant-gardism, both of which were conducted at great personal risk: 'The poets of Young Ireland [. . .] made their lives noble poems also, men who had not merely written about the sword but were ready to bear it, who not only could rhyme to liberty, but could die for her also.' Their poetic achievement was matched by the seditious potential of their revolutionary activity and mobilised the reading public around newly modernised levels of 'national feeling' and separatist consciousness. In particular, Wilde cited the work of his mother's friend, Mary Kelly, who had published under the pseudonym, 'Eva of the Nation'. He described her as the epitome of Young Ireland's fusion of revolutionary political practice and poetics and stressed that her poems were 'permanent in only two things, their love of Liberty and their devotion to Beauty'.[76]

Three decades before the publication of James Joyce's *A Portrait of the Artist as a Young Man*, Wilde acknowledged how the colonised could master and subvert the language of the coloniser. In his San Francisco lecture he raised the issue of linguistic resilience and its relationship to political resistance:

> the poetic genius of the Celtic race never flags or wearies, it is as sweet by the groves of California as by the groves of Ireland, as strong in foreign lands as in the land which gave it birth – and indeed I do not know

anything more wonderful, or more characteristic of the Celtic genius, than the quick artistic spirit in which we adapted ourselves to the English tongue – the Saxon took our lands from us and left them desolate, we took their language and added new beauties to it [. . .]77

Wilde continued by praising the Irish in California, and particularly San Francisco, for being 'now and always so generous to the cause of Ireland', and his lecture amounted to a significant intervention in the political crisis at home. With its stress on the crystallisation of anticolonial art around modern literary and political expression, the Irish revolutionary literature that he praised was shown to bear a direct relationship with his own Aestheticism. Wilde used this opportunity to provide his audience with a clear indication of his views on art's capacity to achieve political liberation as well as its significance for the more privatised experience and consumption of culture, as he had already done in Saint Paul. Both registered on the imagination in profoundly subjective terms, and both were at odds with empire and capital. Like his mother, Wilde did not regard Irish culture as being cut off from the concerns of the diaspora and he concluded his speech by calling for the establishment of a centre for the study of Irish culture in San Francisco, with an appeal to his audience to found a library dedicated to Irish literature and establish a museum for Irish art in the city. In doing so, the Irish of San Francisco could honour their national sentiments by institutionalising them: as he told his audience in Saint Paul, culture found expression in nationalism, or 'the love you bear for every running brook of your native land'. It was also revealed 'in the esteem you bear for the names of the great men whose deeds and works have shed such luster upon Irish history'.78 Wilde's proposals for culture's potential to mobilise and advance the radical cause of Irish independence presented questions about art and Aestheticism in direct relation to the issue of political commitment.

Wilde believed that this correlation would restore the grandeur of Irish art: '[W]hen Ireland gains her independence, its schools of art and other educational branches will be revived and Ireland will regain the proud position she once held among the nations of Europe.'79 The San Francisco lecture confused some, who were now uncertain of the label of 'Irish-Englishman' that had been conferred on Wilde by the British and American press.80 His call for the consolidation of the Irish diaspora echoed his mother's appeals in her pamphlet, 'The American Irish' and with it he associated himself with resistance to British rule. The anticolonial beliefs that Wilde expressed in the United States also bear heavily on his progressive class politics and contextualise the complaint made in 'The Soul of Man Under Socialism', about 'the stupidity and hypocrisy and Philistinism of the English', which he described as the 'unbearable' problem that had also confronted the republican poet, Percy Bysshe Shelley, earlier in the nineteenth century.[81]

Notes

1. Wilde, 'Irish Poets and Poetry of the Nineteenth Century', p. 30.
2. Jerusha McCormack argues that Wilde's interest in Irish matters was limited to a fascination with Celticism and its emphasis on fate rather than agency. See 'Introduction: The Irish Wilde', in Jerusha McCormack (ed.), *Wilde the Irishman* (New Haven: Yale University Press, 1998), pp. 1–8, p. 2.
3. David Lloyd, *Nationalism and Minor Literature: James Clarence Mangan and the Emergence of Irish Cultural Nationalism* (Berkeley: University of California Press, 1987), p. xi.
4. Mary Watson, *People I Have Met: Short Sketches of Many Prominent Persons* (San Francisco: Francis, Valentine and Company, 1890), p. 51.
5. Michael Farrell has noted that between 1800 and 1921, at least 105 separate coercion acts were passed at Westminster. See Michael Farrell, *Emergency Legislation: The Apparatus of Repression* (Derry: Field Day, 1986), p. 5.
6. Ian Small, 'Introduction', in *Complete Works*, vol. 1, pp. ix–xxvi, xi.
7. O'Reilly was also a successful poet and novelist. See Ian Kenneally, *From the Earth, a Cry: The Story of John Boyle O'Reilly* (Dublin: Collins Press, 2011), pp. 205–13.
8. Small, 'Introduction', in *Complete Works*, vol. 1, p. xi.
9. As Martin argues, coercion is recommended as fundamental to governance in Arnold's *Culture and Anarchy*, which was first serialised as a series of essays in *Cornhill* magazine in 1867, the year of the Fenian insurgency and the Hyde Park riots. These and other essays by Arnold form part of his longer-term engagement with Irish politics. See Amy E. Martin, *Alter-Nations: Nationalisms, Terror, and the State in Nineteenth-Century Britain and Ireland* (Columbus: Ohio State University Press, 2012), especially chapter 2: 'Fenianism and the State'.
10. Matthew Arnold, 'The Study of Celtic Literature', in *The Study of Celtic Literature and Other Essays* (London: Dent, 1919), pp. 1–136, pp. 19, 27–8.
11. Ibid. pp. 47, 61, 70, 68.
12. Edward Said, *Orientalism* (London: Penguin, 1995), p. 11.

13. Arnold, 'The Study of Celtic Literature', in *The Study of Celtic Literature*, pp. 68, 75.
14. Ibid. p. 82.
15. Ibid. p. 83.
16. Wilde, 'Mr. Henry O'Neill, Artist', in *Complete Works*, vol. 6, p. 14.
17. Arnold, 'The Study of Celtic Literature', in *The Study of Celtic Literature*, p. 83.
18. Ibid. pp. 118, 119, 83, 84, 103.
19. Oscar Wilde, 'L'Envoi', in *Miscellanies* (London: Methuen, 1908), pp. 31–41, p. 31.
20. John Ruskin, 'Idolatry', in *Aratra Pentelici* (London: George Allen, 1907), pp. 35–68, pp. 52–4.
21. Ibid. pp. 54–5.
22. Mike Sanders, *The Poetry of Chartism: Aesthetics, Politics, History* (Cambridge: Cambridge University Press, 2012), p. 13.
23. Ruskin, 'Idolatry', in *Aratra Pentelici*, pp. 55–7.
24. Lewis and Smith, *Oscar Wilde Discovers America*, p. 137.
25. Ibid. p. 3.
26. Undated, quoted in Richard Butler Glaenzer, *Oscar Wilde in America*, unpublished ms., Folder 5, p. 8. UCLA Clark Library Wilde G543M3 081 [1900–20].
27. Lewis and Smith, *Oscar Wilde Discovers America*, p. 128.
28. See Ibid. pp. 72–3.
29. *Chicago Morning News*, undated, cited Glaenzer, *Oscar Wilde in America*, Folder 6, p. 3.
30. 'Irish Secret Societies', *The Wasp*, 10.357, 2 June 1883, p. 12. In the centrefold illustration, 'Asinine Oblations', Wilde is depicted collecting money for the Fenian movement along with Jeremiah O'Donovan Rossa, Michael Davitt and Charles Stewart Parnell. 'Asinine Oblations', *The Wasp*, 9.333, 16 December 1882, pp. 791–2.
31. *New York Times*, 19 January 1882, quoted in Lewis and Smith, *Oscar Wilde Discovers America*, p. 181.
32. *New York Tribune*, 5 November 1882, recorded in Glaenzer, *Oscar Wilde in America*, Folder 11, UCLA Clark Library, Wilde G54M3 081.
33. *Washington Post*, 22 January 1882. The cartoon is reproduced in Lewis and Smith, *Oscar Wilde Discovers America*, p. 101.
34. Charles G. Sauls to Oscar Wilde, 2 October 1882. Sauls wrote: 'I went to a Minstrel show where they burlesqued you awfully, but I suppose & hope you have good sense enough not to mind that.' UCLA Clark Library, Wilde S256L W672 1882 Oct. 2.
35. Archibald Forbes to Oscar Wilde, 26 January 1882. Clark Library Wilde F692L W6721 1882 Jan. 26.
36. *The Wasp* declared: 'Someone ought to take a smooth-bore club and pound this Wilde will-o'-the wisp upon the caboose pocket until the coroner could draw fee.' It also demanded that he be 'crippled with a bed-slat'. Untitled, *The Wasp*, 9.333, 16 December 1882, p. 797.

37. Lewis and Smith, *Oscar Wilde Discovers America*, p. 102.
38. Elizabeth Marbury to Oscar Wilde, 10 November 1894. UCLA Clark Library Wilde M312L W6721 [1894?] Nov. 10.
39. See David M. Friedman, *Wilde in America: Oscar Wilde and the Invention of Modern Celebrity* (New York: Norton, 2014); Ellmann, *Oscar Wilde*, chapters 5 and 6; Michèlle Mendelssohn, *Making Oscar Wilde* (Oxford: Oxford University Press, 2018).
40. Richard D'Oyly Carte to Howard Paul, 25 December 1881. UCLA Clark Library Wilde, Box 10, Folder 43, C322L P324 1881 Dec. 25.
41. Richard D'Oyly Carte, 'Oscar Wilde's Visit to America', 4 February 1882. UCLA Clark Library Uncat. Wilde mss, pp. 1–2.
42. See Gregory Castle, 'Misrecognising Wilde: Media and Performance on the American Tour of 1882', in Joseph Bristow (ed.), *Wilde Discoveries: Traditions, Histories, Archives* (Toronto: University of Toronto Press, 2013), pp. 85–117, p. 87.
43. See Amy E. Martin, 'Victorian Ireland: Race and the Category of the Human', *Victorian Review*, 40.1, Spring 2014, pp. 52–7.
44. Lewis and Smith, *Oscar Wilde Discovers America*, pp. 215–16, 108, 379.
45. Unfortunately, Engels' project went unfinished, but his draft chapters, outline and notes explain his comprehensive grasp of the reality of colonial violence in Ireland, as practised from the first Anglo-Norman invasions of the twelfth century until the late nineteenth century. See Frederick Engels, 'History of Ireland' and 'The Preparatory Material for the "History of Ireland"', in Karl Marx and Frederick Engels, *Ireland and the Irish Question,* trans. from the German by S. Ryazanskaya, D. Danemanis and V. Schneierson, from the French by K. Cook and from the Italian by B. Bean (London: Lawrence and Wishart, 1971), pp. 170–269.
46. See William Wilde, *Lough Corrib, its Shores and Islands* (Dublin: McGlashan and Gill, 1867).
47. Wilde to James Knowles, October 1881, in *Complete Letters*, p. 115
48. Jane Francesca Wilde (Speranza), 'The American Irish' (Dublin: William McGee, 1882, originally published New York, 1879), pp. 9, 15, 36–7, 28–9, 35.
49. Ibid. p. 1.
50. Ibid. pp. 1–2.
51. Ibid. p. 19.
52. Ibid. p. 2.
53. Ibid. p. 1.
54. Ibid. p. 2.
55. C. M. O'Keeffe to Lady Wilde, 23 June 186–? Clark Library Wilde 04122L W6712 [186–]? Jun. 23.
56. Speranza, 'The American Irish', p. 3.

57. Ibid. pp. 9–11.
58. Ibid. pp. 11, 19–20, 27.
59. *Saint Paul Globe*, quoted in Lewis and Smith, *Oscar Wilde Discovers America*, p. 225.
60. The neoliberal 'shock doctrine' described by Naomi Klein has its origins in this long history of imperialist violence, for which Ireland was a key laboratory. See Naomi Klein, *The Shock Doctrine: The Rise of Disaster Capitalism* (London: Penguin, 2007).
61. *Saint Paul Globe*, quoted in Lewis and Smith, *Oscar Wilde Discovers America*, p. 225.
62. Ibid. pp. 225–6.
63. *The Omaha Bee*, 19 March 19 1882, quoted in Lewis and Smith, *Oscar Wilde Discovers America*, p. 229.
64. See William Warren Rogers, 'In Defense of Oscar Wilde: Mary E. Bulloch on his Savannah Appearance in 1882', *The Georgia Historical Quarterly* 84.3, Fall 1990, pp. 475–85.
65. Mary Watson, *People I Have Met*, p. 50.
66. Robert Pepper, 'Introduction', in Oscar Wilde, *Irish Poets and Poetry*, p. 3.
67. Pepper, Ibid. pp. 15, 41.
68. *The Chronicle* and *Report*, quoted in Wilde, *Irish Poets and Poetry*, pp. 29, 19.
69. Ibid. p. 27.
70. Ibid. p. 33.
71. Jane Francesca Wilde, 'The American Irish', p. 18.
72. Oscar Wilde, 'Irish Poets and Poetry of the Nineteenth Century', p. 27.
73. Quoted Ibid. p. 28.
74. Ibid. p. 28.
75. Anglo-Irish anachronism is confronted through the mode of gothic in Sheridan Le Fanu's story of vampirism, 'Carmilla', and in Bram Stoker's 1897 novel, *Dracula*. Both works represent the Anglo-Irish aristocracy as vampiric and unproductive. The political connotations of these texts have been discussed by Margot Backus, Seamus Deane, Robert Tracey and Joseph Valente. See Backus, *The Gothic Family Romance,* Seamus Deane, *Strange Country: Modernity and Nationhood in Irish Writing since 1790* (Oxford: Oxford University Press, 1997), Robert Tracy, 'Introduction', in Joseph Sheridan Le Fanu, *In a Glass Darkly* (Oxford: Oxford University Press, 2008), pp. vii–xviii, and Joseph Valente, *Dracula's Crypt: Bram Stoker, Irishness and the Question of Blood* (Urbana and Chicago: University of Illinois Press, 2002).
76. Wilde, *Irish Poets and Poetry*, pp. 29–30, 32. Kelly was married to Kevin Izod O'Doherty, who had been transported to Australia for his involvement in the 1848 rebellion. Her *Poems, by 'Eva of The Nation'*, was published in San Francisco in 1877.

77. Wilde, *Irish Poets and Poetry*, p. 34.
78. Ibid. pp. 34, 25–6.
79. Wilde, 'Irish Poets and Poetry of the Nineteenth Century', p. 34; Lewis and Smith, *Oscar Wilde Discovers America*, pp. 225–6.
80. Untitled, *Denver Daily Times*, 11 April 1882, Glaenzer, *Oscar Wilde in America*, Clark Library, Folder 11.
81. Wilde, 'The Soul of Man', p. 239.

Chapter 2

Coercion and Resistance: *Vera . . . or the Land War*

In the first act of Wilde's 1880 play, *Vera; or, The Nihilists*, Russian radicals discuss the gruesome merits of political violence. As they debate the matter, a conspirator declares that '[o]ne dagger will do more than a hundred epigrams'.[1] Centring on the antagonism between what Wilde represented as the systemic and 'bloody work'[2] of state repression and the resistance that it provoked, Wilde's first play dramatises the contemporary political crisis in Ireland and criticises the anachronistic class system that prevailed in the country at the end of the nineteenth century. Its proposal is that terrorism was not the mindless work of apolitical criminals, but the result of political despair and the official violence that he criticised during his 1882 tour of the United States. Although ostensibly portraying the more distant phenomenon of Russian state repression, the ongoing deployment of coercion in Ireland is encoded in *Vera; or, The Nihilists*. While agrarian revolutionary tactics such as boycotting, moonlighting and rent strikes were familiar issues to the news consuming public of the early 1880s, Wilde's first play offers a barely veiled portrait of the politics of the Irish Land War, which it sets in contemporary Russia. By translating the Irish crisis into a revolutionary Russian setting, Wilde partially concealed his objective of collapsing the liberal-imperialist construction according to which late Victorian Britain presented itself as the home of democracy. Wilde's sympathy with Russian insurgents and nihilists opposed to Csarism is evident in *De Profundis*, 'The Soul of Man' and in 'The Critic as Artist', in which he compared revolutionaries in 'wounded Russia' to Symbolist poets. What united the artist and the agitator was their shared interest in suffering and 'the terrible fascination of pain'.[3] Wilde's mother, meanwhile, hoped that some pain could be inflicted on the British establishment with an outbreak of war in Europe that would weaken Britain's international position and present the Irish Fenians with an opportunity to organise another revolution,[4] but the assassination of Alexander II in St Petersburg in March 1881 only intensified the grip of reaction across the continent.

Wilde's seemingly contradictory personality mediated the tensions that were inherent in his experience as an Irish republican working in the British metropolis, where he also expressed opposition to imperialism. As we have seen in Chapter 1, he praised Irish Americans for supporting the anticolonial struggle at home and, by the time he learned about the deaths of Burke and Cavendish, he had already condemned the occupation of his country and the dispossession of its poorest people.[5] Written during the year before his US tour, *Vera; or, The Nihilists* strategically displaces the Irish Land War into its Russian setting and conveys the ideological sympathies that connected nineteenth-century Irish republicans to the broader political struggles of Europe and Russia.

Critics have emphasised the play's structural flaws, contrived dialogue and reliance on unlikely coincidences (Arthur Symons regarded it as a pointless curiosity)[6] but these same melodramatic devices, with greater refinement, would later characterise Wilde's society comedies of the 1890s.[7] The play's innovative transplantation of the Irish crisis into the safer, more distant setting of Slavic unrest invests it with the very immediate question of militant Irish nationalism, providing an early model for the subtler treatments of politics that Wilde dramatised during the 1890s. Thus, the contemporary crisis of Russian autocracy (under much public discussion since the Second Afghan War and the political show trials of members of the progressive Russian Land and Freedom movement of 1877–8)[8] becomes a surrogate setting for the much closer crisis of the Irish Land War. My reading of this play is influenced by Sos Eltis' interpretation of *Vera; or, The Nihilists* as a blueprint for his later, commercially successful works which offer more strategically articulated critiques of empire and capital. By employing these distancing effects Wilde carefully detached the drama from what Eltis describes as the 'delicate political arena' of late Victorian Britain and its colonial and class crises.[9] Throughout the 1890s Wilde refined the ideas that he expressed in *Vera* . . . and rather than abandoning them, translated the very immediate issue of state violence and coercion into the more generally palatable form of the social comedy (Symons claimed that the play's 'excited' content was far more sensational than Wilde's later work).[10] This more explicitly political drama provoked critical hostility before it was even performed, and the antagonism that it aroused explains Wilde's more sensitive treatment of the themes of imperialism, coercion and class in his later plays.

The political message of *Vera; or, The Nihilists* was uncompromising and the play conveys the social and aesthetic reflexivity that was so central to late-nineteenth-century melodrama. Wilde's attempt to popularise political themes by presenting them at a barely concealed remove from contemporary events was not unique. Dion Boucicault, who offered to mentor Wilde and invest in his writing when they met in the United States,[11] had already discovered that, with careful timing, Irish politics could make for marketable entertainment: his romanticised interpretation of the Fenian uprising of 1867, *The Shaughraun*, was staged seven years after the failure of the rebellion, in 1874. Premiered before American audiences a year before its first performance in London, Boucicault's play was followed by his appeal for the release of Irish political prisoners in an open letter published in the *Daily Telegraph* in 1876.[12] The political potential of melodrama also appealed to the Fenians themselves: William Mackey Lomasney, who was the most active of Jeremiah O'Donovan Rossa's dynamiters, wrote a nationalist play of his own, entitled *Irish Hearts*, which was performed at the Standard Theatre in Chicago.[13]

However, Wilde's play did not appear in the wake of an abortive outbreak, but intervened in the Irish Land War, which erupted in 1879 and was ongoing at the point at which he composed and tried to stage the play. *Vera; or, The Nihilists* was a literary intervention in this ongoing, popular insurgency that Wilde intended to be taken seriously, and which he did not want to be perceived as depicting an insincere or 'operatic conspiracy'.[14] However, the play was challenged from the outset by the competitive and thoroughly marketised spectacularity of late-nineteenth-century popular theatre.

In this fast-moving environment, popular dramas that failed to satisfy audience demand for constant innovation or 'hyperstimulus' often struggled commercially.[15] This was a requirement that even Boucicault would fail to meet by the mid-1880s as even his plays began to appear *passé*.[16] Although Wilde also failed to keep pace with melodrama's very rapid evolution and the momentum that continually updated the genre's keynote features of intense action and rapid, crowd-pleasing spectacles, he learned from his experience and brilliantly lampooned these techniques in *The Importance of Being Earnest* over a decade after the curtain had finally gone down on his theatrical nihilists.[17] The outlandishness and ideological referentiality[18] of melodramatic theatre provided the language, form and aesthetic diction through which Wilde dramatised the Irish crisis and contradicted the popular imperialist perception that contemporary revolutionaries were committed to violence for its own sake. As Eltis has shown, *Vera; or, The Nihilists* explores the relationship between state terror and insurgent violence through its complex registration of Wilde's own republican beliefs. The play's necessarily guarded but 'almost revolutionary' critique of state violence contradicts contemporary dramatisations of Russian nihilism as the work of lunatics.[19] Reading the play exclusively as an examination of nihilism, Eltis does not consider it as an adaptation of Irish politics but her interpretation of Wilde's exploitation and frustration of the genre's expectations outlines the deeper, complex and consistently ironic patterns and layers of political meaning that were overlooked by late Victorian critics.

Wilde rather indiscreetly exposed his political ambitions when, after completing the play in September 1880, he informed Edward Smyth-Pigott, the Lord Chamberlain's Examiner of Plays, that he was 'working at dramatic art because it's *the democratic* art'.[20] A year later, he described the play to his university friend, George Curzon, as 'my first attack on Tyranny', indicating that further radical interventions were to come.[21] *Vera; or, The Nihilists* implicitly articulated the 'practical republicanism' that Wilde claimed had made his mother famous,[22] but shortly after making these declarations of its revolutionary purpose the play's London premiere was abandoned due to what the *World*, edited by his brother, Willie, described as its disturbance of 'the present state of political feeling in England'.[23]

When *Vera* was eventually but briefly staged in New York in 1883, *Punch* denounced it as propagandistic 'rot' that exposed Wilde's own, secret 'life Republican', all of which, it declared, was 'Vera bad', indeed.[24] British newspapers reprinted hostile reviews from the New York press denouncing the play as a 'coarse' and 'common' effort, an 'unreal' and 'sickening rant' composed of 'bantam gabble about freedom and the people'. Having offended the ruling class sensibilities that were serviced by the New York *Times*, *Herald* and *Tribune*, Wilde's fusion of class politics and anticolonialism was deemed unacceptable by American conservatives, just as it had been by their British peers.[25] However, he was not without supporters: the play's expressions of democratic sentiment were noted in the *New York Mirror*, which identified its subject matter with the broader, radical objectives of Wilde's Aestheticism and its democratic demands for the 'development of a taste for all that is beautiful on earth'.[26]

The play's critical damnation coincided with the opening act of another kind of radical political performance taking place in Ireland, Britain and the United States. Beginning with an explosion at Salford Barracks in January 1881, the Fenian dynamite campaign continued with attacks targeting military, political and symbolic sites in London and other British cities. With these bombings the Irish crisis assumed a central presence in the late Victorian political imagination. *Vera; or, The Nihilists*, and its preoccupation with Russian political violence already seemed to contemporary reviewers to be hitting much too close to home and Wilde had already acknowledged that his 'unavowedly republican' ideas would not be tolerated in England.[27] His realisation that this radical perspective was not just unacceptable, but 'unthinkable' and, in dramatic terms, unrepresentable in England, led him to warn another correspondent about the unique hazards of staging political theatre in London.[28]

The Mediation of 'Outrage'

Composed over two years, when it was subjected to lengthy revisions and corrections, the play's commercial prospects were not great at a moment when official violence was peaking in Ireland and while Fenians were detonating bombs in Britain.[29] The play implied that state violence was the signature tactic of British policy in Ireland and addresses the imposition of martial law, including the paramilitary policing methods with which it was enforced, the internment of political prisoners and the general suspension of rights. These had been the essentially permanent methods of controlling Ireland following the introduction of the Crime and Outrage Bill in 1847 when Irish peasants were dying of starvation and disease *en masse*. The measure was repeatedly renewed until 1871, when it was updated to include the suspension of *Habeas Corpus*, which had been separately legislated for since 1793. The Bill was again renewed in 1881, while even more draconian powers were imposed by Arthur Balfour's Criminal Law and Procedure Act of 1887. The absolutism legislated by these Acts throughout the nineteenth century underlines the contradictory nature and limited scope of late Victorian parliamentary democracy. Both factions of British power at Westminster updated and renewed them, as Tories and Liberals frequently deployed increasingly violent and totalising methods to repress popular political dissent in Ireland.[30]

The violent reality of coercion was manifested on the night of 5 May 1882, when, as Wilde toured Pennsylvania, the Royal Irish Constabulary opened fire on a mass demonstration in Ballina, County Mayo. Armed with shotguns, fixed bayonets and clubs, a detachment of police attacked a crowd of over 3,000 people celebrating the Kilmainham Treaty and the release from prison of Charles Stewart Parnell, Michael Davitt and other Land League activists. The shooting began when police were jeered for seizing musical instruments from a children's band that had been playing at the head of the procession. Witnesses denied the RIC's claims that stones were thrown before the police started firing, and at the subsequent inquests the commanding officer failed to produce any evidence of the injuries he claimed his men had suffered.[31] Terrible wounds were inflicted on several children and two of them, 13-year-old Patrick Melady and another, named only as Kelly in press reports, died from their injuries. The survivors' injuries included head wounds (in one case, shotgun pellets entered a child's head behind his ear and exited through his eye socket), spinal damage, punctured lungs and severed fingers. At Patrick Melady's inquest, the jury was told that buildings on King Street had been 'riddled' with shotgun blasts that shattered windows and damaged homes and businesses in the town centre, while the RIC commander admitted losing count of how many volleys he ordered his men to fire into the crowd.[32]

Within days, the already diluted coverage of the 'Ballina Tragedy', as the mass shooting was described in the press, was immediately overshadowed by more detailed newspaper reports on the Phoenix Park 'murders'. One night after the RIC attack in Ballina, and just hours after having been sworn into office as the new Chief Secretary for Ireland, Lord Frederick Cavendish was stabbed to death outside the Viceregal Lodge in the Phoenix Park in Dublin by a Fenian splinter group called 'The Invincibles'. His Permanent Under Secretary, Thomas Burke, was also killed. Cavendish's predecessor, William 'Buckshot' Forster had resigned in protest against the Kilmainham Treaty, which he perceived as an affront to British authority; this double killing of the new Chief Secretary and his most powerful advisor at Dublin Castle made newspaper headlines for months. In contrast to press representation of what happened in County Mayo as an inadvertent, even innocent loss of control by the RIC, the media framed this attack as a 'demoniac crime' designed 'to subvert all law and order by the terrorism of assassination'. Portrayed as an example of 'Fenian malignity', the Phoenix Park killings were used from the outset to illustrate the inherent wickedness of Irish nationalism.[33]

Coverage of the attack in the unionist and imperialist press swamped nationalist reports of the RIC shootings in County Mayo, as gruesome details of the stabbings were circulated widely so as to amplify the narrative of Fenian depravity. Focusing on the existential threat posed by the 'evil in Ireland', British and Irish newspapers demanded the rapid suppression of Fenianism in retaliation for this 'enormous crime'. Cavendish's grieving widow was enlisted in a campaign calling for the extermination, or 'putting down' of Irish republicanism and its 'reign of murder' and 'foul assassination'. By constructing an image of the abject and even sublime brutality of anticolonial militancy (*The Times*, in one of its many exhaustive reports, described the deed as 'unspeakably revolting'),[34] the British press redacted imperialist violence from public view by ignoring the frequency and intensity with which coercion was applied. This narrative tactic of reducing Irish insurgency to the level of unimaginable barbarity, violence and 'slaughter'[35] was already very familiar to observers on the left. Writing for the French republican newspaper, *La Marseillaise*, in 1870, Jenny Marx complained about the distorting 'kaleidoscope of the English press' which operated on behalf of the state and 'in accordance with the orders received'. She described its objective as the vindication of official force and the justification of Britain's 'regime of white terror in Ireland'. Providing ideological justification for 'the plundering and even extermination of the tenant farmer and his family by the landlord', she explained that the British press defended state violence in Ireland for representing the final sanction of 'property right', while, in contrast, 'the desperate farmer's revolt against his ruthless executioner is called an agrarian outrage'.[36]

By explaining the killing and maiming of children by the RIC in Mayo as the unfortunate, unintended and, ultimately, insignificant outcome of uncontrollable events for which the state and its agents held no moral or political responsibility, British press coverage of Land War incidents like these distracted the reading public from the structurally violent nature of imperial rule in Ireland. Hyperbolic reports on the deaths of Cavendish and Burke, which persisted for over a year, portrayed the Phoenix Park killings as yet another example of Irish 'outrage' and depicted resistance to coercion as a random, cruel and apolitical phenomenon that bore no relation to state repression. While the violent policing of demonstrations with bayonet charges and shotgun volleys went largely unreported in the Victorian press, insurgent actions were represented as the work of barbarians. This construction of violence as a phenomenon that travelled in a single direction denied the colonial dynamic that produced it and was intended to depoliticise the Irish crisis. One particularly slanted justification for state violence appeared in the *Daily News*, which complained that children's bands like the one fired on by the RIC were 'abominable nuisances' in provincial towns like Ballina, where the police finally dropped their guard and fell victim to the relentless provocations and 'determination of the urchins'.[37] As Niall Whelehan has shown, the exercise of lethal force by European states against their domestic opponents at the end of the nineteenth century places Fenian activity against a wider context of frequent and spectacular displays of state violence. Whereas the press expressed astonishment and disgust over the stabbings of the 'martyred' politician, Cavendish, and his local fixer, Burke,[38] the Phoenix Park killings took place in an era during which states regularly deployed full spectrum coercion as a first resort against popular democratic movements.[39]

Wilde's Views on Insurgency

When asked to respond to the Phoenix Park killings by a journalist from the *Philadelphia Enquirer*, Wilde explained the dialectical relationship between colonial violence and the resistance that it provoked. With considerable irony, he drew attention to the decontextualisation of the crisis in Ireland with an unflattering assessment of Cavendish: 'I do not see why they should wish to assassinate mediocrity, for he was just an easy-going, pleasant, mediocre gentleman, whom no one could have a grudge against.' 'Such, too,' he told his interviewer, 'was Mr Burke.' Dismissing both men as inconsequential figures (Wilde had, by now, learned the necessarily tactical value of ambiguity when discussing current political violence), he added:

> The assassinations were undoubtedly the result of intoxication at what the Irish thought a complete victory (i.e., the releases of Davitt and Parnell). They turned liberty into license. But when liberty comes with hands dabbled in blood, it is hard to shake hands with her, eh? [. . .] But then we forget how much England is to blame [. . .] she is merely reaping the fruit of seven centuries of injustice.[40]

Wilde's views on the need to understand the pressures that give rise to revolutionary violence and which underline the reasons for its 'bloody purpose',[41] explained how the pair functioned within the historical pattern of colonial violence and within which both men personified and managed the structural apparatus of the coercive state. Prefacing his remark with the stock condemnation of insurgent action that is still demanded of public figures, Wilde rationalised the attack by drawing attention to its place within the longer, permanently violent chronology of the Irish experience of occupation, about which he had also recently spoken in San Francisco. Their deaths, Wilde explained, were a consequence of this ongoing crisis: as the British state's key figures in Ireland, they represented imperial power and the injustice upon which it rested. In this very significant statement Wilde also drew attention to colonialism's distortion of reality: disguised, legalised and constantly adapted and modernised over the course of centuries, violence remained the principal technique through which Ireland was being governed.[42]

Even Land League sympathisers in the US, including John Boyle O'Reilly, attempted to distance themselves from the stabbings by describing them as the depoliticised and personalised action 'of a Guiteau or a madman' (Charles J. Guiteau had assassinated President James Garfield over a series of rejected applications for consular posts the previous summer).[43] While Cavendish had been, for a few hours, Ireland's most senior colonial administrator, Thomas Burke, whom Anna Parnell described as 'the real ruler of Ireland',[44] was a close friend of the Wilde family and had dined at their home in Merrion Square. Shortly after the attack, Jane Wilde wrote to her son, describing the atmosphere of uncertainty and fear that had taken hold in the country, lamenting the end of 'Poor Tom Burke' and adding 'What a fate!'[45] While the press claimed that Burke was politically neutral, he was central to the administration of the state: having advised 'Buckshot' Forster on the application of his Protection of Persons and Property Act from its introduction in January 1881, he administered the measure's deployment. Denounced by Michael Davitt as an exercise in 'political tyranny', condemned by Charles Stewart Parnell as a form of 'legalized violence', and viewed by the Land League as legislating for an official 'system of terrorism and [. . .] military violence', the Act allowed for the imprisonment without trial of almost 1,000 people whom Burke's agents, reporting to his offices in Dublin Castle, had identified as radicals.[46]

Moving amid these intersecting spheres of cultural and political influence, wherein rebels and reactionaries regularly crossed the family threshold at Merrion Square, Jane Wilde was closely connected to militant republicans and their opponents within the condensed political atmosphere of Dublin. When news of Burke's fate reached

Oscar Wilde he was very conscious of the overlap between literary and political expression, and of the need to balance them against the delicate framework of Ireland's unstable political grid. This web, in which power, influence and resistance collided, was itself charged with the antagonistic energies of authority and rebellion – the central tensions that underlined public and cultural life in colonial Dublin and were managed by Dublin Castle's meticulous régime of surveillance. Wilde's own radical self-awareness was accentuated by his parents' efforts to structure an intellectual sphere within their salon, where government agents and Fenian sympathisers circulated around discussions of art, literature, politics and history. Burke's visits to the Wilde residence, which was also visited by republicans like Christopher O'Keeffe, reveals, in turn, the strange adjacency of these political opponents in late-nineteenth-century Dublin: Speranza entertained Dublin Castle's principal administrator while, simultaneously, she criticised British rule and cultivated her own profile as Irish nationalism's 'queen of culture'.[47] The often rather slight removes that separated coercionists like Burke from the radicals they pursued and imprisoned gave Oscar Wilde a keen sense of the importance of developing a politically strategic art, along with a sharp understanding of the mechanics of political repression and the dangers of mobilising dissent.

Wilde's own integration into London's powerful cultural circles was not, then, the unexpected appearance of an ambitious upstart who was eager to abandon his Irish identity, as Curtis Marez has claimed. He had been raised within the culturally compressed and politically intimate atmosphere of the colonial city within which his parents had learned the value of networking. Most importantly, these efforts afforded them the freedom to do so publicly – writers like O'Keeffe and his friend, Jeremiah O'Donovan Rossa, who criticised British rule from outside this protective sphere, were imprisoned. Stressing the contradictory impulses that characterised Anglo-Irish feeling in late-nineteenth-century Ireland, Marez emphasises that Wilde's own theoretical paradoxes were the result of this colonial background, a context that was coloured by the waves of political crisis and instability that characterised life there. Arguing that these contradictions distracted him from Irish nationalism to the extent that he always adhered to the 'preconditions [. . .] of Empire', Marez claims that Wilde was motivated by a desire to be assimilated by the English.[48] However this dismissal of his anti-imperialism too readily assumes an abrupt transition from an Irish subjectivity toward a new self-identification as British and, as we have seen with the public criticism to which he was subjected throughout the early 1880s, Wilde's cultural and political status as an outsider, alien and radical was criticised by the imperialist media as often as it challenged his qualifications as a public intellectual.

Vera; or, The Nihilists

Such, then, were the politically-charged circumstances during the lapse between the first publication of *Vera; or, The Nihilists*, in September 1880, and its eventual performance in New York three years later. Stage and society are separated by a fragile boundary in the play, as its barely concealed subject matter – the repression of the Irish peasantry – becomes clear. Its Russian setting is under constant surveillance as the melodrama unfolds in a land where 'every street [. . .] [is] filled with spies, every house with traitors', and the 'dread night of tyranny' mirrors Ireland under coercion.[49] Comparisons of Ireland with Russia were common in contemporary literary and political discussions: in *Moby-Dick*, first published in 1851, Herman Melville compared the Irish to the Russian peasantry. When Ishmael discusses the suffering of captured whales, he asks: 'What are the sinews and souls of Russian serfs and Republican slaves but Fast-Fish [. . .] What to that redoubted harpooner, John Bull, is poor Ireland but a Fast-Fish?'[50] Shortly after the Fenian rebellion of 1867, Karl Marx also observed that Britain's treatment of Irish political prisoners had no parallel except Imperial Russia's persecution of revolutionaries, an analogy that was repeated by Engels in 1872.[51] In 1867 the militant English poet, W.J. Linton, whose work Wilde admired, argued that in Ireland, Russia and elsewhere '[m]isgovernment and oppression and persecution are the same [. . .] whether under the ordering of a Nicholas or a Castlereagh'.[52] In 1886, the Russian nihilist, Sergius Stepniak, praised what he considered the 'deep and lasting influence' of the organisational model provided by the Irish Land League and proposed it as an example for radical movements in Russia.[53]

The play opens with a Prologue in which Vera Sabouroff, a barmaid working at her father's tavern on a road leading to Siberia, discovers that her brother, Dmitri, is being transported to a forced labour camp. When Dmitri appears in a convoy of prisoners that stops at the tavern he asks Vera to avenge his imprisonment. Later, at the beginning of the first Act, set five years after the Prologue, his sister has established herself as the nihilist movement's most deadly assassin. Although she is now in love with her comrade, Alexis, the pair cannot marry as they have pledged their lives to the overthrow of the Czar. When one of their secret meetings is interrupted by the military, Alexis saves the group by revealing that he is in fact the Czarevitch – son of the emperor and heir to the Russian throne. This revelation only intensifies Vera's love for him while antagonising the rest of her comrades: in the second Act, after the Czar and his tyrannical Prime Minister, Prince Paul Maraloffski, criticise Alexis' democratic beliefs, the emperor is assassinated with a shot fired through an open window. Alexis ascends to the throne and exiles Prince Paul to France but instead the Prime Minister infiltrates the nihilists with the intention of provoking them into killing the new, liberal Czar. This task is given to Vera but when she confronts Alexis in the fourth Act he announces his plans to reform the state. When he is confronted by Vera, the Czar asks her to marry him but when she accepts she remembers that she must now prevent the nihilists from initiating their back-up assassination plan. To do so she stabs herself, then throws the bloody dagger out of the palace window to make them believe that the Czar has been killed, then dies as the curtain falls, declaring 'I have saved Russia!'[54]

Despite its Russian setting, the play's discussion of official violence makes it very clear that Wilde's critique of tyranny is aimed at the British state. Wilde's opposition to coercion directed from Westminster and Dublin Castle is thinly ciphered when Vera asks: 'Do you know what martial law means? It means the strangling of a whole nation!' The theme of conflict between the imperial state and its republican opponents is manifested to the point of obviousness, so that when the President of the nihilists declares that '[e]very nation is fit for a republic', Vera's hatred for the 'crowned dog' at the head of the state resonates with anti-British sentiment. The colonial administration in Ireland is barely disguised as the Czar's unstable police state, which the nihilists aim to 'change to a republic'. When one of the revolutionaries announces that 'what Russia needs is a Republic',[55] Wilde again grounds his melodramatic plot in the struggle between the coercive British state and the Irish republican Fenian movement, adding contemporary relevance to its dramatisation of this nearby conflict.

In the first Act, the nihilists claim that revolutionary deeds are of more importance than political words. When the Professor announces the subject of discussion as 'assassination considered as a method of political reform', Michael replies: 'I think little of pen and ink in revolutions. One dagger will do more than a hundred epigrams.'[56] By means of this reflexive and particularly subversive statement, Wilde asks the audience to consider why the cultural and literary endeavours of the liberal intelligentsia appear pointless to those desperate enough to take action against the state. This irony urges us to consider the immediacy of insurgency: as Eltis has shown, the play was written in a dangerously repressive atmosphere in which '[w]ords without deeds were sufficient grounds for imprisonment', and it was staged at a moment when the expression of radical opinion was a hazardous step for any dramatist operating in Britain.[57] This point is encoded along with Wilde's other subversive statements, while the play's melodramatic register performs a distancing function, which becomes apparent when Maraloffski advises the revolutionaries that '[g]ood kings are the only dangerous enemies that modern democracy has'.[58] This direct swipe at Britain's constitutional monarchy exposes the concealment of repressive policies behind the façade of modern liberalism, subverting the play's conventional ending and bringing Wilde's views closer to Jenny Marx's perspective on Ireland.

The Prologue's pastoral setting in a militarised countryside where the threat of political imprisonment is omnipresent also reflects the occupation of Ireland. Policed by the Czar's troops, the peasantry exist on the brink of annihilation and their collective hunger is a reminder of the decimation of rural Ireland during the 1840s and 1850s. The ongoing threat of further mass starvation remained an immediate preoccupation for Irish separatists, bringing the Czar's transformation of Russia into a terrorised 'wide waste'[59] into close proximity with what Wilde described in San Francisco as the 'general wreck'[60] of occupied Ireland. The traumatised country that Karl Marx described as having been shattered through relentless cycles of political and economic destruction and cultural 'sterilisation'[61] is presented to audiences in this allegorisation of Ireland.

The tension between revolutionary ideology and absolutist hegemony is central to the play, and the total power of the coercive state is exposed during Vera's encounter with political prisoners in the Prologue. During this exchange, in which the heroine meets her captive brother on his way to Siberia, Wilde exposes repression in the style of Sergei Nechaev's 1869 manifesto, *Catechism of the Revolutionist*:

> Vera (*advances to the Nihilists*): Sit down; you must be tired. (*Serves them food.*) What are you?
> A Prisoner: Nihilists.
> Vera: Who put you in chains?

Prisoner: Our Father the Czar.
Vera: Why?
Prisoner: For loving liberty too well.
Vera (*to prisoner who hides his face*): What did you want to do?
Dmitri: To give liberty to thirty millions of people enslaved to one man.
Vera (*startled at the voice*): What is your name?
Dmitri: I have no name.
Vera: Where are your friends?
Dmitri: I have no friends.
Vera: Let me see your face!
Dmitri: You will see nothing but suffering in it. They have tortured me.
Vera (*tears the cloak from his face*): Oh, God! Dmitri! my brother![62]

This nihilistic mantra is repeated at the beginning of Act 1, when the conspirators' oath is recited:

'To strangle whatever nature is in us; neither to love nor to be loved, neither to pity nor to be pitied, neither to marry nor to be given in marriage, till the end is come; to stab secretly by night; to drop poison in the glass; to set father against son, and husband against wife; without fear, without hope, without future, to suffer, to annihilate, to revenge.'[63]

Renouncing all connections with any type of bourgeois existence and swearing loyalty to their cause of vengeance, Wilde's nihilists are committed to total but negative revolution. In this sphere, personal relations are abandoned and the very concept of family is rejected, a promise that is also made by Vera, when she promises 'to annihilate and revenge' and dedicates herself to the ideology and practice of terrorism[64] (Vera is modelled on Vera Zassoulich, who attempted to assassinate the Russian Chief of Police in 1878).[65] Her desire to dissolve existing society contrasts with the alienation felt by the nihilist, Evgeny Vasilev, or Bazarov, in Ivan Turgenev's 1862 novel, *Fathers and Sons*. In the midst of the social catastrophe generated by Russian autocracy, Bazarov expresses his disillusionment not only with society but with the potential of language itself when he reflects that, during times of political and moral crisis '[i]t's astonishing how a man can still believe in words'.[66] Turgenev was Wilde's favourite Russian author[67] but their representations of nihilism differ in that Wilde stages the thoroughly negative politics of revenge as the outcome of popular repression. The culture of desperation, of which his nihilists are violent agents, and the terrorism that they practise, are direct results of the political collapse of the state. In Turgenev's novel, Bazarov's deeply individualised and introspective dissent is portrayed rather differently (and less shockingly) as the consequence of a more private logic of despair.

The play's central theme is that mutual destruction is assured under conditions of widespread terror. This materialises on stage with the Czar's impulsive proclamation of martial law, which is met with Vera's call for revolutionary action against the régime:

> Vera: Ay, martial law. The last right to which the people clung has been taken from them. Without trial, without appeal, without accuser even, our brothers will be taken from their houses, shot in the streets like dogs, sent away to die in the snow, to starve in the dungeon, to rot in the mine. Do you know what martial law means? It means the strangling of a whole nation. The streets will be filled with soldiers night and day; there will be sentinels at every door. No man dare walk abroad now but the spy or the traitor. Cooped up in the dens we hide in, meeting by stealth, speaking with bated breath; what good can we do now for Russia?
> President: We can suffer at least.
> Vera: We have done that too much already. The hour is now come to annihilate and to revenge.
> President: Up to this the people have borne everything.
> Vera: Because they have understood nothing. But now we, the Nihilists, have given them the tree of knowledge to eat of and the day of silent suffering is over for Russia.
> Michael: Martial law, Vera! This is fearful tidings you bring.
> President: It is the death warrant of liberty in Russia.
> Vera: Or the tocsin of revolution.
> Michael: Are you sure it is true?
> Vera: Here is the proclamation. I stole it myself at the ball to-night from a young fool, one of Prince Paul's secretaries, who had been given it to copy. It was that which made me so late.
> (*Vera hands proclamation to Michael, who reads it.*)
> Michael: 'To ensure the public safety—martial law. By order of the Czar, father of his people.' The father of his people!
> Vera: Ay! a father whose name shall not be hallowed, whose kingdom shall change to a republic, whose trespasses shall not be forgiven him, because he has robbed us of our daily bread; with whom is neither might, nor right, nor glory, now or for ever.[68]

Terror is represented here as the outcome of the repressive policies and actions of the state. The Czar's plan to control the population through military occupation and the denial of rights is built upon a foundation of total surveillance which is presented as a form of systemic violence. Constantly monitored by the police, soldiers and informers, the revolutionaries are compelled into plotting desperate measures against the Czar, and the violent dialectic within which they are forced to act is itself produced by the 'fearful' moral vacuum created by the state's imposition of censorship and political closure. The great irony here is that revolutionaries like Vera, who speak and act against it, are now found to be reproducing the destructive logic of their oppressor, even to the point of self-destruction. They are portrayed by Wilde as being motivated by their experience of alienation and exclusion, and by the intensity of their own desire to counter the hegemonising and desensitising effects of the official violence of the government. Their answer to the state is their drive toward destruction, which is punctuated with deeds of their own that are designed 'to annihilate and to revenge'.[69]

Wilde's discussion of the Irish crisis is presented at a necessary remove but the seemingly distant 'tocsin of revolution' sounds closer to home as the Czar's declaration of martial law mirrors imperial legislation in Ireland. By associating the official violence of the British state with the tyranny of Czarism, and by suggesting the need to replace monarchical absolutism with the democratic structure of a republic, Wilde situated his Russian terrorists alongside Irish Fenianism and socialist politics in general.

Imperial Patriarchy and Anticolonial Feminism

The Czar's promise to eradicate all opposition to his rule highlights Wilde's critique of the coercive, anti-democratic state. When the Czarevitch declares his republicanism and his loyalty to 'my brothers, the people', his father replies by threatening to raze Saint Petersburg. His antagonism toward the revolutionaries is also gendered as he regards the female revolutionary as particularly threatening:

> 'The people! The people! A tiger which I have let loose on myself; but I will fight it to the death. I am done with half measures. I shall crush these Nihilists at a blow. There shall not be a man of them, no, nor a woman either, left alive in Russia. Am I Emperor for nothing, that a woman should hold me at bay? Vera Sabouroff shall be in my power. I swear it, before a week is ended, though I burn my whole city to find her. She shall be flogged by the knout, stifled in the fortress, strangled in the square! [. . .] For two years her hands have been clutching at my throat; for two years she has made my life a hell; but I shall have revenge. Martial law

[. . .] martial law over the whole Empire; that will give me revenge. A good measure, Prince, eh? A good measure.'[70]

Here, Wilde amplifies the comprehensive and totalising nature of imperialist violence as the severity of state violence against women is matched by the Czar's promise to annihilate an entire city in his pursuit of insurgents. His recourse to exemplary and ritualised force is articulated through a sadistic fantasy in which the coercive action of the state becomes an expression of the personalised desire of a brutal monarch. In this fantasy, violence is perpetrated against Vera through the official means of imprisonment, corporal punishment and, finally, execution. Fearful of the threat posed by radicalised women, the Czar promises a prolonged cycle of violence wherein the complete physical and political destruction of the female revolutionary is achieved within the broader context of the deployment of martial law against all of his subjects. This coercive fantasy is intensified by the Czar's projection of its infliction upon the resistant female subject while it is also charged with a hegemonising thrust directed against the entire population. Total violence in its actual and rhetorical forms is the first resort of the imperial state, both against individual antagonists and those whom Prince Paul derides in an anti-democratic aside as the 'common mob'.[71]

The play's anticolonial content is amplified by this focus on the influence of revolutionary women, and Vera is later described by the Czar's ministers as a revolutionary 'she-devil', while her comrades complain when she is absent that the 'whole fire of revolution seems fallen into ashes when she is not here'.[72] Vera's militancy mirrors the radicalism of the Ladies' Land League which was established in Ireland to provide leadership and direction to forms of agitation that lay beyond the terms of the 1881 Coercion Act.[73] While the state showed that it had no qualms about attacking or imprisoning working women protestors, Michael Davitt predicted that women could not be as easily interned or brutalised by the police or British army but female agitators proved 'more dangerous to despotism than men'.[74] Heather Laird has emphasised the ingenuity, organisational complexity and sheer intensity of Irish women's and girls' resistance to coercion and how this took place across a very broad and active front involving tactics that were developed through a considerable variety of actions. These included boycotting (a tactic that was invented by the women of Ballinrobe, Co. Mayo, and was soon practised by women in other insurgent areas), physically resisting evictions, harvesting crops before they could be seized by the military and police, rioting, disrupting the seizure of livestock, and preventing sheriffs' sales. As Laird has shown, the state retaliated with official violence that transformed their everyday lives into an actual 'war zone': in their homes, on streets and farms and during protests, Irish women were bayoneted, shot, beaten, clubbed, kicked, dragged, strangled, violently tied and manacled (so as to restrict blood circulation to their arms and hands), and arrested and imprisoned. By tying down British Crown forces through inventive and courageous means that placed themselves in direct confrontation with the military, police, land agents and bailiffs, these revolutionary Irish women confounded the state, its armed agents and judiciary with disruptive strategies that undermined the 'familiar notions of power and the political' that informed imperialism.[75]

Vera appears as dangerous as these Irish women revolutionaries. In the Prologue, she is criticised by her father for expressing 'too many ideas' and is censured for the seriousness of her convictions, particularly her compassion for the rural poor. Her social commitment becomes clear when she announces that 'there is so much else to do in the world but love' and rejects any possibility of romance (until she falls for the Czarevitch with fatal consequences). As the military detachment arrives with prisoners at her father's inn, their commanding Colonel warns his men of the dangers of engaging with a literate woman, since reading, writing and thinking independently are hazardous skills: 'No peasant should be allowed to do anything of the kind. Till your fields, store your harvests, pay your taxes, and obey your masters – that is your duty.' When Vera threatens to expose the reality of state violence by asking '[w]ho are our masters?', she is told by the officer that the prisoners are being transported for raising similar questions. Her dismissal by her father as a 'foolish girl' draws the Colonel's observation that '[e]very woman does talk too much'. Here oppression is internalised within the family as Peter's attempt to silence his own daughter echoes the repressive influence of the Russian patriarch, who is hailed as 'Our Father the Czar', and in whose name the prisoners are being held captive.[76]

Patriarchal violence is also manifested through the régime's suppression of reason, which further internalises the authority of the state by isolating the peasants from one another. Driven by a desire to help others that her father cannot understand, Vera's generosity toward her friends and neighbours counters the alienation that Czarism cultivates among its subjects. Peter's own indifference to suffering is revealed by his hard-hearted recollection of the disasters endured by his community:

'Let God and our Little Father look to the world. It is none of my work to mend my neighbour's thatch. Why, last winter old Michael was frozen to death in his sleigh in the snowstorm, and his wife and children starved afterwards when the hard times came; but what business was it of mine? I didn't make the world. Let God and the Czar look to it. And then the blight came, and the black plague with it, and the priests couldn't bury the people fast enough, and they lay dead on the roads – men and women both. But what business was it of mine? I didn't make the world. Let God and the Czar look to it. Or two autumns ago, when the river overflowed on a sudden, and the children's school was carried away and drowned every girl and boy in it. I didn't make the world – let God and the Czar look to it.'[77]

Peter's wilful isolation from his neighbours is the result of long-term hardships that connect this dramatised crisis of the Russian peasantry with the contemporary events of the Irish Land War and the ongoing contestation of Irish political sovereignty. Testifying to the annihilation of rural society through mass starvation, economic crisis, ecological devastation and their destruction of entire families, his catalogue of disasters reflects colonialism's distortion of popular memory and its erosion of popular awareness of the trauma that it inflicts. Imperialism's paralysation of historical memory is confronted by Wilde with Peter's attempt to rinse his own consciousness. His lack of sympathy with the dispossessed, the sick and the dying addresses the state-engineered mass deaths of the 1840s and 1850s – events that remained within the scope of living recollection in 1881.[78] Opening with his recollection of 'the blight' and its disastrous impact upon the peasantry, and culminating with an epidemic of disease and the final horror and indignity of hurried, unconsecrated burials, Peter's recollection of what he has witnessed corresponds with the catastrophic impact of the starvation of Ireland during the 1840s and 1850s. The image of a corpse-strewn countryside echoes contemporary accounts of mass death in Ireland, including Jane Wilde's powerfully indignant poem of 1847, 'The Stricken Land' (to which I will return in Chapter 4) in which the 'charred, uncoffin'd masses' of children, women and men who starved amid plenty are resurrected to confront their imperialist 'murderers, the spoilers of our land'.[79]

Peter's denials allegorise official complicity in the destruction of mid-nineteenth-century Ireland. By callously asking 'what business was it of mine?' and justifying his own denial by stating 'I didn't make the world', he shows his desensitised response to crises, resulting from the state's programme for the political, economic and cultural degradation of Russia. His declarations that the peasantry should 'let God and the Czar look to it' also reflect the indifference of early Victorian British governments and their selectively applied dogmas of *laissez faire*.[80] Their belief in the autonomous sanctity of markets stood in direct contradiction to the analogue imperial doctrine of the direct and total exploitation of resources, which Speranza condemned so powerfully in 'The Stricken Land'. Wilde returns to this issue in the second Act with the Prime Minister's declaration that coercion is not only a politically effective method, but 'an economical one too' that will 'carry off your surplus population in six months'. The Czar's observation that '(t)here are too many people in Russia, too much money spent on them, too much money on courts of justice'[81] also draws attention to the Malthusian doctrines that influenced British policy toward Ireland throughout the nineteenth century.[82]

Peter's acceptance of the political crisis as inevitable and even natural also signals the normalisation of state violence in the popular imagination. From his limited perspective, the poverty, suffering, death and destruction that he has witnessed over the years have no political origin: deprivation, starvation and natural calamity are interpreted as the work of divine providence, and as occurring without any social, political or structural context. Making this claim even as armed agents of the repressive state enter his home with manacled prisoners in tow (including his own son), he rationalises poverty as part of a broader, heavenly programme. His refusal to recognise the relationship between the violent interventions of the state and its abandonment of the poor, along with the restrictions imposed by his own severely limited understanding of the peasantry's vulnerability to these crises, draws attention to the oppressed subject's refusal of reason as he fails to recognise the colonial dynamics of his historical circumstances. As we will see in the following chapter of this study, Wilde returned to this matter in his 1891 essay, 'The Soul of Man'.

The peasantry's endurance of political repression and economic disaster has resulted in this acceptance of want, hunger and suffering that erases awareness of the responsibility of the state. Peter's failure to empathise with the victims of imperial violence is countered in the third Act when one of the nihilists, Michael, remembers Dmitri's suffering, which is captured in the condition of his body when they meet at the inn. The collective state of the oppressed nation is reflected in Michael's recollection of Dmitri's 'young face, pale with famine' and his 'young limbs, twisted with torture; the iron chains they made him walk in'.[83] Here, Wilde describes the condition of Irish political prisoners in language similar to that used by his mother in her essays and poems, as the direct language of Irish anticolonial protest is ciphered in its translation into the dramatic dialogue of this Russian-set play.

Terror and the Coercive State

At the height of the Fenian insurrection of 1867, Karl Marx told an audience in London that the Irish peasantry remained locked in an endless cycle of 'English terrorism' that was legislated for and authorised by coercion laws. He argued that Ireland's subordination rested upon officially constructed food crises, or '[p]artial famines' that left the Irish under the perpetual threat of mass starvation in an agriculturally productive colony that was fully stocked with foodstuffs. The agrarian rebels, Fenians and, later, Land Leaguers, who fought back had to contend with a legislative arsenal of 'Insurrection Acts, Arms Acts [. . .] [and] Coercion Acts' at the disposal of successive Chief Secretaries.[84] The deployment of these repressive measures formed the history of coercion that underlines the play's critique of state violence, which is dramatised as the Czar's 'ban of terror'.[85] In Wilde's melodramatic portrayal of Russia, the weaponisation of subsistence through the withholding of food supply is combined with the colonial state's legalisation of the permanent denial of rights. In this way, the play's seemingly unlikely, melodramatic action depicts the violent atmosphere of official repression that characterised the governance of late-nineteenth-century Ireland.

The paranoid Czar and his tyrannical Prime Minister are obvious stand-ins for the Chief Secretary and Permanent Under Secretary at Dublin Castle. While the Russian monarch issues draconian laws, Prince Paul Maraloffski, in his role as political enforcer, collectively punishes the peasantry with executions and other official reprisals, declaring that 'the best cure for Republicanism is the Imperial crown'.[86] As the play proceeds, this violent authority is challenged by Vera's participation in revolutionary conspiratorial politics.

Introduced in Act 1 in her new guise as the dangerously radicalised 'she-wolf' of the revolution, Vera criticises the wasteful and debt-ridden aristocracy that is exploiting the poor, which it regards as its primary source of capital: as the Marquis de Poivrard asks, 'What is the use of the people except for us to get money out of?'[87]

Sensitive to the condition of the peasantry, the Czarevitch responds to the crisis by questioning the morality of exploitation:

> Czarevitch: The priests have taken heaven from the people, and you would take the earth away too [. . .] Is it so small a thing to strangle a nation, to murder a kingdom, to wreck an empire? Who are we who dare lay this ban of terror on a people? Have we less vices than they have, that we bring them to the bar of judgment before us?
> Prince Paul: What a Communist the Prince is! He would have an equal distribution of sin as well as of property.
> Czarevitch: Warmed by the same sun, nurtured by the same air, fashioned of flesh and blood like to our own, wherein they are different to us, save that they starve while we surfeit, that they toil while we idle, that they sicken while we poison, that they die while we –
> Czar: How dare – ?
> Czarevitch: I dare all for the people; but you would rob them of the common rights of men.
> Czar: The people have no rights.[88]

Wilde's republican and socialist sentiments are articulated very clearly here, echoing his mother's complaint that imperialism 'strangles all life'.[89] The Czarevitch's declaration of the rights of man is stated in defiance of the coercive demands of absolutism, as Russian tyranny is shown to reflect the colonial violence described by Marx: subjected to official terror, the population is denied the freedoms promised to its subjects by the British state. Wilde's dramatisation of Russian autocracy criticises the bourgeois liberal-imperialist position, and the heir apparent's protest is couched in a lightly concealed expression of Irish separatism, communism and humanism. Punishing the peasantry, he warns, will prove to be a self-destructive policy. His father's response, spoken immediately before his assassination, exposes the extremism of British policy in Ireland:

> 'From this day I proclaim war against the people – war to their annihilation. As they have dealt with me, so I shall deal with them. I shall grind them to powder, and strew their dust upon the air. There shall be a spy in every man's house, a traitor on every hearth, a hangman in every village, a gibbet in every square. Plague, leprosy or fever shall be less deadly than my wrath [. . .] I shall have peace in Russia, though it be the peace of the dead [. . .] See, thus shall I crush this people beneath my feet!'[90]

Repeating his threat to oppress the peasantry to the point of extermination, the Czar announces a policy of mass surveillance supported with this network of police agents and informers. Penetrating every community, his model of total control mirrors coercive practice in the colonial laboratory that was nineteenth-century Ireland,[91] and its repressive structures are underlined by the overarching presence of state violence. The state is emblematised here in the image of the gallows and its policy is articulated through the Czar's promise to impose violent pacification. His reliance on spectacularly violent methods echoes William Ewart Gladstone's 1868 promise to 'pacify Ireland', an ambition that was formalised with the passage of the Peace Preservation Act of 1870, which accompanied his first Land Act of the same year. Retrospectively and incorrectly hailed as a champion of rights for Irish nationalists, Gladstone actually intensified coercion in Ireland, exposing the oppressive policies of British liberal imperialism.[92] Wilde's correspondence with Gladstone, like his parents' networking efforts in Dublin, was aimed at situating his work and protecting it within the cultural-political sphere that he criticised so intensively in *Vera; or, The Nihilists*. His strategic praise for Gladstone should be qualified against the context and content of this play, in which a prime minister is given absolute control over the state when appointed imperial *Maréchal*, and then assigned to administer a policy of pacification designed to impose 'the peace of the dead'.[93]

Revolutionary Discourse

The explicitness of the Czar's reliance on coercion is matched by the nihilists' valorisation of revolutionary action, as when Vera describes physical resistance as a necessary response to repression. She argues that by harming seemingly invincible heads of state, violence is not just an expression of force but also a statement of democracy:

> 'Martial law! O God, how easy it is for a king to kill his people by thousands, but we cannot rid ourselves of one crowned man in Europe! What is there of awful majesty in these men which makes the hand unsteady, the dagger treacherous, the pistol-shot harmless? Are they not men of like passions with ourselves, vulnerable to the same diseases, of flesh and blood not different from our own? What made Olgiati tremble at the supreme crisis of that Roman life, and Guido's nerve fail him when he should have been of iron and of steel? A plague, I say, on these fools of Naples, Berlin, and Spain! Methinks that if I stood face to face with one of the crowned men my eye would see more clearly, my aim be more sure, my whole body gain a strength and power that was not my own! Oh, to think what stands between us and freedom in Europe! A few old

men, wrinkled, feeble, tottering dotards whom a boy could strangle for a ducat, or a woman stab in a night-time. And these are the things that keep us from democracy, that keep us from liberty. But now methinks the brood of men is dead and the dull earth grown sick of child-bearing, else would no crowned dog pollute God's air by living.'[94]

Wilde proposes here that the key to successful revolutionary action is the desublimation of monarchical power and the demystification of individuals embodying it. Vera proposes that this can only be achieved with their destruction and, like the Czar, she believes in the necessity of personalising political conflict. According to her logic, nihilists will succeed when they recognise their targets as human and vulnerable. Revolutionaries such as Gerolamo Olgiati, the republican conspirator involved in the assassination of the Duke of Milan in 1476 and Guido, or Guy Fawkes, whose plot to blow up the English parliament was prevented through its last-minute discovery, failed to acknowledge this. Vera's theory of the levelling value of political violence proposes to deliver the Czar and his ministers to the kind of force being inflicted on those they are exploiting and terrorising. She explains to her comrades that the state's weakness lies in the fragility of the system that these figures represent, and Wilde's most subversive gesture in this play is to highlight the defencelessness of these officials when confronted with the challenge of direct action and the agency and determination of the insurgent. All of this occurs within the generally violent context of state repression, through which the everyday 'business' of repression is exposed as 'bloody butchery'.[95] While the Czar's court discusses the containment of the nihilists' rebellion, his authority is shown to depend on violence and the state's indifference to the suffering that it causes. So, the peasantry are dehumanised by ministers who describe them as 'vulgar, illiterate, common and vicious [. . .] no better than the animals in one's preserves, and made to be shot at'.[96]

Conclusion

One of the play's earliest literary critics suspected that *Vera; Or, The Nihilists* 'silhouetted' Wilde's real political views.[97] The American actress, Marie Prescott, who bought its production rights, believed that its staging of the themes of state violence and terrorism, with the closing spectacle of 'power pleading for the poor' would appeal to American audiences.[98] However, Wilde's first melodrama quickly disappeared into obscurity. Set in a corrupt polity verging on disintegration, it explores the coercive state's fusion of legalised violence, economic exploitation, political repression and surveillance. When it is revealed that peasants are starving to death in the empire's southern provinces, a minister describes their plight as an opportunity: 'The more starvation there is among the people the better. It teaches them self-denial, an excellent virtue.'[99] Wilde's dramatisation of Russia closely resembles the colonial condition of Ireland during the nineteenth century, where imperial modernity brought with it 'dispossession, subordination and the loss of sovereignty'.[100] By staging Ireland as Russia, Wilde paralleled nihilism with Irish insurgency, bringing its Russian origins and rationale into proximity with the repeated political crises that afflicted nineteenth-century Ireland. His scarcely veiled transplantation of Britain's nearest colony onto the more distant setting of Russia was a radical step. Its basic encryption of colonial policy in Ireland drew attention to the enduring instability of the imperial project there. As the play concludes, the Czarevitch finds that inheriting his father's crown is a pointless honour, because possession of 'the widest empire' appears degrading 'when matched with love'.[101]

Notes

1. The text that I have drawn from is the 1880 Ranken & Co. edition, republished in Merlin Holland (ed.), *The Complete Works of Oscar Wilde* (London: HarperCollins, 1999). Quotation from Act 1, p. 688.
2. Ibid. p. 687.
3. Oscar Wilde, 'The Critic as Artist', in *Complete Works*, vol. 4, pp. 123–206, p. 186.
4. Jane Francesca Wilde, 'The American Irish', p. 9.
5. With migration, Irish republicanism assumed a global presence and, as Wilde discovered during his American tour, his separatist views were certain to have a sympathetic audience wherever he encountered Irish labour. The internationalism that he contributed to Irish politics had a literary as well as a political impact, manifested in his dedication of the first edition copy of *Vera* . . . that he gave to Walt Whitman 'to a beautiful poet, a sincere republican and a charming friend'. See Wilde, in *Complete Letters*, n. p. 96.
6. Symons, *A Study of Oscar Wilde*, p. 67.
7. Elizabeth Carolyn Miller has responded to these criticisms, raised by Holbrook Jackson, Richard Ellmann, Josephine Guy, Ian Small and Julie Buckler, by pointing to the play's role within the subversive

melodramatic tradition. See Elizabeth Carolyn Miller, 'Reconsidering Wilde's *Vera; or, The Nihilists*', in Joseph Bristow (ed.), *Wilde Discoveries: Traditions, Histories, Archives* (Toronto: University of Toronto Press, 2013), pp. 65–84, p. 65. The anarchist historian, David Goodway, has also dismissed the play. See David Goodway, *Anarchist Seeds Beneath the Snow: Left-Libertarian Thought and British Writers* (Liverpool: Liverpool University Press, 2006), chapter 4, 'Oscar Wilde'.

8. See Norbert Kohl, *Oscar Wilde: The Works of a Conformist Rebel*, p. 34.
9. Sos Eltis, *Revising Wilde: Society and Subversion in the Plays of Oscar Wilde* (Oxford: Clarendon Press, 1996), p. 29.
10. Symons, *A Study of Oscar Wilde*.
11. Dion Boucicault to Mrs George Lewis, 29 January 1882, reprinted in Wilde, *Complete Letters*, n., p. 135.
12. See Deirdre McFeeley, *Dion Boucicault: Irish Identity on Stage* (Cambridge: Cambridge University Press, 2012), especially chapter 5, 'The Politics of Exile: *The Shaughraun* in New York' and chapter 6, '"Audiences are not political assemblies": *The Shaughraun* in London'. Boucicault's letter was published on 10 January 1876.
13. I am very grateful to Gillian O'Brien, who drew my attention to this lost play. See Gillian O'Brien, *Blood Runs Green: The Murder that Transfixed Gilded Age Chicago* (Chicago: University of Chicago Press, 2015), p. 235.
14. Wilde to Richard D'Oyly Carte, undated, reprinted in Mason, *Bibliography of Oscar Wilde*, pp. 255–6, p. 256.
15. Ben Singer, *Melodrama and Modernity: Early Sensational Cinema and its Contexts* (New York: Columbia University Press, 2001) p. 8.
16. McFeeley, *Dion Boucicault*, pp. 170–1.
17. Singer, *Melodrama and Modernity*, p. 2.
18. Ibid.
19. Eltis compares the play to popular melodramas such as *The Russian Bride* (1874), *Russia* (1877), *Fédora* (1882), *Mardo, or the Nihilists of St Petersburg* (1883), *The Red Lamp* (1887), *Vera* (1890) and *The Nihilist* (1897). See Eltis, *Revising Wilde*, pp. 38–43.
20. Wilde to Edward F. Smyth-Pigott, September 1880, in *Complete Letters*, p. 98.
21. Wilde to George Curzon, November 1881, in *Complete Letters*, p. 117. Ironically, Curzon would become the Viceroy of India (1898–1905) and Foreign Secretary (1919–24).
22. Wilde to James Knowles, October 1881, in *Complete Letters*, p. 115. Wilde offered to put Knowles, editor of the *Nineteenth Century*, in contact with Speranza.
23. *The World*, 30 November 1881, p. 12, quoted in Mason, *Bibliography of Oscar Wilde*, p. 254.

24. 'The Play's Not the Thing', *Punch*, 1 September 1883, p. 99.
25. Hostile reviews from the *New York Times*, *New York Tribune* and *New York Herald* are quoted in 'Mr Oscar Wilde's Play', *Derby Daily Telegraph*, 22 August 1883, p. 4
26. 'Vera', *The New York Mirror*, 25 August 1883, reprinted in Mason, *Bibliography of Oscar Wilde*, p. 273.
27. Wilde to Clara Morris, c. September 1880, in *Complete Letters*, p. 97.
28. Wilde to an unidentified correspondent, c. September 1880, in *Complete Letters*, p. 97.
29. Eltis has pointed out that the play appeared in three incarnations: the first, privately printed edition of 1880 was followed by a second, 1882 edition. This included a number of revisions and the addition of a Prologue, and the final edition of 1908 is based on Wilde's further corrections to the 1882 edition. See Eltis, *Revising Wilde*, p. 44.
30. See Farrell, *Emergency Legislation*, p. 5.
31. 'The Ballina Tragedy', *The Freeman's Journal*, 25 May 1882, p. 3.
32. 'The Ballina Tragedy', *The Freeman's Journal*, 24 May 1882, p. 5; 'The Affray in Ballina', *The Freeman's Journal*, 8 May 1882, p. 2.
33. 'The Fenian Murders in Dublin', *Illustrated London News*, 20 May 1882, p. 489; 'The Assassinations in Dublin', *The Times*, 9 May 1882, p. 6; 'Funeral of Lord F. Cavendish at Chatsworth', *Illustrated London News*, 20 May 1882, p. 501.
34. 'Lady Cavendish on the Evil in Ireland', *Evening News*, 13 May 1882, p. 3; 'Funeral of Mr. Burke at Dublin', *Illustrated London News*, 20 May 1882, p. 501; 'Reign of Murder in Ireland', *Manchester Courier*, 9 May 1882, p. 5; 'The Assassinations in Dublin', *The Times*, 9 May 1882, p. 6; 'The Assassinations in Dublin', *The Times*, 12 May 1882, p. 10.
35. 'Lady Cavendish on the Evil in Ireland', *Evening News*, 13 May 1882, p. 3.
36. Jenny Marx (as J. Williams), 'Agrarian Outrages in Ireland', *La Marseillaise*, 2 April 1870, reprinted in Marx and Engels, *Ireland and the Irish Question*, pp. 396–9, pp. 396–7.
37. 'Serious Affray at Ballina', *Daily News*, 8 May 1882, p. 3.
38. 'Funeral of Lord F. Cavendish at Chatsworth', *Illustrated London News*, 20 May 1882, p. 501.
39. Niall Whelehan, *The Dynamiters: Irish Nationalism and Political Violence in the Wider World, 1867–1900* (Cambridge: Cambridge University Press, 2012), p. 3.
40. 'Land League: Proclamation of the President of the American Branch', *Philadelphia Enquirer*, 8 May 1882, p. 1.
41. This is how the Czarevitch describes assassination in this later edition of the play. See *Vera; or, The Nihilists*, Act 2, p. 46.
42. Cavendish's enormous fund of inherited wealth originated in the labour of the Irish peasantry. This was the very class that, throughout

the nineteenth century, existed under the permanent cycle of coercion that Wilde described to audiences and readers in the United States and that had been attacked with such ferocity by the Royal Irish Constabulary on the night preceding the aristocrat's own death. He hailed from the Hartington line, a colonial dynasty in possession of a vast plantation straddling Counties Cork and Waterford and his political appointment was also a matter of heredity: his older brother, Spencer Compton Cavendish, the Marquess of Hartington and principal heir to the estate, preceded him in the office of Chief Secretary for Ireland. From 1870 to 1874, Spencer Cavendish protected landed interests by suspending *Habeas Corpus* in Westmeath and he opposed the reform of Irish university education, warning the cabinet that it would undermine Protestant hegemony. See Jonathan Parry, 'Cavendish, Spencer Compton, Marquess of Hartington and Eighth Duke of Devonshire (1833–1908)', *Oxford Dictionary of National Biography*, Oxford University Press, 2004; online edition, 2008 <http://www.oxforddnb.com/view/article/32331>, accessed 13 January 2017.
43. 'Land League: Proclamation of the President of the American Branch', *Philadelphia Enquirer*, 8 May 1882, p. 1.
44. Parnell's memoir was written in 1907 but went unpublished until 1986. See Anna Parnell, *The Tale of a Great Sham* (Dublin: Arlen House, 1986), p. 135.
45. Jane Francesca Wilde to Oscar Wilde, 8 May 1882. Clark Library Wilde W6712L W6721 [1882?] May 8.
46. Michael Davitt, *The Fall of Feudalism in Ireland, or The Story of the Land League Revolution* (London: Harper & Brothers, 1904), pp. 334, 336–7.
47. Untitled, *Sporting Times*, 8 February 1896, p. 7.
48. Curtis Marez, 'The Other Addict: Reflections on Colonialism and Oscar Wilde's Opium Smoke Screen', *ELH*, 64.1, Spring 1997, pp. 257–87, p. 261.
49. Wilde, *Vera; or, The Nihilists*, Act 3, pp. 711, 708.
50. Herman Melville, *Moby-Dick or, The Whale* (London: Penguin, 2003), pp. 434–5.
51. Karl Marx to Frederick Engels, 16 March 1867, in Marx and Engels, *Ireland and the Irish Question*, p. 149. Frederick Engels, 'Relations Between the Irish Sections and the British Federal Council', 14 May 1872, in Marx and Engels, *Ireland and the Irish Question*, pp. 301–4, p. 303.
52. William James Linton, 'Fenianism and Republicanism', in *Ireland for the Irish: Rhymes and Reasons Against Landlordism* (New York: The American News Company, 1867), pp. 11–26, p. 19. Linton declared that only through the transformative 'Promethean fire of the Republic' could all of Europe be 'revivified': 'Fenianism and Republicanism', p. 22. Wilde admired Linton's work and published a favourable

review of his *Poems and Translations* in the *Pall Mall Gazette* in 1889. See 'The Poet's Corner', *Pall Mall Gazette*, 24 June 1889, p. 3.
53. Sergius Stepniak, *The Russian Storm-Cloud or, Russia in Her Relations to Neighbouring Countries* (London: Swan Sonnenschein, 1886), p. 212.
54. Wilde, *Vera; or, The Nihilists*, Act 3, p. 720.
55. Ibid. Act 1, p. 689; Act 3, pp. 711, 709.
56. Ibid. Act 1, p. 688.
57. Eltis, *Revising Wilde*, p. 15.
58. Wilde, *Vera; or, The Nihilists*, Act 3, p. 709.
59. Ibid. Act 4, p. 717.
60. *St. Paul Globe*, quoted in Lewis and Smith, *Oscar Wilde Discovers America*, p. 225.
61. Karl Marx, 'Outline of a Report on the Irish Question to the Communist Educational Association of German Workers in London, December 16th, 1867', in Marx and Engels, *Ireland and the Irish Question*, pp. 126–39, p. 136.
62. Wilde, *Vera; or, The Nihilists*, Prologue, pp. 684–5.
63. Ibid. Act 1, p. 687.
64. Ibid. Act 1, p. 689.
65. Eltis, *Revising Wilde*, p. 34.
66. Ivan Turgenev, *Fathers and Sons* (trans. from the Russian by Richard Freeborn, Oxford: Oxford University Press, 1991), p. 192.
67. See Oscar Wilde, 'A Batch of Novels', *Pall Mall Gazette*, 2 May 1887, p. 11, reprinted in *Complete Works*, vol. 6, pp. 165–7.
68. Wilde, *Vera; or, The Nihilists*, Act 1, p. 689.
69. A similar logic is shown at work a century later among members of the Red Army Faction in Uli Edel's 2008 film, *The Baader Meinhof Complex*, which charts the gradually hardening attitudes of the group's members during the 1970s. Edel's historical drama, based closely on Stefan Aust's 1985 book of the same title, emphasises how as the group grew increasingly alienated from the state, its campaign became progressively more violent and spectacular. See Uli Edel (dir.), *The Baader Meinhof Complex* (German: *Der Baader Meinhof Komplex*), Entertainment One, 2008. See Also Stefan Aust, *The Baader Meinhof Complex* (trans. from *Der Baader Meinhof Komplex* [Hamburg: Hoffmann und Campe, 1985], London: The Bodley Head, 2008).
70. Wilde, *Vera; or, The Nihilists*, Act 2, p. 702.
71. Ibid. Act 3, p. 707.
72. Ibid. Act 2, p. 701; Act 1, p. 688.
73. Margaret Ward, *Unmanageable Revolutionaries: Women and Irish Nationalism* (London: Pluto, 1995), p. 4.
74. Davitt, *The Fall of Feudalism in Ireland*, p. 299.
75. See Heather Laird, 'Decentring the Irish Land War: Women, Politics and the Private Sphere', in Fergus Campbell and Tony Varley (eds),

Land Questions in Modern Ireland (Manchester: Manchester University Press, 2013), pp. 175–93, quotations from pp. 187, 176.
76. Wilde, *Vera; or, The Nihilists*, Prologue, pp. 683–4.
77. Ibid. p. 682.
78. Terry Eagleton, *Heathcliff and the Great Hunger: Studies in Irish Culture* (London: Verso, 1995), p. 280. Eagleton describes here how colonial modernity hinges on the denial of its inherently violent function.
79. The poem was originally published in *The Nation* on 21 January 1847. See Melville, *Mother of Oscar*, p. 33. For the poem in its entirety, see 'The Famine Year', in Jane Francesca Wilde (as Lady Wilde), *Poems by Speranza* (Glasgow: Cameron and Ferguson, 1871), pp. 10–12.
80. As Christine Kinealy has pointed out, *laissez faire* was conveniently forgotten when it did not suit the British establishment, as when it was abandoned during the Corn Laws and Navigation Acts. See Christine Kinealy, *This Great Calamity: The Irish Famine, 1845–52* (Dublin: Gill and Macmillan, 1994), p. 8.
81. Wilde, *Vera; or, The Nihilists*, Act 2, p. 702.
82. As Christine Kinealy has shown, Malthus's recommendation that population expansion could be controlled through the restriction of subsistence exercised enormous influence over British administrators in Ireland. See also Thomas Malthus, *An Essay on the Principle of Population* (originally published 1798; reprinted London: Penguin, 1985).
83. Wilde, *Vera; or, The Nihilists*, Act 3, p. 712.
84. Marx, 'Outline of a Report', pp. 130, 133.
85. Wilde, *Vera; or, The Nihilists*, Act 2, p. 703.
86. Ibid. Act 2, p. 702.
87. Ibid. Act 1, p. 687; Act 4, p. 715.
88. Ibid. Act 2, p. 703.
89. Jane Wilde to Lotten von Kraemer, 1864, quoted in Melville, *Mother of Oscar*, p. 97.
90. Wilde, *Vera; or, The Nihilists*, p. 705.
91. See Martin, *Alter-Nations*, chapter 2, 'Fenianism and the State'.
92. Upon receiving royal approval to form his first government from Queen Victoria on 1 December 1868, Gladstone declared, 'My mission is to pacify Ireland.' John Morley, *The Life of William Ewart Gladstone* (London: MacMillan, 1903), vol. 2, p. 252.
93. Wilde, *Vera; or, The Nihilists*, Act 2, p. 705. For Wilde's correspondence with Gladstone, see Wilde to W. E. Gladstone, June 1888, 14 May 1887, 17 May 1887, 20 July 1881, in *Complete Letters*, pp. 350, 46, 48, 113.
94. Wilde, *Vera; or, The Nihilists*, Act 1, pp. 689–90.
95. Ibid. Act 2, pp. 696–7.
96. Ibid. Act 2, pp. 698–9.

97. Archibald Henderson, 'The Dramas of Oscar Wilde', *Arena*, 38, August 1907, pp. 134–9, reprinted in Karl Beckson (ed.), *Oscar Wilde: The Critical Heritage* (London and New York: Routledge, 1970), pp. 270–7, p. 272.
98. Marie Prescott to Oscar Wilde, 11 February 1882, reprinted in Karl Beckson (ed.), *Oscar Wilde* (1970), pp. 266–7, p. 267.
99. Wilde, *Vera; or, The Nihilists*, Act 3, p. 715.
100. Joe Cleary, *Outrageous Fortune: Capital and Culture in Modern Ireland* (Dublin: Field Day Publications, 2007), p. 78.
101. Wilde, *Vera; or, The Nihilists*, Act 4, p. 717.

Chapter 3

Class, Criticism and Culture: 'The Soul of Man Under Socialism'

Oscar Wilde believed that authority engineered the twinned crises of capital and empire and he argued that socialism, anticolonialism and Aestheticism were interlinked. His 1891 essay, 'The Soul of Man Under Socialism' (republished shortly after his conviction as 'The Soul of Man') is a key example of the kind of heterogeneous political and cultural discourse that, as Mark Bevir argues, characterised socialist writing of the fin de siècle. Rather than advocating rigid or centralising forms of political determinism for the left, the arguments presented by Wilde and other writers such as H. M. Hyndman, Charlotte Wilson, Louise Michel, Eleanor Marx, John Barlas, Peter Kropotkin and George Bernard Shaw, to cite just a few, reflect the diversity and experimental nature of progressive thought in this period. Wilde's essay, with its suggestions not just for new social and cultural possibilities, but also for new ways of thinking about them, was an important intervention in the overlapping literary and political discussions of the period.[1]

As well as providing Wilde with opportunities to criticise British policy in Ireland, his tour of the United States had allowed him to observe and criticise modern industrial capitalism at first hand. In Philadelphia he explained the 'political-economical importance of aesthetics':

> They believe that the people of the artisan class have toiled long enough on unloved labour amid unlovely, hard, repulsive surroundings. Hence you see the political-economical importance of aesthetics. The toiling thousands of Great Britain are growing more and more dissatisfied every year with their dreary lives filled only with incessant, unattractive toil [. . .] The problem of controlling them is only to be solved by making them happy in their labour.[2]

Wilde's proposal echoes John Ruskin's earlier critique of modern industrial capitalism as a dehumanising phenomenon, and he had already criticised its reliance on the 'vile deification of machinery' in 1877.[3] This claim also raises the point that art is a political phenomenon capable of inspiring working-class sensibilities that were brutalised by prolonged social inequality. Despite Ruskin's disdain for Irish culture, Wilde shared his belief that Aestheticism could draw inspiration from labour and believed that, as a cultural movement, it should speak directly to workers and confront the conditions they struggled with. Just before his arrival in San Francisco, he told reporters in Sacramento that it was among 'the mechanics and workers' of America that he hoped to see 'the triumph that must come'. Believing that culture ultimately belonged to workers, he called on them to become 'creators in art' who would revolutionise it by using their creativity to reflect the achievements of the democratic 'masses' rather than facilitating the 'accomplishment and luxury of the rich'.

Clearly, Wilde hoped that Aestheticism would influence the working classes. As Diana Maltz has shown, there was considerable unease within late Victorian cultural circles over the prospect of working-class participation in Aestheticism[4] but Wilde advocated for workers' involvement in every sphere of art and culture:

> We must teach the people to use their hands in art. All that is artistic must begin in handicraft [. . .] I would dignify labor by stripping it of its degradation and by developing all that is beautiful in the laborer's surroundings and opening his eyes to it [. . .] I would speak to the hardworking people, whom I wish I could reach through the prejudice that shuts them and me away from each other.[5]

By publicly acknowledging and advocating for the connection between art and labour, and by highlighting the ties that bound the experiences of the Aesthete to those of working-class people, Wilde countered press attacks aimed at limiting his exposure to and popularity among workers. Many of these were focused on discouraging workers from attending his lectures. Having appealed to an audience in Cleveland to oppose capitalism by resisting the urge to become 'a mere collection of money-making merchants', Wilde advised them to 'influence us [i.e., Europeans] [. . .] by producing noble art and a noble civilization'. He stated that art, not capital, would be the true measure of American culture: 'we value your American poets much more than your American millionaires'.

He also advised his audience on how American greatness should be measured: 'we estimate you by the amount of great men you have produced, not by your hoarded wealth'.[6]

Regarding Walt Whitman's poetry as superior to the political and economic power of capital, Wilde also complained that, for the wealthy, culture assumed the aura of 'an accomplishment rather than an atmosphere'.[7] In contrast to this, he found living expressions of Aestheticism among the poorest workers in the United States. Before he spoke on Irish art and political separatism, Wilde also observed the Chinese workers of San Francisco, who, to his delight, provided vital examples of the theoretical connections between art, work and pleasure upon which his own Aestheticism was based. 'What was most pleasing about the Chinese,' he told an audience in London, 'was that everything they did and touched was beautiful.'[8] Wilde admired them for investing the most common objects with beauty and praised them for providing models with which Aestheticism could be directly translated into everyday, material practice:

> San Francisco is a really beautiful city. China Town, peopled by Chinese labourers, is the most artistic town I have ever come across. The people – strange, melancholy Orientals, whom many people would call common, and they are certainly very poor – have determined that they will have nothing about them that is not beautiful. In the Chinese restaurant, where these navvies meet to have supper in the evening, I found them drinking tea out of china cups as delicate as the petals of a rose-leaf, whereas at the gaudy hotels I was supplied with a delf [sic] cup an inch and a half thick. When the Chinese bill was presented it was made out on rice paper, the account being done in Indian ink as fantastically as if an artist had been etching little birds on a fan.[9]

Wilde was fascinated with these outsiders: working-class immigrants who 'came here, with pick and shovel', and in whose routines he recognised everyday manifestations of Aestheticism. The very appearance of Chinatown amplified this impression:

> in this monarch city one passed at night time into a little city of winding streets lit not by gas, but by painted paper lanterns, the beautiful lattice-work of the projecting windows reaching sometimes across these little winding thoroughfares through which there was a constant procession of Chinese.[10]

Here, the spectacle of 'navvies' who 'drank their refreshing beverage out of a pretty cup' registered profoundly upon his imagination. His own hotel, in contrast, served coffee in a cup that was so heavy he complained that it could have been used as a weapon.[11] Wilde was fascinated by the sight of these 'rough railway excavators' gently handling teacups while 'fully appreciating the influence of their beauty'. Their lifestyle was a promising example for artists seeking to introduce ideal, democratised practices and forms of art into the everyday world of labour. By describing Chinese labourers to his English audiences as 'navvies' he also associated them with the immigrant workers who were more immediately recognisable to them: the itinerant and largely Irish railroad workforce whose labour was key to the modernisation of Victorian Britain.[12]

Not only was Chinese working-class culture beautiful, it was exemplary: 'If these men could use cups with that tenderness our children would learn by force of the influence of beauty and example to act in a like manner.'[13] He was equally impressed by the modest, undecorated and minimalist stage of the Chinese theatre, which was 'the most beautiful in the world, because it was founded on the imagination'. With 'no scenery at all, and the actors admitting everything they did was art', it revealed to him how Chinese immigrants inhabited a profoundly aestheticised reality despite their poverty and the exhausting intensity of their work:

> Their poetry was far too delightful to be locked up in books which perhaps people would not read, so the poet wrote his sonnets upon fans and pocket handkerchiefs and sometimes embroidered them upon beautiful dresses, and in that way, Chinese poems were much better known to the Chinese than European poems were to the Europeans.[14]

For Wilde, the materiality of such art underlined the Chinese-American worker's ability to cultivate Aestheticism through a creative consciousness that produced delicate and refined alternatives to the vulgar commodities and practices cultivated by industrial capitalism. Such encounters with working-class Americans and immigrants, particularly in the western United States, led him to regard the country as a potential laboratory, or 'conservatory' for the development of art and culture. In contrast, he considered the bourgeoisie, particularly on the east coast, as anachronistic imitators of the cultural and political 'follies of Europe'.[15]

During the summer of 1883, months after his return to England, Wilde's explicit identification with subaltern cultures was criticised by the *Pall Mall Gazette*. Reporting on his public lecture on his impressions of the United States, it complained that 'the proletariate [sic]' would be admitted 'at the modest charge of five shillings a head' to listen to his progressive views on 'woman [. . .] miners, Mormons, Chinese, negroes'.[16] However, Wilde was cheered when he warned his British audiences that these workers were alienated from art 'so bound up in respectability that it had no room for them'. His mission to convince workers of their importance to the project of Aestheticism by informing them of his belief 'that between art and respectability there was really no connection at all' was taken seriously by the British public. Almost a decade before the publication of 'The Soul of Man Under Socialism', audiences in England, Scotland and Ireland responded positively to his reflections on the struggles of working-class people and his sympathy for them.[17]

'A Chinese Sage'

At the beginning of 1890 Wilde again outlined his views on the differences that distinguished the refinements of Chinese culture from the vulgarities of capitalist modernity in an essay written for Wemyss Reid's liberal paper, *The Speaker*. Reviewing the British diplomat and sinologist, Herbert Giles' translation of the writings of the ancient Taoist philosopher, Chuang Tsŭ, Wilde explored the anarchic opinions of this 'very dangerous writer' on the subjects of authority, power, protest and culture. He found subversively colourful alternatives to late Victorian morality in Tsŭ's work, which he regarded as refreshingly disruptive. Many of the ideas that Wilde explored later in 'The Soul of Man Under Socialism' are sketched in this piece, in which property and capital are criticised and the resistant subject celebrated.[18] The review appeared several months before Wilde heard George Bernard Shaw's lecture on socialism to the Fabian Society, upon which Shaw claimed that the ideas presented in 'The Soul of Man Under Socialism' were based.[19] Wilde praised the ancient philosopher's emphasis on individualism, which he described as 'an ideal somewhat needed by an age like ours', and the persuasive, even disruptive force of his remarkably 'destructive criticism'. He hoped that if they were taken seriously, Tsŭ's writings would undermine British imperialist culture by placing 'some check on our national habit of self-glorification'. With the publication of Giles' translation, this philosopher, whose entire life seemed to Wilde a prolonged protest against authority, now had the potential to distress the modern middle classes by 'disturbing [. . .] dinner parties' and appearing 'impossible at afternoon teas'.[20]

Wilde explained the relationship between art and anarchy by emphasising the necessity of disruption, and in the review he easily fused his own aesthetic theories with Chuang Tsŭ's ideas about autonomy. Wilde noted how Tsŭ believed that individual and cultural freedom could be realised through the 'fresh medium of experience'. The potential of the disobedient subject lay in his negation of bourgeois virtue, with Tsŭ's ideas complementing Walter Pater's stress on the power of what Kate Hext terms 'the discrete moment' of the epiphany.[21] Wilde pointed to the ironic commodification of Tsŭ's image on 'the simple tea-trays and pleasing screens of many of our most respectable suburban households', the occupants of which had no sense of the radical content of his writings: 'If they really knew who he was, they would tremble.' While Tsŭ had penetrated middle-class households through the circulation of popular homeware, Wilde was amused by the prospect of his nihilistic and subversive 'worship of Nothing' terrifying bourgeois possessors of goods bearing his likeness.[22]

Wilde emphasised the relevance of Tsŭ's work to late Victorian society, as his 'contempt for utilitarian systems', along with his 'great creed of inaction' and belief in 'the uselessness of all useful things' highlighted the irrelevance of modern consumption. Because fulfilment was to be found in the experience of resistance, Tsŭ's 'idealist' Taoist philosophy had a profoundly contemporary resonance. It spoke directly to the conditioning imperatives of capital: 'Chuang Tsŭ was more than a metaphysician and an illuminist. He sought to destroy society as we know it, as the middle classes know it.' Combining 'the passionate eloquence of a Rousseau' with 'the scientific reasoning of a Herbert Spencer', Tsŭ was a strangely modern writer whose philosophy, Wilde believed, directly addressed the political and cultural challenges of late Victorian capitalism and its alienating forms of modernity.[23]

Unlike Friedrich Nietzsche's profoundly alienated nihilism, Tsŭ's anarchism proposed a more co-operative model for action and Wilde was very interested in his objection to competition. He believed that this was also particularly relevant at the end of the nineteenth century:

> He pities the rich more than the poor, if he ever pities at all, and prosperity seems to him as tragic a thing as suffering. He has nothing of the modern sympathy with failures, nor does he propose that the prizes should always be given on moral grounds to those who come in last in the race. It is the race itself that he objects to [. . .][24]

Wilde believed that Tsǔ's writings could inform a direct challenge to the structural inequalities that formed the basis of modern capitalist society and was sure that his critique of power could be applied to contemporary social, cultural and political problems. Principally, it was Tsǔ's objection to standardised morality that telescoped the centuries separating Wilde from the Taoist philosopher. He found the sage's rejection of charity to be as relevant to contemporary social crises as his opposition to competition:

> Yes; incredible as it may seem, this curious thinker looked back with a sigh of regret to a certain Golden Age when there were no competitive examinations, no wearisome educational systems, no missionaries, no penny dinners for the people, no Established Churches, no Humanitarian Societies, no dull lectures about one's duty to one's neighbour, and no tedious sermons about any subject at all. In those ideal days, he tells us, people loved each other without being conscious of charity, or writing to the newspapers about it. They were upright, and yet they never published books upon Altruism. As every man kept his knowledge to himself, the world escaped the curse of scepticism; and as every man kept his virtues to himself, nobody meddled in other people's business. They lived simple and peaceful lives, and were contented with such food and raiment as they could get.[25]

Here there was 'no chattering about clever men, and no laudation of good men', while the 'intolerable sense of obligation was unknown'. The historical record was not contaminated by accounts of the greatness of power: 'The deeds of humanity left no trace, and their affairs were not made a burden for posterity by foolish historians.' The past left no instruction for the present, liberating it from the prescriptive demands of the powerful. By writing from his own, ancient position of isolation from authority, Tsǔ set an example for the alienated modern subject and his critique of morality, charity and institutionalised power appealed to Wilde's radical sensibility. His claim that official compulsion made contentment impossible underscored his very subversive critique of the 'mischievous idea of Government':

> 'There is such a thing,' says Chuang Tsǔ, 'as leaving mankind alone: there has never been such a thing as governing mankind.' All modes of government are wrong. They are unscientific, because they seek to alter the natural environment of man; they are immoral because, by interfering with the individual, they produce the most aggressive forms of egotism; they are ignorant, because they try to spread education; they

are self-destructive, because they engender anarchy. 'Of old,' he tells us, 'the Yellow Emperor first caused charity and duty to one's neighbour to interfere with the natural goodness of the heart of man.'[26]

Charity camouflaged authority, deflecting critique and inhibiting criticism. As Wilde would complain later in 'The Soul of Man Under Socialism', it excused capitalism from responsibility by suggesting private remedies for its socially destructive practices. By temporarily relieving poverty, charity obscured the structural origins of class violence: having obscured the systemic inequalities of Tsǔ's era, it would never resolve the crisis of social inequality at the end of the nineteenth century. Harmful and authoritarian by nature, governments promoted deceitful and 'artificial virtues' that concealed the repressive practices of the state:

> The results were so dreadful that the Government of the day had to bring in Coercion, and as a consequence of this 'virtuous men sought refuge in mountain caves, while rulers of state sat trembling in ancestral halls'. Then, when everything was in a state of perfect chaos, the Social Reformers got up on platforms, and preached salvation from the ills that they and their system had caused. The poor Social Reformers! 'They know not shame, nor what it is to blush,' is the verdict of Chuang Tsǔ upon them.[27]

With this clear swipe at contemporary state violence in its domestic and colonial settings in England and Ireland, Wilde drew attention to the coercive nature of the 'curse of capital', of which, he believed, Tsǔ had written 'as eloquently as Mr Hyndman'. With this comparison of Tsǔ's ideas with those of Henry Mayers Hyndman, the British socialist and founder of the Democratic Federation (later to become the Social Democratic Federation), Wilde again invested his book review with radical political interest. With these explicit references to the problems of government, capital and coercion, he once more expressed his dissident, anticolonial perspective on the wider problems of authority and empire.

Wilde also drew attention to the contradictions informing Tory strategy in Ireland, where the Salisbury régime's policy of violent pacification was being imposed by another hardline chief secretary, Arthur Balfour. These measures depended on the same intensity of police and military force applied by William Ewart Gladstone's chief secretary, William Forster – violence that Wilde regarded as the common currency of Liberal and Tory imperialism. Combined with the double standards and political insincerity of bourgeois reformism, Wilde's review associates coercion with capital, depicting both issues as jointly forming the key crisis of the age. Wilde also agreed with Tsŭ's complaint that the accumulation of wealth was 'the origin of evil' and the basis of the destructive consequences of capitalism:

> It makes the strong violent, and the weak dishonest. It creates the petty thief, and puts him in a bamboo cage. It creates the big thief, and sets him on a throne of white jade. It is the father of competition, and competition is the waste, as well as the destruction, of energy. The order of nature is rest, repetition, and peace. Weariness and war are the results of an artificial society based upon capital; and the richer this society gets, the more thoroughly bankrupt it really is, for it has neither sufficient rewards for the good nor sufficient punishments for the wicked. There is also this to be remembered – that the prizes of the world degrade a man as much as the world's punishments. The age is rotten with its worship of success.[28]

Having criticised the military, political and economic crimes of the imperial state, Wilde then focused on its cultural shortcomings by proposing that the Paterian energy from which Aestheticism drew its power was imperilled by capitalism's morbid drives. The cultural resources that the state sought to exploit were not to be extracted, packaged and marketed for the instant gratification of consumers but were, instead, meaningful expressions of an organic process requiring creative engagement. Wilde warned that beauty and genius, both of which he regarded as natural phenomena organised by the 'order of nature', were being endangered by capitalism. Its provocation of wasteful disorder, competition and violence eroded the natural system of production and had profound consequences for art, morality and culture. Capitalism's artificiality, he believed, was evident in the bourgeoisie's destruction of humanity's natural patterns and inclinations, which were held as the key measure of its success.

Returning to his argument that charity obscured the wrongs of government, Wilde pointed out that their collusion in obscuring the political, economic and social origins of class conflict only perpetuated and intensified the dishonesty of the powerful:

> Then came Governments and Philanthropists, those two pests of the age. The former tried to coerce people into being good, and so destroyed the natural goodness of man. The latter were a set of aggressive busybodies who caused confusion wherever they went [. . .] As a consequence of all this, the world lost its equilibrium, and has been staggering ever since.[29]

The reality of oppression as experienced by the working class in England and the colonised in Ireland was masked by interests dedicated to diverting public attention from the harm caused by the state. Tsŭ's ideal of the 'perfect man' who 'does nothing beyond gazing at the universe', rejects authority and 'adopts no absolute position' provided Wilde with an alternative to the inherently 'violent' practices and imperatives of the imperial bourgeoisie. He believed that the independent consciousness of the perfect man constituted the 'speculum of creation' as it was immune to the demands of government and capital. Tsŭ's ancient vision and its proposals for balanced and resistant detachment from the authority of the state provided Wilde with what he perceived as a realistic model for the modern, radical imagination and a basis for progressive activity capable of subverting power:

> All this is of course excessively dangerous, but we must remember that Chuang Tsŭ lived more than two thousand years ago, and never had the opportunity of seeing our unrivalled civilisation. And yet it is possible that, were he to come back to earth and visit us, he might have something to say to Mr. Balfour about his coercion and active misgovernment in Ireland; he might smile at some of our philanthropic ardours, and shake his head over many of our organised charities; the School Board might not impress him, nor our race for wealth stir his admiration; he might wonder at our ideals, and grow sad over what we have realised. Perhaps it is well that Chuang Tsŭ cannot return.[30]

In this ironic passage Wilde identifies violence as the signature technique of imperial government. Dependent on the systemic force disguised by the bourgeoisie's cultivation of false morality, the state's basic function is to repress and control the population by means of the distortion of subjective thought, whereby people are convinced 'that it is immoral to be consciously good'. Throughout the essay Ireland is presented as a laboratory for the development of this strategy and at the end of the review Wilde asked his readers to consider the injustice at the core of modern government:

> The doctrine of the uselessness of all useful things would not merely endanger our commercial superiority as a nation, but might bring discredit upon many prosperous and serious-minded members of the shopkeeping classes [. . .] And what would be the fate of governments and professional politicians if we came to the conclusion that there is no such thing as governing mankind at all?[31]

Perhaps, as the Irish had already done, the British might now realise their own potentially ungovernable condition if they also accepted that authority was dangerous and morally corrosive. In this important review, Wilde expressed his belief that, whether imposed domestically and with more insidious means in England, or with the openly aggressive methods used in Ireland, the will of the state always depended upon the final sanction of force.

'The Soul of Man Under Socialism'

The observations on the violent dynamics of government, class and empire that Wilde presented in 'A Chinese Sage' informed the critique of authority that he proposed a year later in his essay, 'The Soul of Man Under Socialism'. Here, he returned to the ideas outlined in the review by arguing that aesthetic and cultural fulfilment were only realisable through the pursuit of radical political and cultural change. The essay presents Aestheticism as a moral endeavour:

> With the abolition of private property, then, we shall have true, beautiful, healthy Individualism. Nobody will waste his life in accumulating things, and the symbols for things. One will live. To live is the rarest thing in the world. Most people exist, that is all.[32]

Originally published in *The Fortnightly Review* in February 1891, as 'The Soul of Man Under Socialism', the essay was later issued in book form by Wilde's friend, Arthur Lee Humphreys. Humphreys published the text just five days after Wilde's imprisonment, in a gesture of solidarity that, as Josephine Guy argues, publicised his radical political beliefs at the very moment of his incarceration for homosexuality.[33] In this insurgent piece, Wilde further developed many of the issues raised in 'A Chinese Sage' by explaining that poverty and repression had become so normalised that no single class could fully comprehend its own social and political condition within the oppressive structures of capitalism. This was not an uncharacteristically radical text, as Wilde's political views had also been expressed in other, earlier reviews such as 'Mr Froude's Blue Book' and 'Mr Mahaffy's New Book', which appeared in the *Pall Mall Gazette* in 1887 and 1889 (and to which I will return in Chapter 6). As Lawrence Danson has pointed out, the essay was a direct response to the political discussions with which Wilde was surrounded and immersed himself in.[34] The relationship between politics and culture is also a theme in his earlier essay on aesthetic theory, 'The Critic as Artist', in which Wilde emphasised the need for sympathy with the dispossessed, noting that readers of Victor Hugo 'run to kiss the bleeding mouth of Fantine'.[35]

Until this point, with the exception of his US lectures and interviews, Wilde had issued his most explicit political claims in book reviews, but he now turned to the political essay as a medium for radical expression. Repeating the claim made a decade earlier in *Vera; or, The Nihilists* that violence, both in its physical and rhetorical formations, was always the first recourse of the state, Wilde openly criticised the brutalising, hegemonic and silencing practices of capitalism in 'The Soul of Man Under Socialism'. The essay marks his accelerating engagement with revolutionary politics. Norbert Kohl's dismissal of the piece as a faddish and mediocre effort was not shared by contemporaries like Jack London, who annotated his own copy at its most militant points.[36] Thomas Hastie Bell felt that the essay's powerful synthesis of socialist collectivism and radical individualism significantly countered conservative publications that linked anarchists with images of terrorism, 'bombs and dynamite'.[37] In his 1906 biography, *The Life of Oscar Wilde*, Robert Sherard also stressed the essay's influence over contemporary revolutionary movements in Europe.[38]

Wilde's defence of revolt and his insistence on the moral necessity of political dissent are underlined by his emphasis on radical self-awareness. His complaint was that society was prevented from recognising state violence due to the modern subject's assimilation of the ideology of authority. He believed that these problems could only be countered through the provocation of dissent, without which the poor would remain complicit in their own repression. Arguing that slavery had been normalised within the collective consciousness of its victims, he claimed that similar forms of political and social conditioning had mobilised French peasants who fought for the Bourbon monarchy in 1793: 'To the thinker, the most tragic fact in the whole of the French Revolution is not that Marie Antoinette was killed for being a queen, but that the starved peasant of the Vendée voluntarily went out to die for the hideous cause of feudalism.'[39]

The essay's complex subject matter ranges from the discussion of cultural rebellion to the politics of hunger and the criminalisation of the poor and it proposes, as Marx had already done, that the automation of 'unintellectual', or manual labour would make forms of 'cultivated' pleasure available to the working class.[40] Positioning political revolt alongside historical examples of literary dissent, Wilde cited George Gordon Byron, Percy Bysshe Shelley, Victor Hugo and Charles Baudelaire as the most completely realised personalities of the nineteenth century.[41] Contentment is cited as the final objective of the human species because 'Utopia is [. . .] the one country at which Humanity is always landing,' and Aestheticism's radical political objective is presented as the democratisation of pleasure, without which there could be no social progress: 'When Humanity lands there, it looks out, and, seeing a better country, sets sail. Progress is the realisation of Utopia.' Without the idealism embodied in the work of these writers, culture and intellect are diminished by their subjection to authority; coerced by power, art 'vanishes, or becomes stereotyped, or degenerates into a low and ignoble form of craft'. Wilde believed that art would fulfil its social and aesthetic potential when it became independent of state and market, rendering it a truly anarchic phenomenon. Until that point, 'the moment that an artist takes notice of what other people want, and tries to supply the demand, he ceases to become an artist, and becomes a dull or an amusing craftsman, an honest or a dishonest tradesman'.[42]

Wilde argued that society should balance the production of art against the manufacture of useful commodities and regarded this as key to achieving social harmony and prosperity. Coerced labour did not generate any pleasure and had become a degrading practice for the worker, necessitating 'disgusting' and psychologically damaging activity that was 'mentally and morally injurious' to the individual.[43] He explained that capitalism depended for its existence on the infliction and prolonging of suffering through its endless and cyclic reproduction of need. This violence was felt very directly within the cultural sphere, as the operation and proliferation of capital and its interests obscured art's subversive function, a key responsibility that he accused contemporary artists of avoiding. Regarding art as the 'most intense form of individualism the world has known', Wilde saw it as a particularly rebellious type of expression. Its authenticity as the 'only real mode of Individualism' served the anarchic purpose and practice of the genuine artist, whose work reflected the independence and detachment of Chuang Tsŭ's perfect subject. The radical artist's refusal to obey the rules of capital indicated the liberating potential of art, culture and pleasure: 'alone, without any reference to his neighbours, without any interference the artist can fashion a beautiful thing; and if he does not do it solely for his own pleasure, he is not an artist at all'. Rather than proposing an Aestheticism centred on social alienation or atomisation, Wilde argued for associative practices that would facilitate cultural and political autonomy in the face of the corrupting and anaesthetising power of the state. This was why he believed that the market could be subverted by artists who 'should never try to be popular'. A transformed and utopian society would accommodate their individualism, and the first step toward achieving this objective was to understand culture within the structural and political contexts that he explained in the essay.[44]

Wilde addressed the 'aggressive, offensive, and brutalising' power of the state and its governing class and the ideological, cultural and economic 'terror' through which it was exercised and administered. As well as instilling fear and manipulating popular opinion, state violence hindered the artistic imagination and secured public consent for authority. It enforced conformity by desensitising the public and preserving the 'general ignorance of the community'.[45] Wilde's anarchic claim that 'Art is Individualism' drew on his idea that culture should facilitate the expression of rebellion: its subversive energy could drive the 'disturbing' and thoroughly 'disintegrating force' of the aesthetically-conscious imagination of the artist-revolutionary.[46] Proposing art as a fusion of revolutionary practice, individual expression and radical political agency, Wilde positioned the artist as a dissident figure whose contribution toward the improvement of culture would challenge the coercive authority of the state.

Wilde also complained that the repressive atmosphere within which artists had to operate facilitated the production of insincere and inferior work. Art that resisted the compelling power of authority, as articulated through hostile reviews in the conservative press (the authors of which Wilde ironically labelled 'the public'),[47] had authentic social value:

> what it seeks to disturb is monotony of type, slavery of custom, tyranny of habit, and the reduction of man to the level of a machine. In Art, the public accept what has been, because they cannot alter it, not because they appreciate it. They swallow their classics whole, and never taste them. They endure them as inevitable, and as they cannot mar them, they mouth about them. Strangely enough, or not strangely, according to one's own views, this acceptance of the classics does a great deal of harm. The uncritical admiration of the Bible and Shakespeare in England is an instance of what I mean.[48]

Socially-engaged art could undermine the system that was dehumanising the individual and regulating cultural practice and criticism through its deadening canonisation of the classics. Wilde's warning that official culture was damaging art conveys his belief that coercion had literary as well as political applications, as does his complaint that the sacralisation of state-sanctioned art eroded the aura and significance of those works selected for inclusion in the canon. The rapid consumption and imposition of culture denied time for reflection upon content and meaning and resulted in the commodification of art in ways that prevented readers of Shakespeare and the Bible from experiencing genuine pleasure or reflecting upon their enjoyment of texts. The objective of political and cultural authority, then, was the obstruction of the growth and development of the individual. While art required wholeness, the state thrived on fracturing and deteriorating progressive art forms and social structures.

Wilde associated this problem of cultural degradation with the experience of alienation, economic distress and misery under capitalism. Stressing that the connection between politics and art lay in humanity's capacity for sympathy, he argued that it was the possession and expression of a critical disposition towards capitalism that distinguished the creative, anarchic and aesthetic individual from the bourgeois managerial 'public' that authority served. In contrast, true individualism cultivated social wellbeing but would not impose itself by assuming power over others. Wilde believed that humanity's natural tendency toward solidarity was restricted by the 'immoral idea of uniformity of type and conformity to rule', a problem that, he felt, had become very pronounced and 'most obnoxious' in England.[49] Associating reactionary culture with the conservative tendencies of the British establishment, which dictated to the artist and society alike, Wilde argued that such interference undermined art's harmonising 'aesthetic effect' by demanding the 'unhealthy', insincere and derivative practices that had become so 'obvious, old-fashioned and common'.[50] Most problematic of all, these techniques and the works produced by them were commercially oriented.

Abusing Art

Wilde maintained that original art had always provoked careless allegations of immorality: 'when they describe a work as grossly immoral, they mean that the artist has said or made a beautiful thing that is true'. The inhibiting form of 'art-abuse' that he regarded as key to the maintenance of the Victorian society of the spectacle and its simulation of culture provoked intellectual crowd-baiting in the press, where reviewers used 'words very vaguely, as an ordinary mob will use ready-made paving stones' in order to confer dissident artists with 'diplomas of immorality'.[51] Wilde claimed that political control depended upon this manipulation of language: 'one of the results of the extraordinary tyranny of authority is that words are absolutely distorted from their proper and simple meaning, and are used to express the obverse of their right signification'. Anarchism with its progressive emphasis on the possibility of socialist individualism could counter this by inspiring a new clarity of expression and thought: 'Under Individualism people will be quite natural and absolutely unselfish, and will know the meanings of the words, and realise them in their free, beautiful lives.'[52] Language, which Wilde described in 'The Critic as Artist' as the origin of consciousness, or 'parent [. . .] of thought'[53] had very direct applications in the struggle for aesthetic meaning and political progress. When used properly by the artist it would liberate society from the obfuscations of power.

Wilde believed that in contrast to the cultural branding by the bourgeois sphere of its officially-approved art, genuine and insurgent art forms would flourish amid anarchy, which he defines in the essay as 'socialism'. Believing that the modern state had destroyed individual style and practice, Wilde concluded that the only 'form of government [. . .] most suitable to the artist is no government at all'.[54] Culture could only flourish if artists developed radical aesthetic and political consciousness, and if they followed their own initiative. By rejecting authority and resisting the imperative to conform to outdated notions of responsibility, the radical artist could contribute toward the improvement of society. This point was reiterated the following year by Peter Kropotkin in his essay 'Well-Being for All', in which he described social wealth as deriving from 'those higher pleasures of art and science which have too long been monopolised by the rich'.[55]

Wilde warned that the natural dynamics of human development and progression were being resisted by all forms of authority: 'To ask whether Individualism is practical is like asking whether Evolution is practical.' What the state offered to the artist and to society was the fearful prospect of cultural and political decay. Repeating the point that he made about coercion in 'A Chinese Sage', he argued that state repression underlined the need for revolutionary action. His belief in humanity's decency in the face of the stagnation and political failure of the state is emphasised in his position on the relationship between art and society, expressed in the claim that: 'What is true about Art is true about Life.'[56]

The Bourgeois Crowd

Inverting the language of anti-democratic Victorian writers like Thomas Carlyle, who equated democracy with the 'total destruction of social order',[57] Wilde also criticised contemporary democracy as a partial and inadequate system that had replaced monarchic absolutism with the equally dangerous and indiscriminate authority of the bourgeois 'mob'. A collective 'despot who tyrannises over the soul and body alike', the bourgeoisie incited a violent energy that was 'blind, deaf, hideous, grotesque, tragic'. Empowered by the authority from which it originated, the bourgeois crowd combined political clout ('the sceptre of the Prince'), claims to moral authority ('the triple tiara of the Pope'), and deception (the 'trick of tyranny').[58] In contrast to the subversive nature of the revolutionary crowd that haunts the bourgeois imagination in *The Importance of Being Earnest* (this subject is also discussed in Chapter 6) the reactionary tendencies of the 'half-educated' middle classes illustrated for Wilde the failure of democracy: by tying the bourgeoisie to capitalist authority, it convinced them to serve as agents of its power. Participating in their own oppression by subduing art and individualism, they behaved as unofficial proxies of the state, proving that acquiescence in 'popular authority'[59] was harmful to social progress. This underlined the political relevance of literature to Wilde: the bourgeoisie's attitude to contemporary writing was, in his view, as dangerous as its involvement in the distribution of political power.

Wilde regarded the press as the establishment's most important tool for the suppression of art. Describing its influence as absolute, he claimed that the journalist had replaced the torturer as the ultimate agent of state power. Authority was channelled through the press's manipulation of mass opinion and its distortion of public consciousness. No longer serving as the 'fourth estate' and now facilitating the privileged élites that Wilde described as Britain's 'only estate', the media contained and restricted public discourse, censored the arts and destroyed the reputations of those it viewed as a threat to the establishment. Its 'terrible force' and discursive violence lay in its strategy of controlling political and cultural life through the publicisation of scandals. Wilde observed that popular consent was continually being manufactured through the conservative press's invention and manipulation of these public spectacles:

> The tyranny that it proposes to exercise over people's private lives seems to me to be quite extraordinary. The fact is, that the public have an insatiable curiosity to know everything, except what is worth knowing.

Journalism, conscious of this, and having tradesman-like habits, supplies their demands. In centuries before ours the public nailed the ears of journalists to the pump. That was quite hideous. In this century journalists have nailed their own ears to the keyhole. That is much worse. And what aggravates the mischief is that the journalists who are most to blame are not the amusing journalists who write for what are called Society papers. The harm is done by the serious, thoughtful, earnest journalists, who solemnly, as they are doing at present, will drag before the eyes of the public some incident in the private life of a great statesman, of a man who is a leader of political thought as he is a creator of political force, and invite the public to discuss the incident, to exercise authority in the matter, to give their views, and not merely to give their views, but to carry them into action, to dictate to the man upon all other points, to dictate to his party, to dictate to his country; in fact, to make themselves ridiculous, offensive, and harmful. The private lives of men and women should not be told to the public.[60]

As Michael Foldy has shown, Wilde had also confronted the press directly in 'The Critic as Artist' with criticisms repeated in 'The Soul of Man Under Socialism'. In both essays he highlighted the construction and mediation of scandal in the interests of the power bases served by the press.[61] This condemnation of scandal refers to the Parnell Commission and is a prescient condemnation of the sensationalised reporting that would mediate Wilde's own trial and destroy his literary reputation. The leader of the Irish Parliamentary Party, Charles Stewart Parnell, successfully sued *The Times* in 1887 when the paper accused him of supporting and even being complicit in the Phoenix Park killings. The accusation drew on a series of forged letters composed by the journalist, Richard Piggott (these were exposed when the texts were found to contain spelling errors consistent with Piggott's own writing). Wilde and his brother, Willie, attended meetings of the Parnell Commission and followed the proceedings closely. Although Parnell was vindicated in court this failed attempt to destroy his political reputation had a sexually-themed sequel when he was named as co-respondent in the divorce of his party colleague and fellow MP, Captain William O'Shea, in 1889. The exposure of Parnell's relationship with Katherine O'Shea ended his career along with the political prospects of the Irish Parliamentary Party as the Irish Catholic hierarchy and opponents within his own party found a ready excuse to undermine the powerful nationalist movement that he had led.[62]

The commodification and politicisation of scandal by the press and its provision of worthless knowledge had become in Wilde's view a form of repression. Scandal was now the currency of power as it had vulgarised journalism and degraded reporters who assumed the values of the 'tradesman'.[63] Having been perfected with the Parnell scandals, the exploitation of private and political sensation also had a distinctly colonial register. Its disruption of privacy was, for Wilde, a strategy that served the needs of the imperial establishment. He regarded the Parnell Commission as an attack on the Irish leader's political activity and viewed press exposure of his private life as evidence of collusion between the press and the state in a campaign to undermine the Irish nationalist movement. Wilde's own exposure under trial in 1895, when the 'The Soul of Man Under Socialism' was in press as a pamphlet, drew similar criticism of the politics of scandal from British anarchists.[64]

Wilde argued that by presenting lies as facts the conservative press was compelling the public to conform to the agenda of the coercive state while establishing targets for popular hostility in the raft of 'indecent' newspapers being published in Britain. These were dedicated to the cultivation of an uninformed public opinion that 'tries to constrain and impede and warp the man who makes things that are beautiful in effect, and compels the journalist to retail things that are ugly, or disgusting, or revolting in fact'. This exploited popular sentiment by creating the 'unhealthy conditions' necessary for the circulation of hostile news reports targeting creative individuals active within the spheres of politics and art. This circular logic satisfied the popular appetite for scandal that it generated, leaving the public demanding more sensational stories and intensifying the kind of 'gross' cultural consumption that Wilde found so objectionable. In this way, the modern 'monster' of misinformed public opinion had been invented and customised by the state and its agents in the popular press.[65]

The Normalisation of Authority and the Need for Revolt

Publicly declaring Wilde's anarchism, 'The Soul of Man Under Socialism' drew on Chuang Tsŭ's ideas about the political tension between authority and culture. Announcing that 'Individualism [. . .] is what through Socialism we are to attain,' Wilde proposed that 'the State must give up all idea of government' because, as the Chinese philosopher had already shown, 'there is no such thing as governing mankind'. The fact that humanity could not be dictated to by any organising power meant that '[a]ll modes of government are failures'. Wilde included deterministic and 'Authoritarian' socialism in his catalogue of despotisms,[66] and the essay is equally critical of late Victorian democracy for its 'bludgeoning of the people, by the people, for the people'. Warning that 'all authority is quite degrading' and as harmful to those exercising it as for those being subjected to it, he noted that state violence was ironically beneficial because its excess of force actually mobilised resistance. However, the true potential of power was realised when authority insinuated itself into the popular consciousness. Once internalised, it assumed a more threatening and insidious dynamic:

> When it is violently, grossly, and cruelly used, it produces a good effect, by creating, or at any rate bringing out, the spirit of revolt and Individualism that is to kill it. When it is used with a certain amount of kindness, and accompanied by prizes and rewards, it is dreadfully demoralising. People, in that case, are less conscious of the horrible pressure that is being put on them, and so go through their lives in a sort of coarse comfort, like petted animals, without ever realising that they are probably thinking other people's thoughts, living by other people's standards, wearing practically what one may call other people's second-hand clothes, and never being themselves for a single moment. 'He who would be free,' says a fine thinker, 'must not conform.' And authority, by bribing people to conform, produces a very gross kind of over-fed barbarism amongst us.[67]

Because it was exercised through subtler and softer processes of indoctrination, the hegemonic influence of authority was more dangerous than direct violence because it exercised a more powerful hold over the popular imagination. It distracted attention from the exercise of state power and prevented society from realising its true extent. In this way, authority seized popular consciousness by simulating liberty and permitting minimal freedoms. Once consent was achieved through these means, authority co-opted democracy by controlling every aspect of the individual's existence and thought. Society's assimilation of coercive power hindered its capacity for critical reflection and left people unconscious of the relationship between the material and psychological workings of the state. Wilde believed that, in contrast, art would enlighten, inspire and even 'dominate' the imagination of the spectator in a liberating reversal of this process.[68] A dynamic aesthetic turn would, as Wilde also claimed in 'The Critic as Artist', impose meaningful form upon the destructive chaos of capitalist modernity. It would counter capitalism's isolating tendencies and heal the discord, disruption and alienation that it induced. By encouraging the subject's exploration of his or her own individualism, selfhood and personality, all of which constituted being and identity, art promised to foster a radical and insurgent popular consciousness.

Violence, Property, Capital and Revolt

Wilde's justification of rebellion centres on his valorisation of the universal 'spirit of revolt', which he regarded as fundamental to human agency and identity. He described isolated acts of violence against authority as expressions of despair: lacking direction, they did not constitute 'the ultimate mode of perfection' because they amounted to transitory and temporary expressions of frustration that were created by the hideousness of their circumstances. He pointed out that violence was a 'reference' to, or direct proof of, the 'wrong, unhealthy, unjust surroundings' that produced it: 'When the wrong, and the disease, and the injustice are removed, it will have no further place.' In contrast to this culture of desperation, a more constructive individualism would be expressed by a society capable of functioning in an organic manner and prepared to assume its purpose 'intensely, fully, perfectly'. However, Wilde did not dismiss resistance because 'the very violence of [. . .] revolution', even when passing and momentary, indicated that '[b]ehind the barricade there may be much that is noble and heroic'.[69]

Wilde believed that the state went to great lengths to circumvent humanity's predisposition to resist and as a result capitalist modernity was qualified by the intensity of its suppression of the rebellious 'soul of man'. Complaining that English law valued capital over people by elevating 'what a man has' so that it had become 'more than what a man is', he identified the very conception of property as the material origin of crime. Enduring endless cycles of 'misery, rage and depression', the poor were now retaliating with theft. By rationalising their despair, Wilde politicised the issue of poverty by presenting it as the result of a repressive class system and the very basis of capitalism's management of entire populations. Criticising the state's repression of individual subjectivity, through which obedience was secured with the incitement of fear and the infliction of want and starvation, he focused on the constant battle with hunger that led to crime. Those classified as offenders were 'not criminals at all' but a reflection of the bourgeoisie, representing 'merely what respectable, commonplace people would be if they had not enough to eat'.[70] With this reasoning, Wilde theorised the political origins of the comparatively minor economic crimes of the poor at a time when anarchists were resisting capitalism by means of *la reprise individuelle*. His essay equated this privatised activity with the more organised and explicitly subversive direct actions of revolutionaries like the French anarchist, Ravachol (whose crimes included grave robberies as well as bombings in the name of *l'Anarchie*), by claiming that the rejection of the concept and practice of private property would finally remove the rationale and necessity for theft.[71]

Wilde believed that the accumulation of property had a disciplinary effect. While the poor were distressed by their own lack of wealth, possessing it also generated profound anxiety for the middle classes whose efforts in acquiring further capital and commodities prevented them from achieving the very liberation that capitalism promised. In such an atmosphere, in which the poor were denied all dignity, rebellion was both a duty and the basis of genuine subjectivity, because 'a poor man who is ungrateful, unthrifty, discontented, and rebellious, is probably a real personality, and has much in him'. Radical selfhood could only develop if spared from the rigours of alienation because, unlike the commodity, it was an authentic phenomenon that never diminished in worth: 'Its value will not be measured by material things. It will have nothing. And yet it will have everything, and whatever one takes from it will be, it will still have, so rich will it be.'[72]

Wilde's attacks on Victorian charity, bourgeois sentimentalism and political reformism also pointed to the dangerous culture of patronage that characterised class discourse in late Victorian Britain, that ignored the material and political causes of poverty and the cultural and intellectual sterility that underlined them. These problems, in turn, highlighted the broader patterns of dependency that threatened creative and productive individualism. This system, which necessitated the disastrous practice of 'living for others', distorted all relationships and characterised capitalist normality by creating a totalising system of class repression that pressed with violence 'upon almost everybody'. Life for the majority was qualified by the experience of poverty, ugliness and starvation, rendering existence in an 'incomplete state'. Driven by discord, it was unstable, unequal, defective and uncivilised.[73]

Having recently discussed the connections between affect and action in 'The Critic as Artist', Wilde again warned that despair had a dangerous immediacy because '[t]he emotions of men are stirred more quickly than any man's intelligence'. This was because 'it is much more easy to have sympathy with suffering than it is to have sympathy with thought'. Sentimentality, not socialism, was the bourgeois response to poverty and inequality, and its insincerity was 'part of the disease' of capitalism. Victorian reformism was not a remedy for poverty but instead aggravated the crisis because by distorting popular perception it prolonged the misery of the poor. Revolutionary socialism's promise to transform property relations was the only possible solution since it was the responsibility and 'proper aim' of the socialist to reimagine and 'reconstruct society on such a basis that poverty will be impossible'. Anything less than the complete, political renovation of existing conditions was pointless because charity, in ignoring the structural causes of poverty, 'degrades and demoralises' the poor while constantly inventing new categories of sin. The operating principles of capitalism could never be reformed because, as a structural combination of economic, political and moral repression, they made it impossible to 'use private property in order to alleviate the horrible evils that result from the institution of private property'. Wilde promised that under a socialist reorganisation of society, people would no longer be subjected to the experience and spectacle of poverty. A state of communism would exist in which everyone would share in and contribute to a general and common condition of 'prosperity and happiness' while maintaining the uniqueness of their identities. This raised for Wilde a theoretically interesting proposal: 'Socialism itself will be of value simply because it will lead to Individualism.'[74]

Wilde's Anarchism

Inspired by Peter Kropotkin's notion that people are instinctively co-operative, Wilde's definition of socialism drew heavily on the Russian anarchist's theory of mutualism. He regarded this as the basis of genuine and radical individualism and the problem, as he saw it, was that capitalism, with its ideology of property, had established a flawed conception of selfhood and even reality. Wilde also believed that the revolutionary figure of the artist was paralleled in the historical figure of Christ, whose suffering and martyrdom reflected the ideals of the modern, anarchic subject 'who resists society absolutely'.[75] Perfection lay in the realisation of this pure and uncontrolled identity, which Wilde regarded as Christ's great achievement.

Wilde believed that artists and revolutionaries were natural allies because they represented this condition of 'true Individualism'.[76]

Kropotkin himself regarded art as a radical practice 'synonymous with creation' and intrinsically connected to revolutionary politics.[77] After Wilde's death he told Robert Ross that the 'The Soul of Man Under Socialism' was a foundational revolutionary text that should be 'engraved, like verses from the Koran are engraved in Moslem lands'.[78] Earlier, in his 1892 book, *The Conquest of Bread*, Kropotkin asked readers to consider how people would behave 'in a society, whose members are properly fed', and elaborated on the cultural possibilities that such a society would cultivate. He believed that anarchism could accommodate every aesthetic need through its resolution of material want and, like Wilde, regarded popular access to art and the 'higher delights' of culture as fundamental to social harmony. The privileging of 'art, and especially of artistic creation' held as important a place in Kropotkin's political vision as it did in Wilde's. The Russian anarchist included it as a key demand alongside improved wages, the abolition of rent, reduced working hours, freely provided food and clothing, and the final erosion of all class distinction. Art would not be produced for commercial consumption in the future that Kropotkin envisioned but would instead be created by anyone interested in doing so, and would satisfy a democratised demand for pleasure. This would require the careful cultivation of 'all individual feeling, all artistic tendency, and all development', so that society would produce 'all that is necessary to material life' and satisfy 'all manifestations of the human mind'.[79]

For Kropotkin, anarchist communism had its closest analogues in the activities of contemporary literary clubs and learned societies, where knowledge was already being freely circulated for these very reasons 'by those who love them, and for those who love them'. Cleansed of the profit motive, publishing could become a 'popular' and creative process, as authors would evolve into writer-producers capable of printing their own books and pamphlets; meanwhile workers presently involved in the setting and printing of texts could learn how to compose their own creative works. Involving everyone, these mutually supportive or 'blended' endeavours would lead to the proliferation of clearly written and accessible texts that would encourage attentive reading and increase the general enjoyment of literature. Despite his own admiration for Ruskin, Kropotkin believed that capitalism's key cultural problem was its accommodation of long-winded writers and the circulation of bloated texts. He claimed that radical collective methods were already afoot in the socialist press, where writers were setting type, printing texts and laying the basis for a literary 'road of liberty'.[80] Works by these authors were 'drawn from life', providing alternatives to texts reflecting the false consciousness of the bourgeoisie. Accurate to 'a thousand intermediate degrees' and infused with the shared consciousness of genuine artist-radicals and their readers, this new and practical integration of literature with the experience of labour would resolve feelings of cultural and political dislocation by finding inspiration in commonly-held progressive ideals. Holding that the relationship between capitalism and its proletarian 'slave' was disastrous for the production of art, Kropotkin promised that this harmonisation would improve culture by replacing fractious, ego-driven art with 'collective works' that were socially responsible and politically focused.[81]

Wilde also believed that by converting private wealth into a collective, public resource, socialist co-operation would replace competition, transforming labour's degraded function into a foundation for collective and responsible action. By removing the 'Tyranny of want', socialism would provide society with its 'proper environment' and 'highest mode of perfection'.[82] Wilde argued that anarchist socialism would solve the combined problems of life, art, politics and work, and argued that the utopia it proposed offered the only possibility of contentment. Other fin de siècle anarchists also demanded an end to property along with the 'destruction' of authority and the establishment of complete individual autonomy.[83] Like Wilde, they argued that their political ideas had cultural as well as aesthetic applications:

> The more miserable and oppressive life is, the more man must contemplate or hear of noble works of art, in order to save himself from despair [. . .] the desire of the poor to participate in the enjoyment of the common productions of culture must in every way be respected. It is even our duty to arouse a taste for artistic pleasures among those who lack them and to unite the isolated sparks into one great flame of love for the grand and the beautiful.[84]

For Jean Grave, the most 'common productions of culture' were as aesthetically valid as those produced by the privileged.[85] Echoing Wilde, he believed that the key to political renovation lay in the inclusion of aesthetic pleasure in his movement's programme. Wilde's proposals for a democratic cultural practice that would liberate the alienated and dispossessed through art reflected views that were often expressed in the writings of contemporary anarchists.

Class, Culture, Pleasure and Resistance

For Wilde, Aestheticism was a socially driven phenomenon and he regarded bourgeois individualism as limited and affording only partial independence to the professional middle class. In this class were found the artists, poets, philosophers, scientists and other 'men of culture' around whom society was focused. Like Kropotkin's revolutionary authors, these were 'real men [. . .] who have realised themselves, and in whom all Humanity gains a partial realisation'. Through their work, they could access meaningful and constructive forms of pleasure. Wilde contrasted the autonomy of the artist who resisted the influence of capital by standing 'outside his subject' with the static helplessness of the bourgeoisie.[86] Burdened by property, they led miserable existences qualified by constant anxiety and needless labour while capitalism's erosion of the intellect ensured that the best personalities among the wealthy went undeveloped. As the ultimate source of political authority, property provided an incomplete measure of meaning and identity:

> In a community like ours, where property confers immense distinction, social position, honour, respect, titles, and other pleasant things of the kind, man, being naturally ambitious, makes it his aim to accumulate this property, and goes on wearily and tediously accumulating it long after he has got far more than he wants, or can use, or enjoy, or perhaps even know of.[87]

This would lead to individual self-destruction and the deterioration of humanity's capacity for pleasure, which Wilde connected to capitalism's denial of freedom. This consequence of property accumulation restricted human development and subjected everyone to a chaotic and disorganised existence:

> One's regret is that society should be constructed on such a basis that man has been forced into a groove in which he cannot freely develop what is wonderful, and fascinating, and delightful in him – in which, in fact, he misses the true pleasure and joy of living. He is also, under existing conditions, very insecure.[88]

Wilde regarded capitalist authority as modernity's greatest and most destructive irony. Even its adherents were denied subjectivity, as '[w]hat a man really has' and 'what is in him' did not equate. He believed that the abolition of private property represented the only possibility for progress as its values were external to the individual and artificial. This would become the basis of a new dispensation with 'true, beautiful, healthy Individualism' as its goal, while capital would lose its grip on the popular imagination: 'Nobody will waste his life in accumulating things, and the symbols for things. One will live.'[89]

Wilde regarded liberation from these constraints as 'the rarest thing in the world' and maintained that freedom could be achieved through immersion in culture. By countering alienation, culture already afforded a sense of wholeness to people of means. Wilde argued that the working class also deserved to enjoy its benefits and insisted that the freedom afforded to culturally active professionals should be extended to all. Until this could be achieved, the experience of intellectual and cultural fulfilment would remain the preserve of the élite and could never be accessed by workers: human 'beasts of burden' who were prevented from enjoying the pleasures made possible by their own labour. Leading an existence that was even more erratic and degrading than that of the bourgeoisie, they were capitalism's principal victims. Their exclusion from pleasure explained why Wilde saw no evidence of 'civilisation in culture, or refinement in pleasures, or joy of life' among the working class.[90]

By refusing to distribute culture among all the classes, capitalism diminished society as a whole. This denial of pleasure to the poor was the problem that charity, with its conservative ideological purpose and 'sentimental dole' would never resolve. Without any structural solution to the crisis, bourgeois normality would always exist precariously on the edge of revolt because 'the best among the poor are never grateful'. The unconquered poor remained 'ungrateful, discontented, disobedient, and rebellious' and would resist because '[w]herever there is a man who exercises authority, there is a man who resists authority'.[91] This dialectic is central to Wilde's discussion of the realities of poverty and hunger and his literary explorations of their presence in late Victorian culture; and in the essay's most insurgent passage he asked:

> Why should they be grateful for the crumbs that fall from the rich man's table? They should be seated at the board, and are beginning to know it. As for being discontented, a man who would not be discontented with such surroundings and such a low mode of life would be a perfect brute. Disobedience, in the eyes of anyone who has read history, is man's original virtue. It is through disobedience that progress has been made, through disobedience and through rebellion. Sometimes the poor are praised for being thrifty. But to recommend thrift to the poor is both grotesque and insulting. It is like advising a man who is starving to eat less.[92]

Just as his mother had argued decades earlier in her 1847 poem, 'The Stricken Land', Wilde depicted the starvation of the poor not as a natural or insoluble problem but as the outcome of deliberate and conscious strategies of power that were developed to isolate the dispossessed and contain their anger. He regarded their capacity for resistance as the measure of their humanity and depicted capitalism's creation of hunger as the most striking crisis of his era. Pointing to the model of abolitionism and its successful campaigns against slavery, he advised the poor to engage in retaliatory actions including theft because 'it is finer to take than to beg'. The 'virtuous poor', or those who had chosen not to rebel, steal or retaliate, had already surrendered by making 'private terms with the enemy' that 'sold their birthright', but the best and most resistant would never submit. Only those wealthy enough to exist in conditions of aesthetic possibility could experience beauty and pursue the benefits of intellectual life, but their privilege did not justify their acquiescence in the injustice and social violence of capitalism.[93]

Notes

1. For a detailed analysis of the diversity of socialist writing and thought in this period, see Mark Bevir's *The Making of British Socialism* (Princeton: Princeton University Press, 2011).
2. Oscar Wilde, interview with *The Philadelphia Enquirer*, 1882, quoted in Lewis and Smith, *Oscar Wilde Discovers America*, p. 66.
3. Oscar Wilde, 'The Grosvenor Gallery', *Dublin University Magazine*, 90 (July 1877), pp. 118–26, in *Complete Works*, vol. 6, pp. 1–11, p. 10. See also Ruskin's *Essays on Political Economy*, originally published in *Cornhill Magazine* from 1862 to 1863, reprinted in *Unto This Last and Other Essays on Art and Political Economy* (London: Dent, 1913).
4. Diana Maltz, *British Aestheticism and the Urban Working Classes, 1870–1900: Beauty for the People* (Basingstoke: Palgrave, 2006), p. 34.
5. *Sacramento Daily Record-Union*, 1882, quoted in Lewis and Smith, *Oscar Wilde Discovers America*, p. 183.
6. Cleveland *Herald*, undated, quoted Lewis and Smith, *Oscar Wilde Discovers America*, p. 183.
7. Here Wilde was referring to well-heeled Bostonians. 'The American Invasion', originally published in *Court and Society Review*, 23 March 1887, reprinted in Robert Ross (ed.), *Collected Works*, vol. 14: *Miscellanies* (Boston: John Luce & Co., 1908), pp. 77–82, quotation from p. 77.
8. 'Mr. Oscar Wilde on America', *The Freeman's Journal*, 11 July 1883 (no page no.), UCLA Clark Library, *Wildeana*, Box 10: 'Wilde in America', 10.18 A.

9. Wilde, 'Impressions of America', pp. 8–9.
10. 'Mr. Oscar Wilde on America', quoted in Lewis and Smith, *Oscar Wilde Discovers America*, p. 249.
11. Uncited newspaper source, quoted in ibid.
12. See Edward Palmer Thompson, *The Making of the English Working Class* (London: Penguin, 1968), pp. 473–85.
13. Quoted in 'Oscar Wilde's Lecture', *The Evening Light* (San Antonio), 22 June 1882, p. 1.
14. 'Mr. Oscar Wilde on America', in Lewis and Smith, *Oscar Wilde Discovers America*, p. 249.
15. Quoted in 'Art and Aesthetics', *The Tribune* (Denver), 13 April 1882, p. 8.
16. *Pall Mall Gazette*, 7 July 1883 (untitled, no page no.), UCLA Clark Library, *Wildeana*, Box 10: 'Wilde in America', 10.15A.
17. 'Mr. Oscar Wilde on America', cutting from *The Freeman's Journal*, 11 July 1883 (no page no.), UCLA Clark Library, *Wildeana*, Box 10: 'Wilde in America', 10.18 A. See also Matthew Sturgis, *Oscar: A Life* (London: Head of Zeus, 2018), pp. 297–8.
18. Oscar Wilde, 'A Chinese Sage', in *Complete Works*, vol. 7, p. 242.
19. Goodway, *Anarchist Seeds Beneath the Snow*, p. 73.
20. Wilde, 'A Chinese Sage' in *Complete Works*, vol. 7, p. 242.
21. Kate Hext, *Walter Pater: Individualism and Aesthetic Philosophy* (Edinburgh: Edinburgh University Press, 2013), p. 28.
22. Ian Small has pointed out that Wilde was commenting on generic images of Chinese immortals painted on cheap houseware items. Wilde, 'A Chinese Sage', in *Complete Works*, vol. 7, p. 238. Also *Complete Works*, vol. 7, *Journalism* 2, p. 516, n. for pp. 18–23.
23. Wilde, 'A Chinese Sage', in *Complete Works*, vol. 7, p. 238.
24. Ibid. p. 238.
25. Ibid. pp. 238–9.
26. Ibid. p. 239.
27. Ibid.
28. Ibid. p. 240.
29. Ibid. pp. 240–1.
30. Ibid.
31. Ibid. p. 242.
32. Wilde, 'The Soul of Man', in *Complete Works*, vol. 4, pp. 229–68, pp. 238–9.
33. Josephine Guy, 'Introduction', in *Complete Works*, vol. 4, p. lxxviii.
34. See Lawrence Danson, *Wilde's Intentions: The Artist in his Criticism* (Oxford: Oxford University Press, 1987), chapter 4: 'The Soul of Man Under Socialism'.
35. Originally published as a pair of essays in autumn, 1890, and then as a single piece in *Intentions* a few months after the original publication of 'The Soul of Man Under Socialism'. See Wilde, 'The Critic as Artist', in *Complete Works*, vol. 4, pp. 123–206, p. 172.

36. Kohl, *Oscar Wilde: The Works of a Conformist Rebel*, p. 133. Oscar Wilde, 'The Soul of Man Under Socialism' (New York: The Humboldt Publishing Company, n.d.). London's annotated copy is held in the Huntington Library's Jack London Collection (Ephemera: Pamphlets, W-Z, JLE 2208).
37. Bell, *Wilde without Whitewash*, p. 93. Bell met Wilde in Paris and was deeply impressed by his political views.
38. Sherard, *The Life of Oscar Wilde*, pp. 131–2. Sherrard noted its popularity among 'the most desperate of the helots of Europe, the Jews of Russia and Poland'.
39. Wilde, 'The Soul of Man', in *Complete Works*, vol. 4, pp. 229–68, p. 236.
40. Wilde, Ibid. p. 237. Marx also believed that machine technology would reduce labour to a minimum, freeing the artistic as well as scientific potential of humanity. See Karl Marx, *Grundrisse: Foundations of the Critique of Political Economy (Rough Draft)*, trans. from *Grundrisse der Kritik der Politischen Ökonomie (Rohentwurf)* by Martin Nicolaus (London: Penguin, 1973), pp. 690–711.
41. Wilde, 'The Soul of Man', in *Complete Works*, vol. 4, pp. 229–68, p. 237.
42. Ibid. pp. 247–8.
43. Ibid. p. 246.
44. Ibid. p. 248.
45. Ibid. p. 249.
46. Ibid. p. 250.
47. Gagnier, *Idylls of the Marketplace*, p. 20.
48. Ibid. pp. 250–1.
49. Ibid. p. 265.
50. Ibid. p. 252.
51. Ibid. pp. 251–2.
52. Ibid. pp. 263, 264.
53. Wilde, 'The Critic as Artist', in *Complete Works*, vol. 4, p. 147.
54. Wilde, 'The Soul of Man', in *Complete Works*, vol. 4, pp. 229–68, p. 261.
55. This essay appeared in English in Kropotkin's book, *The Conquest of Bread*, in 1906, which was originally published in French in 1892 as *La Conquête du Pain*. As David Priestland has shown, the essays in this collection were drawn from Kropotkin's writings for the journals *La Révolté* and *La Révolte*, so the connection between artistic, cultural and political discourse was well-established in anarchist thought by the early 1890s. See Peter Kropotkin, *The Conquest of Bread* (London: Penguin: 2015), p. 28 and David Priestman, 'Introduction', Ibid. xx.
56. Wilde, 'The Soul of Man', in *Complete Works*, vol. 4, pp. 229–68, p. 263.
57. Thomas Carlyle, *The French Revolution: A History* (originally published, 1837; Oxford: Oxford University Press, 2019), p. 559.

58. Ibid. p. 261.
59. Ibid. p. 259.
60. Ibid. pp. 255–6.
61. See Michael S. Foldy, *The Trials of Oscar Wilde* (New Haven: Yale University Press, 2007), especially chapter 3: 'The Reception of the Trials in the Press'. Nicholas Freeman has examined Wilde's trials against the broader practice of sensational journalism. See Freeman, *1895: Drama, Disaster and Disgrace*.
62. See Francis Stewart Leland Lyons, *Charles Stewart Parnell* (London: Fontana, 1978), chapter 13: 'Ireland in the Strand'.
63. Wilde, 'The Soul of Man', in *Complete Works*, vol. 4, pp. 229–68, p. 255.
64. See my *Blasted Literature*, pp. 162–5.
65. Wilde, 'The Soul of Man', in *Complete Works*, vol. 4, pp. 229–68, pp. 255, 259.
66. Ibid. pp. 244, 236.
67. Ibid. p. 244.
68. Ibid. p. 258.
69. Ibid. pp. 244, 267, 255.
70. Ibid. p. 245.
71. See Butterworth, *The World That Never Was*, pp. 300–5.
72. Wilde, 'The Soul of Man', in *Complete Works*, vol. 4, pp. 229–68, pp. 235, 240.
73. Ibid. pp. 231, 236.
74. Ibid. pp. 232–3.
75. Ibid. p. 265.
76. Ibid. p. 237.
77. Peter Kropotkin, *The Conquest of Bread*, pp. 109, 101.
78. Peter Kropotkin to Robert Ross, 6 May 1905, in Ross (ed.), *Robert Ross, Friend of Friends*, pp. 112–14, p. 113.
79. Kropotkin, *The Conquest of Bread*, pp. 100–1.
80. Ibid. pp. 106, 109, 103, 111. For an account of these practices, see Helen and Olivia Rossetti's barely disguised autobiographical novel, *A Girl Among the Anarchists,* which was published under the pseudonym of Isabel Meredith in 1903 (Lincoln: University of Nebraska Press, 1992).
81. Kropotkin, *The Conquest of Bread*, pp. 105, 109–12, 92.
82. Wilde, 'The Soul of Man', in *Complete Works*, vol. 4, pp. 229–68, p. 233.
83. Jean Grave, *Moribund Society and Anarchy* (trans. from *Société mourante et l'anarchie* by Voltairine de Cleyre, San Francisco: Free Society Library, 1899), p. 120.
84. Emile Reich, 'Art and the People', *Free Society* (San Francisco), New Series No. 22, Whole No. 158, Sunday, 10 April 1890, pp. 5–6, p. 5.
85. Grave, *Moribund Society*, pp. 1–7, p. 3.

86. Wilde, 'The Soul of Man', in *Complete Works*, vol. 4, pp. 229–68, pp. 233, 253.
87. Ibid. p. 238.
88. Ibid.
89. Ibid. pp. 238–9.
90. Ibid. pp. 239, 233.
91. Ibid. pp. 234, 239.
92. Ibid. p. 234.
93. Ibid. p. 235.

Chapter 4

Fairy Tales for Revolutionaries

The best way to make children good is to make them happy.[1]

In a series of essays published in the *The Nineteenth Century* between 1890 and 1896 and collected later in his 1902 volume, *Mutual Aid*, the anarchist theorist Peter Kropotkin warned that humanity never progressed under conditions of competition. Arguing that co-operation was the sole driver of social, political and cultural evolution, he claimed that people were motivated by their natural affinity toward one another. Their instinctive solidarity formed the basis of morality while the self-destructive 'gunpowder civilization' of capitalism was centred on violence, disruption and instability. Believing that the human species was genetically programmed for co-operation, Kropotkin warned that capitalism divided societies and cultures by provoking artificial crises that alienated people from one another.[2]

While utopian political thought looks forward toward a future of human perfection, Kropotkin found many of his models for social harmony and collective co-operation in the past.[3] Pointing to examples of happiness, justice and equality that he found in his research on supposedly primitive but morally advanced cultures, he described their co-operative practices. Kropotkin argued that the practice of solidarity, or 'mutual aid', was the key driver behind human evolution and the historical foundation of civilisation. However, the history of this 'higher form of commonwealth' had been erased from popular memory. Historically, sociability had been the key to human evolution as reason, compassion, co-operation and voluntary association led to the successful development of societies. Kropotkin equated political, economic, technological and social progress with moral advancement and predicted that the most humane societies, not the most brutal, would prevail: civilisations and even animal species that failed to co-operate were doomed to failure (he devoted an entire chapter of his book to the study of mutualism among animals). Rejecting Thomas Malthus' interpretation of social development as the outcome of struggle and antagonism, he warned his readers: 'Don't compete!' Advocating combination over conflict, he derided modern capitalism and its deliberate cultivation of 'stony hearts' for causing widespread social atomisation and provoking wars. For Kropotkin, mutualism's natural 'genius' and constructive thrust shaped the cultural and intellectual conditions of progressive societies. As Engels had already done, he also cited Irish Brehon law as a key example of historical communism.[4]

Addressing the issue of cultural production, Kropotkin believed that the communal art of pre-capitalist societies expressed an 'eminently social' aesthetic filled with possibility. Arguing that the finest work had always resulted from collective effort, he particularly favoured ancient Greek art and medieval architecture. He believed that these achievements contrasted dramatically with contemporary monuments to capital, such as the 'meaningless scaffold' of the Eiffel Tower and the ugly artificiality or 'sham structure', of Tower Bridge, both of which he regarded as reflections of the disengaged 'particularism' of capitalist ideology. A new and radical alternative of truly civic art and architecture could reflect the possibility of social union and collective creation by realising the modern French revolutionary principles of liberty, equality and fraternity. Such art was 'worthy [. . .] of Paradise'.[5]

Kropotkin's views on literature were equally politicised and in 1901 he advocated a 'new art-criticism', including literary criticism, that would 'analyse [. . .] not only the aesthetic value of a work of art, but, above all, its leading idea – its "philosophical", – its social meaning'. For Kropotkin, the value of literature lay in its fusion of aesthetic and social innovation: 'A poet who is satisfied with his own self, and does not pursue aims of general improvement, is of no use to his contemporaries.' In a series of lectures delivered in 1901, he also pointed to the connection between political and literary innovation in Russia, where the exploration of the relationship between beauty and truth was considered subversive. The content and technique 'of really good art', along with 'its value, its purport, its comprehension' were to be found in its involvement in 'politics, in social questions, and in humanitarian aspirations'. Here, the connection between revolutionary and literary activity proved that 'true poetry *is* real', serving as the expression of 'life and reality', while the work of any genuine artist (Kropotkin regarded Gogol, Pushkin, Chekhov, Turgenev, Dostoevsky and Tolstoy as exemplary authors) 'bore the stamp of his most sympathetic personality'.[6]

Wilde's views mirrored Kropotkin's anarchist theory of art and literature. As outlined in the previous chapter, Wilde also objected to capitalism's atomising influence, and warned that it was harmful to culture. Like Kropotkin, Wilde discussed the radical potential of literary art in 'The Soul of Man Under Socialism' and in his short story collections, *The Happy Prince and Other Tales* (1888), *A House of Pomegranates* and *Lord Arthur Savile's Crime* (both 1891), he committed this theory into literary action. In these collections he used the folk tradition, the gothic and political satire to criticise late Victorian imperialism, property relations and authority, a practice that, as Caroline Sumpter has shown, was not uncommon among socialist writers.[7] His essay discussed the liberating potential of art and insisted that cultural practice was inherently radical. It explained how art could improve the condition of humanity by providing revolutionary alternatives to the structural violence of capital and poverty. Wilde also encoded and transmitted his radical beliefs through the medium of short fiction, particularly the fairy tale.

The relationship between the fantastic and the political is alluded to in *De Profundis*, in which Wilde also described Kropotkin in religious-visionary terms as a radical embodiment of divinity, possessing 'the soul of that beautiful white Christ coming out of Russia'.[8] Exploring the tension between capitalism and the human desire for co-operation upon which contemporary anarchist philosophy was based, he drew upon what he regarded as the key injustice of his age: the violence done to innocence by capitalism and imperialism. These stories, with their visions for an alternative and morally-focused dispensation, recommend mutualism as both a realistic and progressive social practice.

This chapter explores two of Wilde's better-known stories, 'The Happy Prince' and 'The Selfish Giant' in relation to the less familiar tale, 'The Young King'. 'The Canterville Ghost' (which also enjoys greater recognition) and another, more obscure tale, 'The Star-Child', are also discussed in relation to their treatment of the themes of class dialectics, imperialism and Wilde's own proposals for an anarchic subjectivity modelled on his radical interpretation of Christianity. In these works Wilde presented the anarchist practice of mutualism as a radical utopian possibility – an idea that he amplified through the more openly political content of 'The Soul of Man Under Socialism'. The proposals that these tales articulated for a non-hierarchical and revolutionary counter-sensibility drew on his knowledge of colonialism in Ireland and the influence of contemporary anarchism. In doing so, Wilde advanced ideas that he had already outlined during the 1880s in lectures and reviews that highlighted the persistence of violent colonial practices and policies, along with the aggressive characteristics they shared with capitalism.

Celticism and the Radical Fairy Tale

In an approving review of William Butler Yeats' first collection of poems, *The Wanderings of Oisin and Other Poems*, which was published in the *Woman's World* in 1889, Wilde noted the 'fragmentary' and 'incomplete' images and motifs that informed the young poet's Celticism. This appeared to him 'like stray scenes out of unfinished plays, like things only half remembered, or, at best, but dimly seen'.[9] Yeats' early poetry was inspired by what he perceived as the anti-modern characteristics of the Irish peasantry and he was fascinated by their capacity for belief in the unknown and the unworldly (Wilde's mother stated of them in 1878 that '[n]o people have more intense faith in the unseen').[10] The Irish Literary Revival of the late nineteenth century attempted to counter the imperatives of imperial and capitalist modernity by cultivating a national identity informed by a collective cultural repository drawn from myth, legend and folklore. Through these means it sought to offer its Irish readers radical possibilities for understanding themselves independently of the political and psychological frameworks of imperial culture. Wilde viewed the aesthetic and cultural logic of the Revival, with its emphasis on the fractured and residual elements of the Irish past, as reflecting the movement's exclusively idealistic thrust and its 'romantic temper'. The result was that, in Yeats' collection, '[t]he *spirit* that dominates the whole book is perhaps more valuable than any individual poem or particular passage'.[11]

The Irish Literary Revival sought to counter the misrepresentation of Ireland and the Irish by authors such as Ruskin, Charles Kingsley and Robert Louis Stevenson, along with the racist and imperialist distortions that saturated the columns of the British popular press.[12] Wilde had already suggested in 1886 that non-modern and subaltern forms such as folklore, myth and popular ballads (the cultural forms that Thomas Davis and the Young Ireland movement, of which Wilde's mother was a member, promoted in their journal, *The Nation*) were 'in the highest degree imaginative' and therefore had a unique potential. Rather than viewing them as outdated matter of use only to cloistered archivists, collectors and mythologists, he found potentially liberating patterns in these forms. They suggested constructive outlines for a more consciously modern cultural expression through the means of a socially engaged national literature:

> For the Folk-tale is the father of all fiction as the Folk-song is the mother of all poetry; and in the games, the tales and the ballads of primitive people it is easy to see the germs of such perfected forms of art as the drama, the novel and the epic. It is, of course, true that the highest expression of life is to be found not in the popular songs, however poetical, of any nation, but in the great masterpieces of self-conscious Art; yet it is pleasant sometimes to leave the summit of Parnassus to look at the wildflowers in the valley, and to turn from the lyre of Apollo to listen to the reed of Pan. We can still listen to it.[13]

Wilde reminded late Victorian aesthetes that they should not reject the origins of their art, which, he believed, lay in these forms, and argued that early models of cultural expression could provide artists with ideas and subject matter through which they might explore modern experience. He found a basis for the exploration of his own dissident political perspective on capitalism and empire in the collective cultural expressions of those peoples portrayed by Ruskin in his 1870 lecture, 'Idolatry', as being so primitive that they were doomed to cultural extinction. Wilde's own fairy and folk-based tales, along with those with more contemporary settings, have distinctly modern political resonances, exposing what he described in 'The Canterville Ghost' as '[t]he vugarity [. . .] and the gross materialism'[14] of capitalism.

Wilde's belief in the 'purity' of innocence[15] counters what he paradoxically regarded as the alluring but corrupting influence of the commodity. This antagonism is played out in the tension that emerges in these works. His discussions of innocence in 'The Canterville Ghost', with its recognisably contemporary setting, and 'The Selfish Giant' with its atemporality, present the child as the embodiment of human perfection. In the latter story, the mythical child personifies the infant Christ, resembling the aura of divinity that Wilde later conferred on Kropotkin. While Kropotkin preferred the genre of literary realism, Wilde's fantastic stories draw on the same political and material bases that he insisted were so important to literary writing. Despite their melancholic tone these ultimately hopeful texts challenge bourgeois authority by proposing radical possibilities, as when the Charity Children in 'The Happy Prince' glimpse divinity in the form of angels seen in their dreams.

'The Happy Prince' and the Structural Violence of Capitalism

Published in 1888, *The Happy Prince and Other Tales* has remarkable literary range, varying from the titular moral fable to the sophisticated 'The Portrait of Mr. W.H.', which doubles both as a fiction and a pioneering work of queer theory.[16] In his 1954 essay, 'The Gorgon's Head', Louis Marlow described 'The Happy Prince' as an open statement of Wilde's radicalism that depicted the social origins of poverty as 'the work of man'. Marlow stressed that the tale's originality lay in its portrayal of class violence and its infliction 'upon the weak by gross, greedy, vain, insensitive, unimaginative people'. Despite its fantastic plot, he believed that it conveyed the very bleak reality under which the working poor and their children laboured and subsisted:

> Defenceless sufferers from poverty, hungry children in black streets, beggars, little match-girls without shoes or stockings, it was from compassion for these that Wilde wrote *The Happy Prince*: and from indignation, characteristically touched with irony, against the guilty ones, against the symbolic Mayor who thinks the Prince's statue, when stripped of gold and jewels, 'little better than a beggar', and who decides that 'we must have another statue, and it shall be a statue of myself'.[17]

For Marlow the story exposed the poverty and suffering that existed beneath conspicuous displays of capital and were concealed by its agents, such as the Mayor. This revelation disrupts the logic of capital as the Swallow's disarticulation of the statue of the Happy Prince reveals to the reader Wilde's belief in the baseness of the capitalist spectacle. Stripped of its surface beauty by the bird as it removes the decorative gold leaves and jewels that have made it an object of wonder and admiration in the city, the monument is gradually devalued. So, too, is capital, as the story's moral lies in its corresponding exposure of the violence on which the bourgeois power of the Mayor depends.

The Swallow and the Prince accomplish change through their practice of mutualism, with which Wilde emphasises the moral connections binding empathy to generosity. This is the 'good action' that the Prince describes when he asks the bird to distribute jewels and gold among the poor.[18] Moral agency is drawn from his sympathy with the dispossessed and its social potential is conveyed through the Prince's realisation that the pleasures he enjoyed while alive involved elaborate displays of capital. The dead Prince recollects how his own enjoyment of wealth was contained by the authority that he represented when alive:

> When I was alive and had a human heart [. . .] I did not know what tears were, for I lived in the Palace of Sans-Souci, where sorrow is not allowed to enter. In the daytime I played with my companions in the garden, and in the evening I led the dance in the Great Hall. Round the garden ran a very lofty wall, but I never cared to ask what lay beyond it, everything about me was so beautiful. My courtiers called me the Happy Prince, and happy indeed I was, if pleasure be happiness. So I lived, and so I died. And now that I am dead they have set me up here so high that I can see all the ugliness and all the misery of my city, and though my heart is made of lead yet I cannot choose but weep.[19]

The Prince is exposed to the reality of capital when he witnesses its effects from his position upon the column on which his statue rests. His death has not liberated him from the spectacle but has instead trapped his consciousness within it as his soul is now commodified and contained within the lead heart sealed inside the monument. The palace's title, 'Sans-Souci', meaning 'without care', suggests the establishment's refusal to identify with the dispossessed, and the Swallow discovers that the Prince's statue is as hollow as the political order he represents: '"What! Is he not solid gold?" said the Swallow to himself.'[20] Elevated above the city, the Prince sees through the class border forming the wall around his palace garden and which diminished his own consciousness when alive. His discovery of economic violence masked by the spectacle of bourgeois pleasure is the focus of the tale's political allegory, which follows the Happy Prince's transition from condition of stasis toward becoming a moral agent of 'good action'. His beneficiaries include a seamstress who cannot afford fruit for her ill child, a match girl threatened with physical abuse and an impoverished writer whose predicament conveys the difficulty of creating art under conditions of poverty.

These local interventions are punctuated by the Swallow's Orientalist reminiscences of its flights to Egypt. Its account of these travels underline the vacuity of imperial pleasure:

> All the next day he sat on the Prince's shoulder, and told him stories of what he had seen in strange lands. He told him of the red ibises, who stand in long rows on the banks of the Nile, and catch goldfish in their beaks; of the Sphinx, who is as old as the world itself, and lives in the

desert, and knows everything; of the merchants, who walk slowly by the side of their camels and carry amber beads in their hands; of the King of the Mountains of the Moon, who is as black as ebony, and worships a large crystal; of the great green snake that sleeps in a palm-tree, and has twenty priests to feed it with honey-cakes; and of the pygmies who sail over a big lake on large flat leaves, and are always at war with the butterflies.[21]

In this passage Wilde deploys a very self-reflexive critique of Orientalism to criticise art that has no social impact. The colonial beings and commodities encountered by the Swallow are decadent representatives of excessive consumption, static knowledge, misdirected devotion and pointless struggle. Each symbolises participation in the capitalist spectacle, the strangeness of which is amplified through the bird's fascination with what it has witnessed. For all of their beauty and elegance, these exotic people, creatures and objects remain distant and unreal, as the corruption of their splendour is made clear by the Swallow's encounters with the poverty that was concealed from the Prince when he was alive. The fantastic excess of these scenes fails to interest him as he is now absorbed by the material consequences of consumption, and he sends the Swallow on another mission to witness and then report to him about the reality of poverty:

'Dear little Swallow,' said the Prince, 'you tell me of marvellous things, but more marvellous than anything is the suffering of men and of women. There is no Mystery so great as Misery. Fly over my city, little Swallow, and tell me what you see there.
 So the Swallow flew over the great city, and saw the rich making merry in their beautiful houses, while the beggars were sitting at the gates. He flew into dark lanes, and saw the white faces of starving children looking out listlessly at the black streets. Under the archway of a bridge two little boys were lying in one another's arms to try and keep themselves warm. 'How hungry we are!' they said. 'You must not lie here,' shouted the watchman, and they wandered out into the rain.[22]

The Swallow's accounts of colonially-oriented Decadence and domestic poverty collapse the distinction and distance between imperial rapacity and bourgeois consumption, as Wilde's critique of socially disengaged Aestheticism becomes clear: art lacking in the imaginative sympathy and political resonance that he would also explore in *De Profundis* appears empty, pointless and corrupt in the presence of suffering. Its illusion is disrupted by the violent reality of deprivation that becomes visible across the city and is countered with a final act of responsibility. On learning more about the despair that surrounds him, the Prince instructs the Swallow to strip his statue of its gold leaf 'and give it to my poor'.[23] The statue is transformed with this final act into a suitably hollow monument to capital, as its dismantling by the bird brings hope to the poor through a radical gesture of redistribution. The Swallow's relief missions echo again the anarchists' direct action of *la reprise individuelle*, while having a literary resonance at the same time: the removal of the statue's valuable components is also reminiscent of Fantine's sale of her own body parts in Victor Hugo's *Les Misérables* (1862), a socially-committed novel that Wilde revered, in which the desperate mother sells her hair and teeth to support her child, Cosette.[24] Stripped of its expensive ornamentation, the statue of the Prince is diminished. What remains of it is then destroyed when the utilitarian Art Professor announces that '[a]s he is no longer beautiful he is no longer useful'.[25]

Wilde's critique of the complicity between capitalism, utilitarianism and socially-disengaged art points to the corrupting nature of bourgeois power, which is characterised by the Mayor and Town Councillors, who quarrel over whether a monument to one of themselves should replace the Prince's statue. The ideological, economic and cultural ties that bind capital are exposed with the story's indictment of establishment culture: when art validates capital and the authority upon which it rests, it bears responsibility for its violent consequences. Once art serves injustice by assuming a place within power's symbolic networks, its cultural worth is compromised by the suffering that it conceals.

Following the Swallow's death from exhaustion and the Mayor's destruction of the statue, God asks for the most precious things in the city, and is given the bird's body and the monument's worthless lead heart, which the Mayor's workmen have been unable to melt down. On receiving their material remains, God then announces that both characters have assumed their places in Paradise: 'in my garden the little bird shall sing for evermore, and in my city of gold the Happy Prince shall praise me'.[26] With their redemption the story ends on a revolutionary and hopeful note, as Wilde informs the reader that Paradise, which is greater than the jurisdiction of capital, exists in the radical imagination. What has real value for humanity, and continues to exist in the heavenly city where suffering does not is the capacity for generosity and co-operation that the Prince and the Swallow have realised and experienced through their combined efforts to relieve the suffering of the poor. Capital is subverted, as the beauty of the gold from which Paradise has been rendered represents the principles of a compassionate and radical deity. As Louis Marlow argued, the story's political potency lies in its celebration of the progressive agency exercised through the Prince's conscience-driven action. Wilde's critique of establishment culture continues in 'The Nightingale and the Rose', which was published in the same collection, in which he criticised socially conservative art for exhibiting 'style without sincerity', and complained that its moral and aesthetic emptiness was the result of its failure to convey the value of love, which he regarded as being 'better than Life' and 'mightier than Power'.[27]

Radical Christianity and 'The Selfish Giant'

In 'The Soul of Man Under Socialism', Wilde proposed that radical self-awareness was the ultimate condition of the Christian: '"Know thyself" was written over the portal of the antique world. Over the portal of the new world, "Be thyself" shall be written. And the message of Christ to man was simply "Be thyself." That is the secret of Christ.' Wilde believed that capital prevented self-realisation and that Christ's example had political implications for late Victorian society:

> When Jesus talks about the poor he simply means personalities, just as when he talks about the rich he simply means people who have not developed their personalities. Jesus moved in a community that allowed the accumulation of private property just as ours does, and the gospel that he preached was not that in such a community it is an advantage for a man to live on scanty, unwholesome food, to wear ragged, unwholesome clothes, to sleep in horrid, unwholesome dwellings, and a disadvantage for a man to live under healthy, pleasant, and decent conditions. Such a view would have been wrong there and then, and would, of course, be still more wrong now and in England [. . .][28]

As we have already seen, Wilde believed that capital inhibited human development and intensified inequality. The crises of modernity were profoundly complex because 'our society [. . .] displays far greater extremes of luxury and pauperism than any society of the antique world'. However poverty could be met, countered and defeated through a realisation of selfhood that was based on Christ's radical individualism:

> What Jesus meant, was this. He said to man, 'You have a wonderful personality. Develop it. Be yourself. Don't imagine that your perfection lies in accumulating or possessing external things. Your affection is inside of you. If only you could realise that, you would not want to be rich. Ordinary riches can be stolen from a man. Real riches cannot. In the treasury-house of your soul, there are infinitely precious things, that may not be taken from you. And so, try to so shape your life that external things will not harm you. And try also to get rid of personal property. It involves sordid preoccupation, endless industry, continual wrong. Personal property hinders Individualism at every step.[29]

The selfhood of the fully-realised individual could be measured in her or his capacity to resist authority, and the soul of the conscious rebel could never be violated by capitalism's artificial and 'external' phenomena. Wilde believed that affection, sympathy, understanding and solidarity were to be found within the individual and not in the lifeless symbols and mechanisms of capital. These constituted the 'real riches' found in the 'treasury-house' of the human soul: while possessions could be taken from a person, their subjectivity could not be erased with this loss. The soul or human agency was, he argued, resistant to the inauthentic matter of commodities, or 'things' and their false value, and capitalism could be countered by adhering to Christ's insistence on the value of personal agency. This would allow the modern subject to resist the materialistic imperatives of capital by maintaining a sense of the importance of the individual consciousness, whereby:

> man reaches his perfection, not through what he has, nor even through what he does, but entirely through what he is [. . .] It is within you and not outside of you, that you will find what you really are, and what you really want.[30]

Wilde believed that Christ's simple advice was that 'Man is complete in himself.' The autonomous and rebellious spirit of the complete man could endure violence, imprisonment and public criticism because the individual's creative and resistant capabilities formed the basis of human personality. These characteristics were connected to art because 'in one divine moment, and by selecting its own mode of expression, a personality might make itself perfect'.[31]

The bourgeoisie's self-infliction of misery and service as the agent and guardian of property are central themes of Wilde's best-remembered fairy tale, 'The Selfish Giant'.[32] In this socialist and anticolonial story, a cruel giant returns to his castle after a lengthy absence and proceeds to expel children who have been playing in his garden. After he evicts them (in a clear allegorisation of landlord violence during the Irish Land War),[33] the Giant is boycotted by nature, which goes on strike while the autumn refuses to yield any fruit and the flowers and trees refuse to blossom until he allows the children to return. The garden freezes as a permanent winter sets in but the Giant is redeemed and spring returns when he realises that he no longer wishes to exclude the children.

In this story Wilde explores the possibility of resisting the destructive influence of capital through the presence of the infant Christ, who appears in the Giant's garden. This child, the Giant's favourite, appears for one day when he readmits the children and he returns again at the end of the story to admit the Giant into Paradise. Mutualism counters selfishness and true pleasure is experienced in the sharing of a resource that has become collectivised and returned to common ownership. Like the children brutalised by hunger in 'The Happy Prince', the Christ child has also been harmed, with wounds on his hands and feet clearly symbolising the violence of the crucifixion along with the trauma of contemporary capitalism and imperialism. As Steven Arata has shown, Jesus Christ was put to use at the fin de siècle for a wide and complex range of aesthetic and ideological purposes.[34] Wilde's radical Christian vision is based upon his particularly modern critique of private property, as the story equates the wounded Christ with the suffering of the contemporary poor and colonised. This is rendered with particular intensity and emotional force, as it is directly associated with the suffering of children (Wilde's son, Vyvyan Holland, recalled that his father could not read the tale to him without crying).[35]

Having destroyed the boundary wall separating the community from his garden, the Giant is redeemed through his rejection of the bourgeois and imperial logics of separation, partition, enclosure and denial. No longer a figure of violent authority, he is welcomed into the radical Paradise entered by the Swallow and the Happy Prince. The Giant's experience of mutualism changes him from an isolated individual into a socially aware person and Wilde's proposition here is, again, that genuine and transformative beauty can be found in the liberation of consciousness from the restricting dogmas of capital and empire. The Giant's acknowledgement of the children's pleasure is the key to his own freedom: when he knocks down the wall surrounding his garden, permitting the children to play in it, he realises that they are the 'most beautiful flowers of all'. When the Christ child finally returns years later he becomes angered at the sight of wounds on the little boy's hands and feet – a revelation that within the political context of this fantastic tale conveys the violent reality of imperialist and capitalist authority. As in 'The Happy Prince', this divine intervention occurs within – and against – the context of structural violence, which announces itself at the beginning of the tale with the Giant's declaration that 'TRESPASSERS WILL BE PROSECUTED'. Like the Swallow and the Prince, the child is also resistant to power, which explains why he bears his injuries as redeeming 'wounds of Love'.[36] As the reader recognises the suffering of Christ in the returned child, the Giant is led toward his redemption, death and acceptance into Paradise. Like 'The Happy Prince', 'The Selfish Giant' explores the social and moral potential of acknowledging suffering as the Giant is redeemed by his acknowledgement of the innocence of the most vulnerable victims of capitalist modernity.

Despite its fantastic setting, the story's historically focused, materially conscious and politically insurgent message expresses Wilde's view that liberation can be achieved by identifying with the powerless, and that this identification is more enduring than the power, authority and appeal of capital. This idea is also advanced in 'The Canterville Ghost', which concludes with the newly married Virginia Otis telling her husband that the ghost of Sir Simon de Canterville has taught her 'what Life is, what Death Signifies, and why Love is stronger than both'.[37] A similar idea is also expressed in the conclusion to 'The Soul of Man Under Socialism', in which Wilde insists that pain, suffering and inequality can be countered with a resistance that is grander than the violence of authority.

Imperial Violence and the Politics of Starvation in 'The Young King'

Wilde warned in 'The Soul of Man Under Socialism' that '[s]tarvation and not sin, is the parent of modern crime'. In his story, 'The Young King', first published in *The Lady's Pictorial* in December 1888, and collected in *A House of Pomegranates* in 1891, he depicted the contemporary Irish experience of hunger through a fantastic lens in order to expose its modern origins. Michael Davitt recalled how in 1879 the return of the prospect of mass starvation mobilised popular resistance to landlordism in Ireland and gave rise to the Land War of the 1880s, and described British policy in Ireland as a form of terrorism that was 'preached with impunity, or practised through fear'.[38] Wilde's story explores the fusion of terror, coercion and starvation by the modern imperial state as the horrors witnessed by the young King that mirror the conditions of contemporary Ireland and draw attention to the material conditions and to the political causes and consequences of state-inflicted hunger. The story's lack of geographical specificity does not mask its political immediacy and Wilde was not the first Irish writer to address the Great Hunger of the 1840s and 1850s through the fantastic mode: the very title of Fitz-James O'Brien's 1859 tale of lodging house terror, 'What Was It? A Mystery', conveys the epistemological crisis that ensued from the shock of the violence done to the Irish peasantry during these decades. In O'Brien's tale a group of New York lodgers are attacked by an invisible vampiric creature which they eventually capture and starve to death, its strange condition corresponding with what Terry Eagleton has described as the 'undecidable' status of nineteenth-century colonial Ireland.[39]

Wilde's mother addressed this crisis in more direct terms than O'Brien had done. In 1882 she warned that having already exploited Ireland economically, the British were also sapping the country of its 'currents of thought and energy [. . .] draining the life-blood of Ireland to fill the veins of England', so that 'all that makes a nation great and strong and self-respecting' was being culturally 'annihilated'. The motif of vampirism was deployed by both sides during the Land War and here we find it being applied to underline the parasitism of the occupier. As a result of this exploitation, contemporary Ireland appeared to Speranza as a static cultural slum, frozen like the Selfish Giant's garden with 'decay stamped in her cities and her institutions'. Ireland's function in the 1880s was to serve as 'a mere cattle-pen for England' while satisfying the 'universal decadence' of the imperialist ruling class.[40]

Speranza also addressed the starvation of the Irish in her 1847 poem, 'The Stricken Land', which drew attention to the fact that British troops guarded the shipment of foodstuffs out of Ireland. First published in *The Nation* in 1847, the poem was reprinted as 'The Famine Year' in the 1864 volume, *Poems by Speranza*, which she dedicated, 'To my sons, Willie and Oscar Wilde' with the epigram: I taught them indeed, / Speak plain the word COUNTRY. I taught them, no doubt, / That a country's a thing men should die for at need!'[41] The poem depicts the mass starvation of the Irish as the outcome of consciously and deliberately implemented colonial policies. Speranza directly blamed the British for the genocide of the 1840s: 'Accursed are we in our own land, yet toil we still and toil; / But the stranger reaps our harvest – the alien owns our soil.'[42] The Irish peasantry die from hunger on their 'native plains' while crops are exported under armed guard by British troops:

> Weary men, what reap ye? – Golden corn for the stranger.
> What sow ye? – Human corses that wait for the avenger.
> Fainting forms, hunger-stricken, what see you in the offing?
> Stately ships to bear our food away, amid the stranger's scoffing.
> There's a proud array of soldiers – what do they round your door?
> They guard our masters' granaries from the thin hands of the poor.[43]

The poem concludes by highlighting the divinity of these innocent victims of British imperialism:

> We are wretches, famished, scorned, human tools to build your pride,
> But God will yet take vengeance for the souls for whom Christ died.
> Now is your hour of pleasure – bask ye in the world's caress;
> But our whitening bones against ye will arise as witnesses,
> From the cabins and the ditches, in their charred, uncoffin'd masses,
> For the angel of the Trumpet will know them as he passes.
> A ghastly, spectral army, before the great God we'll stand,
> And arraign ye as our murderers, the spoilers of our land.[44]

Bourgeois-imperial pride is contrasted with the innocence of the Irish victims of what Speranza described as the British government's deliberate 'extermination' policy, and her poem exposes the state's guilt and complicity in their deaths. 'No nation ever endured greater horrors,' she wrote, 'and no people but the Irish could have survived them.'[45]

Terry Eagleton has noted how the Great Hunger 'strains at the limits of the articulable, and is truly in this sense the Irish Auschwitz'.[46] Yet Speranza confronted this violence directly and, like his mother, Wilde was also haunted by the catastrophe. He also engaged with the still-present threat of mass starvation and with the evictions against which the Irish peasantry mobilised themselves during the Land War, and these matters are addressed in 'The Young King'. The tale is informed by Wilde's consciousness of the fact that so many had been forcibly starved to death amid abundance, and that they died as a direct result of the colonial policies criticised in his mother's poem. His consciousness of what Joe Cleary has termed Britain's 'early

Victorian holocaust' and the official cruelty that led to it was, as Owen Dudley Edwards has argued, the greatest intellectual legacy that Wilde's parents bequeathed to him.[47]

'The Young King' explores the moral and human cost of imperialist decadence and the concealment of labour is another constant presence in the story. This also has a culturally autobiographical thrust: the young King at the centre of the story is a guilt-ridden aesthete who redeems himself and his kingdom by achieving a condition of radical divinity. The child of a princess and an artist, he is raised by peasants after his grandfather, the King, has his parents murdered. The young King returns to the court after his grandfather bequeaths the kingdom to him but the boy repeats the kind of class transgression encoded in his parents' relationship as he falls under the influence of the 'strange passion for beauty' that he inherits from them, and which is 'destined to have such an influence over his life'.[48] The story centres on the tension between the monarch's political responsibilities and the aesthete's search for perfection in art, highlighting the necessity of balancing social commitment with the pleasures of experiencing culture. Although the young King delights in the expensive materials used to produce artworks, he is equally fascinated by the image of a slave of the Roman Emperor, Hadrian, whose statue is recovered from a riverbed. Again, unbridled Orientalism stands in for late Victorian consumption and is revealed to be the source of the young King's pleasure:

> All rare and costly materials had certainly a great fascination for him, and in his eagerness to procure them he had sent away many merchants, some to traffic for amber with the rough fisher-folk of the north seas, some to Egypt to look for that curious green turquoise which is found only in the tombs of kings, and is said to possess magical properties, some to Persia for silken carpets and painted pottery, and others to India to buy gauze and stained ivory, moonstones and bracelets of jade, sandal-wood and blue enamel and shawls of fine wool.[49]

As well as acquiring these imperial commodities, the young King has his chambers dedicated to the worship of art:

> The walls were hung with rich tapestries representing the Triumph of Beauty. A large press, inlaid with agate and lapis-lazuli, filled one corner, and facing the window stood a curiously wrought cabinet with lacquer panels of powdered and mosaiced gold, on which were placed some delicate goblets of Venetian glass, and a cup of dark-veined onyx. Pale

poppies were broidered on the silk coverlet of the bed, as though they had fallen from the tired hands of sleep, and tall reeds of fluted ivory bare up the velvet canopy, from which great tufts of ostrich plumes sprang, like white foam, to the pallid silver of the fretted ceiling. A laughing Narcissus in green bronze held a polished mirror above its head. On the table stood a flat bowl of amethyst.[50]

This is more than an obsessive listing of luxury items as the moral price of the young King's accumulation of colonial stuff becomes clear when he realises the human cost of his expensive collecting. His relentless materialism, articulated through his worship of these elaborate goods, is shown by Wilde to have profound moral, social and political costs. The investment of his possessions with the labour that has produced them is acknowledged when he insists upon being served by the 'toil'[51] of the best artists, for whose work administrators scour the empire to find suitable materials.

As the tale proceeds, the lifelessness of the commodity is contrasted with the ebbing vitality of the kingdom's colonial and domestic subjects. As in 'The Happy Prince', colonialism is associated very directly with consumption, wealth and cultural decadence, as Wilde portrays indulgence in these imperial luxuries as an immoral pleasure. The young King has a series of haunting dreams during which he is exposed to the suffering of workers. Starting with a nightmare in which he sees children being forced to work in a mill, he begins to become conscious of the human cost of excessive consumption:

He thought that he was standing in a long, low attic, amidst the whir and clatter of many looms. The meagre daylight peered in through the grated windows, and showed him the gaunt figures of the weavers bending over their cases. Pale, sickly-looking children were crouched on the huge crossbeams. As the shuttles dashed through the warp they lifted up the heavy battens, and when the shuttles stopped they let the battens fall and pressed the threads together. Their faces were pinched with famine, and their thin hands shook and trembled. Some haggard women were seated at a table sewing. A horrible odour filled the place. The air was foul and heavy, and the walls dripped and streamed with damp.

The young King went over to one of the weavers, and stood by him and watched him. And the weaver looked at him angrily, and said, 'Why art thou watching me? Art thou a spy set on us by our master?'

'Who is thy master?' asked the young King.

'Our master!' cried the weaver, bitterly. 'He is a man like myself. Indeed, there is but this difference between us—that he wears fine clothes while I go in rags, and that while I am weak from hunger he suffers not a little from overfeeding.'[52]

As in late Victorian Britain, possession is the mark of status while deprivation and hunger are the realities that capitalism conceals. Ruling-class luxury is made possible by the misery and suffering of the children working at the mill, while their exploitation is underpinned by a régime of industrial and political surveillance. These integrated forms of oppression make possible 'the Triumph of Beauty' represented on tapestries hanging in the royal palace, while repression is normalised through the simulation of freedom by the authoritarian state:

> 'The land is free,' said the young King, 'and thou art no man's slave.'
>
> 'In war,' answered the weaver, 'the strong make slaves of the weak, and in peace the rich make slaves of the poor. We must work to live, and they give us such mean wages that we die. We toil for them all day long, and they heap up gold in their coffers, and our children fade away before their time, and the faces of those we love become hard and evil. We tread out the grapes, and another drinks the wine. We sow the corn, and our own board is empty. We have chains, though no eye beholds them; and are slaves, though men call us free.'[53]

Wilde's criticism of contemporary capitalism is clear, highlighting the gap between the material reality of the weavers' precarity and the state's claim that they are living in a liberal kingdom. Capitalism is shown to rely on the invisible ideological formations and normalised forms of structural violence with which the state disguises its exploitative practices and are depicted here as strategies of class warfare. Violent authority and the obedience that it enforces form the basis of the system but while the workers' 'chains' are concealed from the bourgeoisie, they must live with the imposition of inequality. This is materialised through hunger and child mortality: 'pinched with famine', the workers are a haunting reminder of the starvation of the Irish peasantry and of the working class in Britain.

The weavers' struggle to exist under these circumstances has desensitised them and destroyed their sense of empathy and capacity for love. Wilde makes it clear that this brutalisation is a form of violence in its own right which is as destructive as other, more obvious forms of oppression because it has been internalised by its victims:

> 'Is it so with all?' he asked.
>
> 'It is so with all,' answered the weaver, 'with the young as well as with the old, with the women as well as with the men, with the little children as well as with those who are stricken in years. The merchants grind us down, and we must needs do their bidding. The priest rides by and tells his beads, and no man has care of us. Through our sunless lanes

> creeps Poverty with her hungry eyes, and Sin with his sodden face follows close behind her. Misery wakes us in the morning, and Shame sits with us at night. But what are these things to thee? Thou art not one of us. Thy face is too happy.' And he turned away scowling, and threw the shuttle across the loom, and the young King saw that it was threaded with a thread of gold.
>
> And a great terror seized upon him, and he said to the weaver, 'What robe is this that thou art weaving?'
>
> 'It is the robe for the coronation of the young King,' he answered; 'what is that to thee?'[54]

Crushed by this combination of economic and political oppression, the weavers are traumatised by hunger, poverty, misery and death, while the collusion of the clergy alleviates the state of responsibility for their suffering. The young King witnesses their fear, misery and helplessness before discovering the trace of capital and, with it, his own guilt, which is symbolised in the golden thread being spun on the loom. Again, Wilde emphasises the proximity of wealth to the suffering that it causes in this exposure of the structurally violent processes through which commodities are generated and for which they provide distracting symbolic identifications.[55] With its golden threads, the coronation robe contains visible traces of the labour coerced from the working class through terror, surveillance and economic deprivation. Its manufacture is made possible by this comprehensive system of violence connecting the spectacle of state and capital to the less visible processes upon which it depends.

In his next dream, the young King witnesses his slaves harvesting pearls. After anchoring his galley at an unnamed location in the Middle East or North Africa, the ship's master kills a local Arab who resists him, before compelling one of the slaves to repeatedly dive for pearls in the shark-infested sea until he dies from exhaustion. Unable to intervene, the young King watches; and in his next dream finds himself in another nightmarish colonial setting:

> He thought that he was wandering through a dim wood, hung with strange fruits and with beautiful poisonous flowers. The adders hissed at him as he went by, and the bright parrots flew screaming from branch to branch. Huge tortoises lay asleep upon the hot mud. The trees were full of apes and peacocks.
>
> On and on he went, till he reached the outskirts of the wood, and there he saw an immense multitude of men toiling in the bed of a dried-up river. They swarmed up the crag like ants. They dug deep pits

in the ground and went down into them. Some of them cleft the rocks with great axes; others grabbled in the sand.

They tore up the cactus by its roots, and trampled on the scarlet blossoms. They hurried about, calling to each other, and no man was idle.[56]

The workers are reduced by the degrading conditions of their labour, while environmental havoc is wrought in their search for jewels. This destruction underlines the spectacle of the young King's crown and its symbolic capital again conceals the real, global cost of its manufacture, along with the brutality of the régime that it represents. The hostile environment in which the dream is set also suggests that, when removed from any moral consideration of its material origins, the production of beautiful commodities can be a dangerous activity. This becomes increasingly apparent as the young King observes the spectres of Death and Avarice discussing the catastrophic suffering of the miners:

From the darkness of a cavern Death and Avarice watched them, and Death said, 'I am weary; give me a third of them and let me go.' But Avarice shook her head. 'They are my servants,' she answered.

And Death said to her, 'What hast thou in thy hand?'

'I have three grains of corn,' she answered; 'what is that to thee?'

'Give me one of them,' cried Death, 'to plant in my garden; only one of them, and I will go away.'

'I will not give thee anything,' said Avarice, and she hid her hand in the fold of her raiment.

And Death laughed, and took a cup, and dipped it into a pool of water, and out of the cup rose Ague. She passed through the great multitude, and a third of them lay dead. A cold mist followed her, and the water-snakes ran by her side.[57]

In the true spirit of capitalism, Death and Avarice refuse to co-operate and wastefully compete over the young King's most valuable resource: labour. As they bicker, Wilde also suggests that capitalism is analogous with empire:

And when Avarice saw that a third of the multitude was dead she beat her breast and wept. She beat her barren bosom, and cried aloud. 'Thou hast slain a third of my servants,' she cried, 'get thee gone. There is war in the mountains of Tartary, and the kings of each side are calling to thee. The Afghans have slain the black ox, and are marching to battle. They have beaten upon their shields with their spears, and have put on their helmets of iron. What is my valley to thee, that thou shouldst tarry in it? Get thee gone, and come here no more.'

'Nay,' answered Death, 'but till thou hast given me a grain of corn I will not go.'

But Avarice shut her hand, and clenched her teeth. 'I will not give thee anything,' she muttered.

And Death laughed, and took up a black stone, and threw it into the forest, and out of a thicket of wild hemlock came Fever in a robe of flame. She passed through the multitude, and touched them, and each man that she touched died. The grass withered beneath her feet as she walked.

And Avarice shuddered, and put ashes on her head. 'Thou art cruel,' she cried; 'thou art cruel. There is famine in the walled cities of India, and the cisterns of Samarcand have run dry. There is famine in the walled cities of Egypt, and the locusts have come up from the desert. The Nile has not overflowed its banks, and the priests have cursed Isis and Osiris. Get thee gone to those who need thee, and leave me my servants.'

'Nay,' answered Death, 'but till thou hast given me a grain of corn I will not go.'

'I will not give thee anything,' said Avarice.[58]

The geopolitical ambitions of contemporary imperialists are represented in the tension and intransigence that pit Death and Avarice against one another as both spectres exercise influence over territories occupied by the British military at the end of the nineteenth century. The scene resonates with the actual violence of the Afghan War of 1878–80 and the Anglo-Egyptian War of 1882, which were fought with the objectives of securing strategic control over the Suez Canal and the North-West Frontier Province. Britain's global political dominance is fictionalised in this pair of apocalyptic figures whose Symbolist discussion of violence concludes with a fantastic, coded representation of the destructive reality of imperialist occupation:

> And Death laughed again, and he whistled through his fingers, and a woman came flying through the air. Plague was written upon her forehead, and a crowd of lean vultures wheeled round her. She covered the valley with her wings, and no man was left alive.
>
> And Avarice fled shrieking through the forest, and Death leaped upon his red horse and galloped away, and his galloping was faster than the wind.
>
> And out of the slime at the bottom of the valley crept dragons and horrible things with scales, and the jackals came trotting along the sand, sniffing up the air with their nostrils.
>
> And the young King wept, and said: 'Who were these men, and for what were they seeking?'
>
> 'For rubies for a king's crown,' answered one who stood behind him.

And the young King started, and, turning round, he saw a man habited as a pilgrim and holding in his hand a mirror of silver.

And he grew pale, and said: 'For what king?'

And the pilgrim answered: 'Look in this mirror, and thou shalt see him.'

And he looked in the mirror, and, seeing his own face, he gave a great cry and woke, and the bright sunlight was streaming into the room, and from the trees of the garden and pleasaunce the birds were singing.[59]

Responsibility for imperialist violence is reflected back at the metropolitan consumer as capital is shown to form the basis of imperial occupation and conquest. The disastrous condition of the young King's empire is maintained through its ruthless exploitation of economic resources; its proliferation of war, starvation and disease; and the environmental destruction caused by resource extraction. Widespread suffering and mass death accompany the creation of his gown and crown, both of which advertise and symbolise the young King's imperial power. Turning Symbolism against empire, Wilde's subversive point is that these corrupt commodities are invested with the suffering endured by those on the receiving end of the young King's authority.

The kind of opulence associated with the corrupted decadence of Jean des Esseintes in Joris-Karl Huysmans' 1884 Decadent novel, *À Rebours*, which enjoys a cameo appearance in *The Picture of Dorian Gray*, is situated against its real cost, as this story complicates contemporary and posthumous constructions of Wilde as an amoral consumer.[60] Here, Wilde explores the cost of the production of such beauty. While Huysmans' novel portrays the damning consequences of opulence, des Esseintes is not exposed to the labour that is invested in the creation of the commodities to which he is addicted. In Wilde's story he advances decadence's critique of its own excesses by situating it in relation to the presence and reality of exploited labour. Wilde's radical Aestheticism explores what he terms as the 'the magic and the mystery of beautiful things' by proposing that the commodities enjoyed by the bourgeoisie are produced at a terrible human cost.[61] The extraction of resources from rivers, seas and the earth, and their refinement and manufacture as commodities is directly associated with violence in factories, mines and colonies.

When he awakens from his dreams the young King is presented with his sceptre, crown and golden robe but rejects them now that he has become aware of the suffering and death behind their production. His realisation that they are invested with suffering is countered by his ministers who advise that his visions 'are not real things'. They counter the imperial state's collective guilt by asking: 'What have we to do with the lives of those who toil for us? Shall not a man eat his bread till he has seen the sower, nor drink wine until he has talked with the vinedresser?' Wilde believed that for beauty to be sustainable it must be separated from empire, war and exploitation, all of which, as the young King discovers, form the political fabric of his power: 'On the loom of sorrow, and by white hands of Pain, has this my robe been woven. There is Blood in the heart of the ruby, and Death in the heart of the pearl.' Rejecting the symbols of his authority, he addresses the public in his shepherd's robe and carries his wooden staff. He is challenged by one of his subjects who claims that the existing class dialectic is the natural and necessary order of things and asks: 'Knowest thou not that out of the luxury of the rich cometh the life of the poor?' The King replies by asking: 'Are not the rich and the poor brothers?' The man's answer explains the violence that maintains imperial and class divisions: 'Ay [. . .] and the name of the rich brother is Cain.' When he is condemned by the clergy for degrading his royal office, the young King asks his bishop: 'Shall joy wear what Grief has fashioned?' The cleric replies that suffering is part of the routine of existence, even if the poor must 'eat their food with the dogs' and demands that the young King should tolerate the suffering caused by his empire: 'Is not He who made misery wiser than thou art? [. . .] The burden of this world is too great for one man to bear, and one world's sorrow too heavy for one heart to suffer.'[62] As he turns toward a statue of Christ ornamented with gold and jewels, the young King is challenged by a mob of armed nobles who announce their determination to kill 'this dreamer of dreams [. . .] this boy who brings shame upon our state', but he is transformed before they can harm him:

> And lo! through the painted windows came the sunlight streaming upon him, and the sun-beams wove round him a tissued robe that was fairer than the robe that had been fashioned for his pleasure. The dead staff blossomed, and bare lilies that were whiter than pearls. The dry thorn blossomed, and bare roses that were redder than rubies. Whiter than fine pearls were the lilies, and their stems were of bright silver. Redder than male rubies were the roses, and their leaves were of beaten gold.[63]

The story concludes with this Symbolist expression of revolutionary Aestheticism which challenges the destructive momentum of capital. Commodity fetishism and alienation are countered by the young

King's radical consciousness of the true worth of things and by his awareness of the suffering invested in them. His social awareness and acceptance of moral responsibility leads to the replacement of the symbols of political power and material wealth with much grander emblems of spiritual finery. These are greater than the goods made for the satisfaction of empty pleasure and produced by the chronically violent authority of the state. His shepherd's staff, flowering with its miraculous growths of roses and lilies, now represents the possibility of a new, radical morality. The story ends with the young King's revolutionary faith illuminating the cathedral:

> He stood there in the raiment of a king, and the gates of the jewelled shrine flew open, and from the crystal of the many-rayed monstrance shone a marvelous and mystical light. He stood there in a king's raiment, and the Glory of God filled the place, and the saints in their carven niches seemed to move. In the fair raiment of a king he stood before them, and the organ pealed out its music, and the trumpeters blew upon their trumpets, and the singing boys sang.
>
> And the people fell upon their knees in awe, and the nobles sheathed their swords and did homage, and the Bishop's face grew pale, and his hands trembled. 'A greater than I hath crowned thee,' he cried, and he knelt before him.
>
> And the young King came down from the high altar, and passed home through the midst of the people. But no man dared look upon his face, for it was like the face of an angel.[64]

In contrast to the morbid commodities encountered in his dreams, the young King's faith in humanity causes his staff to flower and illuminates the cathedral with the power of his new, subversive self. The story carries much of the charge contained in Wilde's review of Isaac Sharp's volume of religious poems, *Saul of Tarsus*, in which Wilde criticised the state of theological doctrine: 'Ordinary theology has long since converted its gold into lead, and words and phrases that once touched the heart of the world have become wearisome and meaningless through repetition. If Theology desires to move us, she must rewrite her formulas.'[65] In 'The Young King', dominant formulas of religion, politics, authority and economics are revised, revolutionised and democratised as Christ's symbolic function as a champion of the poor and oppressed outmatches the official power of the state. Wilde connects the relentless privileging of imperial 'stuff' that, as Nicholas Daly has shown, is intensively theorised in late Victorian imperial fiction. Connecting art, culture and politics directly to the material realities of imperialist and capitalist violence, 'The

Young King' offers a sharp audit of the cost of capitalist imperialism.[66] By drawing attention to the uneven distribution of power and wealth between colonial peripheries and the imperial centre Wilde criticised imperial relations and class inequality while also confronting conservative Aestheticism.[67]

'The Star-Child'

A House of Pomegranates also includes the story, 'The Star-Child', in which a group of freezing woodcutters discuss how 'life is for the rich' and how 'much is given to some, and little is given to others. Injustice has parcelled out the world nor is there equal division of aught but sorrow'. Like 'The Selfish Giant', this tale also counters capitalist doctrine by celebrating innocence. When the woodcutters find an infant who has fallen from the sky in a star rather than the gold that they had been hoping to discover, one asks 'what doth a child profit to a man?' Rather than leave the child to die, his companion decides to adopt it, but is criticised by his friend for displaying 'foolishness and softness of heart'. However, while the little boy grows up to become a popular and handsome young man he turns out to be a sadistic narcissist. When he rejects his birth mother, who appears to him as a beggar, she curses him and he is transformed into a repulsive human-reptile hybrid. After leaving his adoptive family, he is abducted by a magician and compelled to search a forest for a piece of enchanted gold in return for his freedom. His redemption occurs through his experience of mutual aid: when he helps a snared hare to escape, it returns the favour by helping him complete his quest. When the Star-Child observes that '[t]he service that I did to thee thou hast rendered back again many times over, and the kindness that I showed thee thou hast repaid a hundred-fold', the hare answers 'Nay [. . .] but as thou dealt with me, so I did deal with thee.' Motivated by pity, he gives the gold to a leper and when he fails to bring it to his master, he is helped again by the animal, which does so because 'thou hadst pity on me first'. After helping the leper twice more the Star-Child returns to his human form and is revered by palace guards, priests and officers who recognise his divinity: 'Thou art our lord for whom we have been waiting, and the son of our King.'[68] He is forgiven by his parents, the King and Queen, who had originally appeared to him as the leper and beggar, and his own reign is marked by kindness. His death marks the end of compassionate rule, and his succession by a tyrant proves that the state is incapable of continuing his benevolence.

Like 'The Happy Prince', 'The Star-Child' also proposes the necessity of mutualism and suggests that collective and co-operative responses to suffering will counter the aesthetic and political mores of the bourgeoisie. In both stories, radical consciousness is acquired as a result of compassion and solidarity, while capitalism is portrayed as dangerously dehumanising. This is the problem also faced by the young Fisherman in 'The Fisherman and His Soul', when he asks: 'Of what use is my soul to me? I cannot see it. I may not touch it. I do not know it.' Merchants warn him that the soul is 'not worth a clipped piece of silver [. . .] for to us it is nought, nor has it any value to our service.'[69]

As these stories make clear, Wilde believed that mutualism had practical applications offering realistic possibilities for social change. On a biographical note, his renowned generosity was in itself a radical practice; the repeated instances of his lending or giving away money was a rejection of capital rather than mismanagement of it. Robert Sherard recalled in his memoir how Wilde would give him money, telling him 'to take what I needed. "It's as much yours as mine," he said. "You know I have no sense of property."'[70] Sherard's recollection underlines Wilde's frequent, practical implementation of the ideas about property and capital that he outlined in 'The Soul of Man Under Socialism', and in these stories he explored the ideas around which his essay was structured in 1891.

Notes

1. 'Literary and Other Notes', *Woman's World*, 1.2, December 1887, pp. 81–5, in *Collected Works*, vol. 7, pp. 22–33, p. 33.
2. Peter Kropotkin, *Mutual Aid: A Factor of Evolution* (originally published London: William Heinemann, 1902; reprinted Mineola, NY: Dover, 2006), pp. xv, 32.
3. For a discussion of contemporary utopian writing, see Matthew Beaumont, *Utopia Ltd.: Ideologies of Social Dreaming in England, 1870–1900* (Chicago: Haymarket Books, 2009).
4. Kropotkin, *Mutual Aid*, pp. xix, 47, 55, 61, 86, 132, 111–12. Drawing on an impressive range of primary and antiquarian sources, Engels noted that the Brehon laws and their protection of communal land ownership survived in Ireland until the final destruction of the Gaelic clan system at the beginning of the seventeenth century. See Frederick Engels to Karl

Marx, 29 November 1869, in Marx and Engels, *Ireland and the Irish Question*, pp. 279–80. See also Engels' completed chapters and draft outline of his planned *History of Ireland*, trans. from the German by Angela Clifford, in Marx and Engels, *Ireland and the Irish Question*, pp. 171–269, in which he noted that with the recent emergence of the Fenian movement, 'the fighting is not yet over'. Unfortunately Engels did not complete this ambitious and extensively researched project as his energies were diverted from it by an attack on another, contemporary manifestation of communism – the French state's destruction of the Paris Commune. See L. I. Golman, in Marx and Engels, *Ireland and the Irish Question*, p. 449, n.178.
5. Kropotkin, *Mutual Aid*, pp. 174–5.
6. Peter Kropotkin (as 'Prince Kropotkin'), *Ideals and Realities in Russian Literature* (New York: Knopf, 1915), pp. 287–9.
7. Sumpter has revealed a rich seam of socialist fairy tale telling in the left wing papers of the fin de siècle, including the *Clarion*, *Labour Leader* and the *Labour Prophet*, which distributed the *Cinderella Supplement* for children. See Caroline Sumpter, *The Victorian Press and the Fairy Tale* (Basingstoke: Palgrave, 2008), especially chapter 4.
8. Wilde to Alfred Douglas, January-March, 1897, in *Complete Letters*, pp. 683–780, p. 754.
9. Oscar Wilde, 'Some Literary Notes', *Woman's World*, March 1889, in *Complete Works*, vol. 8, *Reviews* 2, pp. 433–47, p. 437.
10. Jane Francesca Wilde, 'The American Irish', p. 39.
11. Oscar Wilde, 'Some Literary Notes', in *Complete Works*, vol. 8, *Reviews* 2, pp. 433–47.
12. In 1861 Kingsley described the Irish as 'white chimpanzees' while in 1888 Stevenson called for Land Leaguers to be mown down with Gatling guns. See Gregory Castle, *Modernism and the Celtic Revival* (Cambridge: Cambridge University Press, 2001), especially chapter 2, '"Fair Equivalents": Yeats, Revivalism, and the Redemption of Culture'. For analyses of Victorian racist stereotyping of the Irish, see L. Perry Curtis, *Apes and Angels: The Irishman in Victorian Culture* (Washington, DC: Smithsonian Institute, 1997) and Amy E. Martin, 'Victorian Ireland: Race and the Category of the Human', *Victorian Review*, 40.1, pp. 52–7. Kingsley, quoted Martin, p. 52. For Stevenson's call for the deployment of machine guns in Ireland, see Robert Louis Stevenson, 'Confessions of a Unionist: An Unpublished "talk on things current"' (Cambridge, MA: Privately Published, 1921).
13. Oscar Wilde, 'The Poetry of the People', in *Complete Works*, vol. 8, *Reviews* (Boston, MA: Wymann-Fogg, 1910), pp. 63–6. Quotation from p. 63.
14. Oscar Wilde, 'The Canterville Ghost', in *The Complete Short Stories*, p. 45. All of the stories cited hereafter are drawn from this volume.
15. Ibid. p. 56.

16. James Campbell reads 'The Portrait of Mr. W.H.' as a dual text, in which both the story and the theory are inflected through gnosis, or the idea of a secret, non-obvious meaning that lurks beneath the more readily apparent. The story operates simultaneously as theory, fiction and quasi-religious text in which belief is frustratingly at once desirable and impossible. (See James Campbell, 'Sexual Gnosticism: The Procreative Code of "The Portrait of Mr. W.H."', in Joseph Bristow (ed.), *Wilde Discoveries: Traditions, Histories, Archives* (Toronto: University of Toronto Press, 2013), pp. 169–89, p. 170.)
17. Louis Marlow, 'The Gorgon's Head', *Adam International Review*, 241–3 (1954), p. 15.
18. Oscar Wilde, 'The Happy Prince', in *The Complete Short Stories*, p. 74.
19. Ibid. pp. 72–3.
20. Ibid. p. 73.
21. Ibid. pp. 76–7.
22. Ibid. p. 77.
23. Ibid.
24. See Wilde, 'The Critic as Artist', in *Complete Works*, vol. 4, *Criticism*, pp. 124–206, p. 172. See also Victor Hugo, *Les Misérables* (Paris: Gallimard, 2017).
25. Wilde, 'The Happy Prince', in *The Complete Short Stories*, p. 78.
26. Ibid.
27. Oscar Wilde, 'The Nightingale and the Rose', in *The Complete Short Stories*, p. 81.
28. Wilde, 'The Soul of Man', in *Complete Works*, vol. 4, pp. 229–68, p. 240.
29. Ibid. pp. 240–1.
30. Ibid. p. 241.
31. Ibid.
32. Ann Markey has discussed the story's literary and cultural influences in close detail, pointing to sources ranging from the Christian Bible to Irish mythology, while also exploring its linguistic complexities, all of which combine to 'create [. . .] an artful effect of disarming ingenuousness'. See Ann Markey, *Oscar Wilde's Fairy Tales: Origins and Contexts* (Dublin: Irish Academic Press, 2015), chapter 4 (quotation from p. 111).
33. Jarlath Killeen has read the story as an allegorisation of the Irish Land War. See Jarlath Killeen, *The Fairy Tales of Oscar Wilde* (Aldershot: Ashgate, 2007), chapter 3.
34. See Steven Arata, 'Oscar Wilde and Jesus Christ', in Joseph Bristow (ed.), *Wilde Writings: Contextual Conditions* (Toronto: University of Toronto Press, 2013), pp. 254–72.
35. Vyvyan Holland, *The Son of Oscar Wilde* (Oxford: Oxford University Press, 1987), p. 54.
36. Wilde, 'The Selfish Giant', in *The Complete Short Stories*, pp. 85, 88.

37. Wilde, 'The Canterville Ghost', in *The Complete Short Stories*, p. 63.
38. Davitt, *The Fall of Feudalism in Ireland*, p. 187.
39. Eagleton, *Heathcliff and the Great Hunger*, p. 132.
40. Jane Francesca Wilde, 'The American Irish', pp. 33, 35, 42.
41. Lady Wilde, *Poems by Speranza* (Dublin: James Duffy, 1864), frontispiece.
42. 'The Famine Year', in Ibid. pp. 5–7, p. 6.
43. Ibid. p. 5.
44. Ibid. p. 7.
45. Jane Francesca Wilde, 'The American Irish', p. 29.
46. Eagleton, *Heathcliff and the Great Hunger*, p. 13.
47. Cleary draws on Mike Davis' *Late Victorian Holocausts: El Niño Famines and the Making of the Third World* (London: Verso, 2000). See Cleary, *Outrageous Fortune*. Quotation from p. 78. See also Owen Dudley Edwards, 'Impressions of an Irish Sphinx', in J. McCormack (ed.), *Wilde the Irishman*, pp. 55–6.
48. Wilde, 'The Young King', in *The Complete Short Stories*, p. 142.
49. Ibid. p. 143.
50. Ibid. pp. 143–4.
51. Ibid. p. 143.
52. Ibid. pp. 144–5.
53. Ibid. p. 145.
54. Ibid.
55. See Slavoj Žižek, *Violence: Six Sideways Reflections* (London: Profile, 2008).
56. Wilde, 'The Young King', in *The Complete Short Stories*, p. 147.
57. Ibid.
58. Ibid. pp. 147–8.
59. Ibid. pp. 148–9.
60. Joris Karl Huysmans, *À Rebours* (Paris: Gallimard, 1983).
61. Wilde, 'The Young King', in *The Complete Short Stories*, p. 144.
62. Ibid. pp. 149–51.
63. Ibid. p. 152.
64. Ibid. pp. 152–3.
65. Oscar Wilde, 'The Poet's Corner', *Pall Mall Gazette*, 6 April 1888, p. 3, reprinted in *Complete Works*, vol. 7, pp. 78–81, p. 81.
66. As Daly argues, late Victorian popular fiction provided readers with narrativised commodity theories. See Nicholas Daly, *Modernism, Romance and the Fin de Siècle: Popular Fiction and British Culture, 1880–1914* (Cambridge: Cambridge University Press, 1999), chapter 3: '"Mummie is become merchandise": The Mummy Story as Commodity Theory'.
67. This is evident in 'The Model Millionaire', in which Alan Trevor only appreciates the poor as a resource for art. As he tells Hughie Erskine: 'What you call rags I call romance. What seems poverty to you is

picturesqueness to me.' Oscar Wilde, 'The Model Millionaire', in *The Complete Short Stories*, p. 67.
68. Oscar Wilde, 'The Star-Child', in *The Complete Short Stories*, pp. 203–4, 212–14.
69. Wilde, 'The Fisherman and His Soul', in *The Complete Short Stories*, pp. 173, 175.
70. Robert Harborough Sherard, *Oscar Wilde: The Story of an Unhappy Friendship* (London: Greening & Co., 1909), pp. 88–9.

Chapter 5

The Politics of Art and *The Picture of Dorian Gray*

Oscar Wilde's critique of capital is central to his 1891 novel, *The Picture of Dorian Gray*, in which Dorian, in his youthful perfection, is simultaneously preserved and corrupted by his addiction to commodities. This dependency proves as lethal to Wilde's villainous protagonist as does his indulgence in the radical sexual practices with which the novel's contemporary critics became so fixated. Dorian certainly falls victim to his own pathological tendencies, as Wilde made clear in his letters to the *St James's Gazette* and the *Scots Observer* defending the original incarnation of the novel that was published in the July 1890 edition of *Lippincott's Magazine*.[1] Yet Dorian's violent alienation from aristocratic society is also driven by his destructive craving for things. Emphasising the broader social context within which *The Picture of Dorian Gray* was published and then quickly slated by a largely hostile press, Regenia Gagnier claims that negative reviews of the novel were issued in retaliation against the criticism that Wilde levelled in his essays against conservative journalism. As Gagnier has shown, consumption certainly determined Aestheticism but Wilde also urged his readers to resist this tendency in 'The Soul of Man Under Socialism'. In contrast to the self-aware and socially committed subject projected in the essay as the ideal and responsible modern type, Dorian is a dedicated consumer. As Gagnier argues, this is embedded in the cultural significance of his detached, 'modern (that is historyless) face'.[2]

As Kirsten MacLeod has shown, Wilde pitched Aestheticism against the anachronistic class leanings of Decadence[3] and *The Picture of Dorian Gray* is, at once, a gothic novel and a highly theorised critique of the harmful dynamics of capitalism. Its immersive theoretical excursions underline what Gagnier describes as Wilde's belief in 'the impossibility of separating creation from criticism, doing from talking, and, ultimately, life from art'. Gagnier also locates

Wilde's radical strategy against the novel's articulation of the contemporary social tensions that informed Aestheticism, citing advertising and consumerist culture as its primary influences. This adds political thrust to Lawrence Danson's claim that Wilde advocated an especially 'dissident modernity'. Through these engagements, Gagnier argues, he ironised 'the commercial image of the dandy-artist' and, in doing so, subverted and complicated the image of the bourgeois gentleman.[4] The novel is concerned with the limits of bourgeois morality, which are encapsulated in the lifelessness of the commodities that Dorian collects, and as he assumes their sterility his image in the hidden portrait continues to age, conveying his corruption. Its reflection of this 'monstrous soul-life' and the 'hideous warnings' that it contains[5] are charged with Dorian's contamination by the exhaustively collected and curated objects with which he surrounds himself. This transference of the distortions of capital into the self is symbolised further in the expensive frame with which he surrounds the painting and its shocking image of his true, consumer's identity. Like Karl Marx, who identified the commodity's 'repulsive' capacity to transform 'not only soul, but body' into degraded forms, Wilde depicts the absorption and transformation of the self by capital as a purely destructive process.[6]

John Barlas and Democratic Criticism

Contemporary criticism of *The Picture of Dorian Gray* is most often remembered in relation to the hostility that it elicited from the mainstream press, but its message was best understood by Wilde's anarchist friend, John Evelyn Barlas, a poet and militant anarchist who appreciated the value of the novel's rich Symbolism in relation to the interplay between class, capital and morality. In his self-consciously aesthetic essay, 'Oscar Wilde: A Study', which was published in the *Novel Review* in April 1892, Barlas explained how Aestheticism's 'astral music' was inherently revolutionary, both as art-practice and cultural discourse. Praising the novel's self-reflexive and theoretically complex expression of Wilde's 'symbolic' consciousness, he also emphasised the significance of its abstract discussions of literary artifice. Barlas pointed to this fusion of literary, cultural and theoretical concerns as evidence of Wilde's brilliance which proved his credentials as a characteristically modern writer whose 'high genius' had already been established by 'placing criticism at the summit' during his years as a reviewer prior to the novel's publication. Barlas believed that

Wilde had now advanced fiction to a new level of expression: 'From the first he was a critic *in* art, and he is now the artist *of* criticism.' He regarded the novel's theoretical content as its most vital component as this conveyed to the reader, 'in strange disguise', Wilde's 'Titan-like defiance' of cultural and political authority. For Barlas, there was no distinction between Wilde's political and literary avant-gardism, which established his radical credentials along with his reputation as the fin de siècle's 'prince of poets':[7]

> Concentration and universality are great gifts not often found together; the gift of the creative artist is not often united in one person with the gift of the sterile critic. Oscar Wilde has both: he can make beautiful things of a distinct type; he can enjoy beautiful things of every type. The milk and honey of Palestine, the wine and olives of Hellas, the jade-green wormwood of modern France, are familiar food to him, and through the palate thrill the soul [. . .][8]

By means of the democratic practice combining literary and cultural theory with 'art creation', Wilde's aesthetically focused and socially involved writing drew upon the bitter experience of modernity as much as it did upon his knowledge of Orientalist classicism. This reflected to Barlas the material conditions upon which Wilde's work was based. He also believed that progressively experimental writing like the kind exhibited in *The Picture of Dorian Gray* was also 'necessary to the divine in man' because it encouraged the creative instinct in reader and writer alike: 'We all must make something,' he insisted. For Barlas, Aestheticism carried an inherently democratic charge as art involved an equal exchange between the artist and those who enjoyed his work. Stressing the need for the subject to experience art as pleasure, he argued that Wilde treated criticism as being equally as important as the creative act. The process of experiencing art was as vital as the enjoyment of producing it because Wilde 'holds the critic greater than the artist; holds him who dwells in the palace greater than him who builds it. And indeed, to enjoy may be better than to create, for full enjoyment may come after creation'. Criticism that ignored the autonomy of the artist's imagination failed to acknowledge the influence of this creativity.

Drawing on the biblical analogy of the Book of Genesis, Barlas also stressed the centrality of labour to the value and experience of art:

> After making the world God rested on the seventh day, and blessed all that He had made. And that day He hallowed. He who enjoys the palace is greatest, but he must make it himself.

> Yet God began, doubtless, to create again upon the Monday: there were other worlds to make or direct.
>
> Criticism is repose after creation, but creation is the six days' work of God – creation and destruction.[9]

Barlas regarded criticism that was unconscious of the intensity of genuine creative effort as a pointless exercise. His apocalyptic note stressed that avant-garde creativity necessarily occurred through the eradication of what already existed by the divine figure of the artist and critic.[10] As Vincent Sherry has argued, Wilde's 'alternative, emancipatory' practices were a form of cultural renovation that made him the 'instigating figure' of literary modernism. Barlas' emphasis on his critical and creative significance indicated that, as an anarchist, he recognised the potential for social, literary and critical progress contained in Wilde's work. Revolutionary upheaval was key to artistic innovation, and Barlas regarded *The Picture of Dorian Gray* as a deeply poetic novel combining the political interests of Victor Hugo with the prose style of Théophile Gautier and the intense Symbolism of Gustave Flaubert. Echoing these French influences, its experimental form established Wilde as 'the first poet-novelist in England':

> criticism pure and simple makes only the middle period of Oscar Wilde's development. He began as a critical poet in verse, and he ends as a symbolic poet in prose. He is the first poet-novelist in England. Fielding, Dickens, Thackeray were novelists, but not poets. Shelley wrote some novels when he was young, but left prose for poetry. The poetry of Scott is better seen in his poems and novels. In France it is otherwise. Hugo, Flaubert, Gautier were poets of prose. The creator of Gilliatt's heroic love and Jean Valjean's holy sufferings was a poet; he who saw the snake-skin slippers of Salammbô by the marble bath-tank in her scarlet room, and waded through the massacre of the valley of the Battle-axe, and beheld lions crucified, was a poet; he who loved a woman he had never seen, gave to her the hands of Magdalen, the body of sleeping Antiope, the raiment of an Eastern queen, and who found her in the flesh in strange disguise, and made her his own for but a single night, was a poet; and he who has clothed the mystery of the Phoenix in *The Picture of Dorian Gray* is a prince of poets [. . .] The personality of the man we know is already there: the love of colours, of bright birds, and beautiful gems.[11]

For Barlas, *The Picture of Dorian Gray* combined the themes of empathy, sensuality, violence and politics found in these earlier works. Believing it to be reminiscent of the experimental Symbolism of *Salammbô*,

Gustave Flaubert's Decadent tale of slave rebellion in fourteenth-century Carthage, and of the moral precision of Victor Hugo's socially-engaged fiction, Barlas identified with the fusion of sensation and morality in Wilde's subtly political novel. As with these earlier works, its significance lay in the force and clarity of its images and impressions, which Barlas linked to the novel's political content. He believed that Aestheticism was inherently progressive because 'a man who is all this, and whose fate has cast him upon these latter days, cannot fail to be a revolutionist'. The aesthete, or 'voluptuous artist', deployed style as a revolutionary tactic by means of his subversive methods of paradox and wit. Barlas saw this as an improvement on the destructive methods of contemporary terrorists, because Wilde was:

> a very Michael, or rather, a Raphael, for he does not use physical means, but spiritual. Nor are his spiritual weapons of the coarser kind, noisy [. . .] He does not use dynamite, but the dagger – a dagger whose hilt is crusted with flaming jewels, whose point drips with the poison of the Borgias. That dagger is the paradox. No weapon could be more terrible.[12]

In applying radical, literary weapons rather than the methods of physical force, the kind of literary subversion found in *The Picture of Dorian Gray* demolished tradition because it 'stabbed all our proverbs' and undermined the political and cultural authority that they represented, because 'our proverbs rule us more than our kings'. For Barlas, who was himself a poet and victim of state violence, the conjoined spheres of art and politics constituted a very real battlefield where the cause of revolution was served by Wilde's advanced consciousness as a literary prophet. As David Weir maintains, 'modernism itself can be read as a translation of politics into culture',[13] and an articulation of this overlap is found here in Barlas' claim that the novel's radicalism lay in its capacity to challenge the reader's perception of authority. Turning again to a metaphor of destruction, Barlas explained this was an immensely political issue:

> With a sudden flash of wit he exposes to our startled eyes the sheer cliff-like walls of the rift which has opened out, as if by a silent earthquake, between our moral belief and the belief of our fathers. That fissure is intellectual revolution.[14]

Regarding *The Picture of Dorian Gray* as a political work wherein Aestheticism expresses the artist's revolutionary imagination, Barlas found radical political as well as aesthetic value in its experimental literary expression. Key to this was the novel's shocking content, and he regarded it as a fiction that would advance the twin causes of literary and political freedom. For Barlas there was no tension between revolutionism and Aestheticism as he found the word-deed continuum that exercised such a profound hold over the late-nineteenth-century anarchist imagination to be central to *The Picture of Dorian Gray*.

He was not the only radical writer who recognised the connection between aesthetics and politics. Edward Carpenter, who complained that 'life [. . .] [is] a mere empty blob without freedom' regarded the struggle for democracy and equality as 'the essence of all expression, and the final surrender of Art'. For Carpenter this political cause gave form and meaning to experience and underlined 'the divine' objective for which all artists 'have struggled and still struggle'. In *Towards Democracy* (1883), his experimental anthology of memoir, poetry, literary analysis and utopian socialist writing, Carpenter explained his own understanding of how the desire for political liberation was instinctual. This impulse toward freedom constituted the basis of the human condition:

> Of that which exists in the Soul, political freedom and institutions of equality, etc., are but the shadows (necessarily thrown); and Democracy in States or Constitutions but the shadow of that which first expresses itself in the glance of the eye or the appearance of the skin.[15]

Carpenter also criticised British imperialism and praised anticolonial efforts in Ireland, where he saw 'liberty's deathless flame leaping on her Atlantic shore'.[16]

Like Wilde, Carpenter combined his desire for sexual, artistic and anticolonial liberation in his writings. His radical understanding of the relationship between art, culture and revolutionary consciousness underlines how socialist *littérateurs* were convinced that their political experimentation had direct analogues in the sphere of art. Barlas' interpretation of *The Picture of Dorian Gray* conveys a similar understanding of the relationship between the practices of literary Aestheticism and the language and practice of revolutionary politics.

As explained in Chapter 3, Wilde indicated the connections that bound anarchist politics to literary practice in his review of Herbert Giles' translation of the writings of the ancient Chinese philosopher, Chuang Tsŭ. Tsŭ's anti-utilitarian sentiment is echoed at the very beginning of *The Picture of Dorian Gray*, where Wilde proclaimed in his Preface to the 1891 text that '[a]ll art is quite useless'.[17] Struck by Tsŭ's critique of wealth and impressed by his insistence on the importance of subjective consciousness, Wilde admired his adoration of 'the *purum nihil* and the Abyss'. This placed him firmly in the tradition of the aesthetic and political radicalism with which Wilde self-identified, as his ideas were firmly at odds with those of the late Victorian bourgeoisie. Tsŭ's notion of productive 'contraries' appealed to Wilde because such radical paradoxes, he believed, could not be accommodated within the bourgeois imagination.[18]

Politics, Pleasure and the Literary

The Preface to *The Picture of Dorian Gray* includes a statement on the potentially threatening nature of art:

All art is at once surface and symbol.
Those who go beneath the surface do so at their peril.
Those who read the symbol do so at their peril.[19]

This declaration, which was written in response to criticism of the original text of the novel published in *Lippincott's*, introduces the reader to a text that serves as a manifesto in which art, politics and subjectivity are discussed in unusual detail. If all art is, as Wilde argues here, simply 'surface and symbol', what, then, could lie underneath? This dangerous territory is explored in this complex and highly theoretical novel with its sophisticated fusion of literary, cultural and political ideas.[20] These subversive notions are explored at an early stage in the text, during two very self-conscious discussions of the nature of the relationship between art, politics and subjectivity, all of which rests just beyond the surface of the text's ostensible appearance as a gothic romance. As Wilde warns the reader in the Preface, interpreting the symbolic meanings of this or any other worthwhile text can be hazardous but also rewarding, a claim that was also the basis of Barlas' highly politicised review of the novel. The discussions that take place between the artist, Basil Hallward, his aristocratic friend, Lord Henry Wotton, and the initially innocent Dorian Gray introduce the reader to a wider discourse on the relationship between art, society and the individual. All of this is encapsulated in the novel's deliberately provocative atmosphere of innuendo and suggestion, within which Wilde encoded the sensitive topic of revolutionary politics.

Rather than offering another reading of *The Picture of Dorian Gray* as a text that celebrates and explores the queering of sexual identity, which it very clearly does, I want to emphasise, as Barlas did, the contemporary relevance of Wilde's equally important subversion of late Victorian conceptions about art, politics and subjectivity. This is accomplished through the novel's anarchic Aestheticism, through which Wilde underlines his very risky treatment of both the subject and value of the symbol. As a literary text and an extended statement about aesthetic and political practice, *The Picture of Dorian Gray* provides a subversive manifesto for alternative modes of being and observing. It proposes that existence and perception are intimately linked, and if the reader is open to considering radical alternatives, then the risky experience of looking beyond surfaces for the deeper meanings of symbols will be a rewarding one. Invested with Wilde's anarchic understanding of the relationship between art and society, the novel offers insights into the relationship between aesthetic and political radicalism, its implications for the private, subjective self and its relevance to the wider cultural-political sphere. Although Wilde does not treat politics explicitly within the novel, his radicalism underlines his awareness of the dangers facing those whose ideas and actions defied the boundaries imposed by the bourgeois and imperial frameworks of the late Victorian state. As Wilde insists in the Preface, art reflects the interests of the spectator as well as mirroring life – a claim that he believed held equally true for radical readers as much as it did for the novel's conservative critics. By opening with this observation *The Picture of Dorian Gray* underlines his belief in the need for complementary artistic *and* political renovation.

Another claim made by Wilde in the Preface is that '[d]iversity of opinion about a work of art shows that the work is new, complex, and vital',[21] which stresses how the value of art is qualified by the heterogeneity of the responses that it provokes. Its function, he suggests, is to provoke disagreement and dissent and not to service some centralised critical authority, as he believed critics of the original text of his novel had done in 1890. In his 1887 review of John Collier's *A Manual of Oil Painting*, Wilde had already complained that 'the real difficulty of modernity in art is that the artist passes his life with respectable people, and that respectable people are unpictorial'.[22] The 'respectable' but wholly artificial aspects of bourgeois normality were, he felt, uninteresting, and these false values were targeted again in *The Picture of Dorian Gray*. According to Christopher Millard, the socialist who helped Robert Ross edit Wilde's posthumously published *Collected Works*, this subversive quality underlined the novel's 'strangeness of colour' and its aura of 'passionate suggestion'. This animated both the text and its subject matter by 'flickering like lightning through the gloom of the subject'.[23]

The attack on criticism that appeared in 'The Soul of Man Under Socialism', which was published several months after the 1890 text, conveyed Wilde's defensive reaction to hostile reviews. In this essay, as we have already seen, his fusion of political and artistic criticism associated creativity within radical individualism and explained why, as he previously argued in his 1890 dialogue, 'The Critic as Artist', 'you must intensify your own individualism'.[24] Announcing anarchism as the path to cultural liberation, he insisted that the truthful appreciation of beauty (itself a key cultural exercise) was a purely subjective matter. In these essays Wilde regarded Aestheticism as an inevitable consequence of anarchism because the capitalist state prevented the individual from achieving intellectual and social fulfilment.

This of course, did not alter the fact that mainstream reviewers negatively influenced public perceptions of *The Picture of Dorian Gray*, which, despite the success of the *Lippincott's* serialisation, sold poorly when published as a book.[25] Doubtless, readers were put off by reviews warning that the novel contained 'matters only fitted for the Criminal Investigation Department',[26] a claim that Wilde countered by trying to distance his fiction from the mass literary market. By distinguishing his work from the commercial imperatives described by Gagnier and which he regarded as coarse and unchallenging, Wilde confronted the conservative aesthetic and ideological practices that informed popular literature by deliberately placing his fiction in dialectical opposition to the critical mainstream.[27]

Wilde responded to such criticism by explaining that the novel's literary value lay in its engagement with bourgeois culture, and insisted that its key theme was his negative portrayal of middle-class values.[28] In asserting that '[r]omantic art deals with the exception and with the individual', he argued that Dorian's significance lay in his exceptionality:

> Good people, belonging as they do to the normal, and so, commonplace type, are artistically uninteresting. Bad people are, from the point of view of art, fascinating studies. They represent colour, variety, and strangeness. Good people exasperate one's reason, bad people stir one's imagination.[29]

Wilde also claimed that Aestheticism's right to represent unruly but fascinating subjects was under attack from a culturally conservative press bent on controlling the content of literature: 'The poor public,' he complained to the editor of the *St. James's Gazette*, 'hearing from an authority so high as your own, that this is a wicked book that should be coerced and suppressed by a Tory government, will, no doubt, rush to it and read it.' Wilde also warned, however, that the moral contained within the book was the lesson that indulgence was not the path to freedom because 'excess [. . .] brings its own punishment'.[30]

Fenianism and *The Picture of Dorian Gray*

The Picture of Dorian Gray is an anarchic novel about the destructive consequences of capital which prove to be personally and morally disastrous for Dorian. The liberal *Daily Chronicle* complained that it promoted 'unbridled indulgence in every form of secret and unspeakable vice', but these experiences only become available to Dorian precisely because he acquires access to 'every resource of luxury and art' – the very excesses that hostile reviewers criticised Wilde for celebrating.[31] Wilde insisted that this was the novel's core meaning and the 'terrible moral' of Dorian's eventual fate and damnation. In subsequent exchanges with the press, he stressed that the 'monstrous theory' of censorship was profoundly repressive as it allowed governments to exercise political authority 'over imaginative literature'. Adopting an Irish outsider's position in relation to British culture, Wilde openly expressed in his correspondence with the press his own anxiety over 'the possibility of any general culture in England', where, he believed, influential fanatics were distorting 'the artistic instinct of the English'.[32]

Wilde agreed with his critics that the novel explored the dangers of luxury, but he also defended it by pointing to the kind of corruption that results from Dorian's excessive behaviour. To hostile reviewers preoccupied with Dorian's and, by extension, Wilde's own 'loathsome'[33] queerness (one described his 'feminine' and 'twisted' writing as the work of a 'literary lady'),[34] Wilde stressed that his protagonist's disintegration was primarily a social, economic and political collapse, rather than a case of simple sexual degeneracy. *The Christian Leader*, which praised the novel's 'mingled culture and corruption', grasped its social critique very clearly: 'We can only hope that it will be read and pondered by those classes of British society whose corruption it delineates with such thrilling power.' Wilde also responded to the charge that his novel was 'defiling English society' by stressing the importance of Dorian's misguided subjectivity which, following his unsuccessful 'attempt to kill conscience', emerges badly damaged: failing to realise his potential as a subject who must engage with society and realise Chuang Tsŭ's ideal of 'self-culture' and individualism, he retreats from society and 'kills himself' instead.[35]

Aestheticism was regarded by Wilde's conservative critics as an attack on late Victorian capitalist culture. By concentrating on what they perceived to be the novel's celebration of Dorian's transgression of sexual mores, they deflected attention from Wilde's desire to reveal the true nature of bourgeois normality with 'curious colours, subtle in their loveliness and fascinating in their almost mystical tone'. With this unusual literary scheme, Wilde planned to express Aestheticism's principal objection to establishment culture, which he described as 'our reaction against the crude primaries of a doubtless more respectable but certainly less cultivated age'. The novel's themes are expressed in relation to art and culture, and with it Wilde aimed to undermine authority by changing popular, received notions about culture, identity and responsibility. Its setting within aristocratic and ruling-class circles is vital to the meaning of the tale, and Dorian's rapid moral decay results from his exposure to this environment: writing to the *Scots Observer*, he described how '[i]t was necessary [. . .] for the dramatic development of the story, to surround Dorian Gray with an atmosphere of moral corruption. Otherwise the story would have had no meaning and the plot no issue'.[36]

The hostility continued and in reviews of Robert Ross' *Collected Works* (1908) the *Times* condemned the novel as a 'perverted' and 'deplorable' text, while the *Sunday Times* described it as 'but a tour de force in morbidity'.[37] But as well as being described in such terms as the work of 'a literary dung-fly',[38] *The Picture of Dorian Gray* was also associated with Irish political violence, much as Wilde himself had been in the pages of *Punch* a decade earlier. This accusation was levelled by 'H', an anonymous correspondent believed by Wilde to have been W.E. Henley the arch-imperialist and editor of the *Scots Observer*, the newspaper in which the accusation was printed.[39] 'H' intervened in the excited debate about art and morality by pointing to Wilde's republicanism, describing *The Picture of Dorian Gray* as a politically seditious text , or 'treasonable perfomance' celebrating 'crime, vulgarity, Radicalism, and obscenity'. For 'H' proper literary taste, political conservatism and loyalty to the British Empire were one and the same, and he compared the novel's politically subversive potential to that of T.D. Sullivan's Fenian ballad, 'God Save Ireland' and its 'blackguard doggerel about three cowardly murderers' (the song celebrates the 'Manchester Martyrs' – three Fenian prisoners whose hanging in Salford Gaol in 1867 were among the last public executions in England). As the controversy over the content of *The Picture of Dorian Gray* developed into a political row in which the novel's sexual content was equated with the 'infamous matter' of Irish republicanism,[40] conservatives began to read Aestheticism as a cultural encoding of the political objectives of Fenianism and socialism. 'H' also attacked Wilde's:

> assertion that when a man writes a book or paints a picture the critic ought not to discuss what he says in the book or what the picture is of, but only whether the book is well or ill written, or the picture well or ill painted. The proposition amazes me [. . .][41]

In contrast to this, 'H' believed it was 'the clear and obvious duty' of the literary critic to:

> discuss both the subject treated and the treatment of the subject, and if he considers that one is praiseworthy and the other is not, to say so as plainly as possible. When he is discussing the subject he must say anything there is to be said about its morality or immorality, and when he is discussing the treatment there is no morality or immorality for him to say anything about.[42]

For 'H', aesthetic taste and political morality were one and the same – no work of fiction could be dissociated from the established political beliefs of its author. In Wilde's defence, the literary journalist and art reviewer, Charles Whibley, replied that 'H's detestation of the novel and his outrage over its expression of Aestheticism was motivated by his own opposition to Home Rule.'[43] Wilde also responded by describing 'H' an 'unreal' example of the 'infinite varieties of Philistines' found in Britain and countered his view that 'the test of art should be the political opinions of the artist' with another subtle swipe at British rule in his home country: 'if one differed from the artist on the question of the best way of misgoverning Ireland, one should always abuse his work'.[44] In this way, the political crisis in Ireland was perceived as being central to Wilde's claim that the moral purpose of *The Picture of Dorian Gray* was to reveal 'to each man what he is to himself'. Wilde believed that the crisis exposed the British political unconscious by reflecting colonial misrule back at the imperial observer, because '[i]t is the spectator, and not life, that art really mirrors'. As Linda Dryden has argued, the novel's critique of late Victorian society is 'overtly subversive'.⁴⁵ Wilde believed that the real value of *The Picture of Dorian Gray* lay in its capacity to reveal to the reader the opposing side of his or her identity, whether that alternative be Irish, queer, artist or anarchist. These anxious and aggressive responses to his novel reveal much about late Victorian Britain's political and sexual unconscious.

Subverting Romance

With its recognition of the novel's dialectical confrontation between beauty and decay, the *Christian Leader* accepted that the deterioration of Dorian's image in the portrait reflected the degrading and degenerating condition of bourgeois subjectivity. Walter Pater agreed and, in his review carried in the *Bookman*, pointed out that Wilde's 'wholesome dislike of the common-place' was 'rightly or wrongly identified by him with the bourgeois, with our middle-class'. His ideological conflict with this class and its material 'habits and tastes' politicised the text and drove Wilde 'to protest emphatically against so-called "realism" in art'. Arguing that the novel offered the bourgeoisie 'anything but a homely philosophy of life', Pater identified its subversive aesthetic in Wilde's 'pleasant' rendering of 'accessory detail, taken straight from the culture, the intellectual and social interests, the conventionalities, of the moment'. Set firmly within the reality of the bourgeois sphere and allegorising its culture, Pater believed that the novel hinged on the portrait's function as a carrier of brutal truth that exposes the moneyed classes. This, he suggested, allowed Wilde to radically undermine capitalist ideology from within, as Dorian's moral slippage revealed the void beneath the surface of middle-class experience; the novel's appeal, he felt, would lie in its consciously modern treatment of the gothic theme of the double precisely because it was invested within one of this culture's important 'accessory details'. Dorian's *doppelgänger*, he pointed out, differed from other literary manifestations of the double because it appeared within the novel as a material object and art commodity.

Pater believed that readers would care less for the story's moral than for 'the fine, varied, largely appreciative culture of the writer' precisely because of this:

> Its interest turns on that very old theme, old because based on some inherent experience or fancy of the human brain, of a double life: of Döppelgänger [sic] – not of two *persons*, in this case, but of the man and his portrait.⁴⁶

Clearly, *The Picture of Dorian Gray* was read by contemporaries as violating the established political and sexual ideologies of late Victorian Britain and hostile reviewers read it as a text that contained a range of radical ideas. Wilde's defence of the novel was structured around his own refusal to be drawn on its ultimate meaning, adding to what conservative editors like W. E. Henley regarded as its abominable and even satanic quality.[47] In trying to establish some distance between himself and the novel's ultimate meaning, Wilde left its content open to interpretation, but the 1891 Preface contradicted bourgeois approaches to art, as well as the assumption that fiction ought to be commodified. By declaring the uselessness of art within capitalist society, Wilde bound Aestheticism to contemporary radicalism. His refusal of such values in April 1891, when the novel was first published in book form, was followed eight months later by the practical help that he offered to John Barlas when he was arrested for firing a revolver at the Speaker's House in Westminster. Barlas' favourable review of Wilde's work appeared in print the following spring.[48]

Wilde's rejection of capital also informs the novel's manipulation of genre. As Talia Shaffer has pointed out, a range of Aesthetic fictions exploited the conventions of the romance, but *The Picture of Dorian Gray* also proposed a number of significant and subversive changes to it. Lord Henry Wotton raises this point at the very beginning of the novel, when he tells the artist, Basil Hallward, that nothing succeeds like melodrama because '[n]owadays a broken heart will run to many editions'.[49] As Shaffer points out, Wilde unravelled the romance and its requirement for 'feverish heroism' because '*Dorian Gray*, the most famous of the aesthetic novels, carries the cumulative and complex traces of its history of negotiations with its genre.'[50] The expectations generated by the romance are subverted by Wilde, who suggested an alternative role for fiction that is articulated through the novel's exploration of the nature of the relationship between art and anarchy.

Wilde's message did not, however, promote the virtues of unlimited indulgence and his youthful anti-hero turns out, in the end, to be a demented liability who refuses to place any limits on his behaviour. As Shaffer points out, Wilde was keen to deny familiar but ideologically-oriented structures like the marriage plot and subverted the romance's logic of admirable self-sacrifice, but his protagonist cannot be reconciled to bourgeois moral, political or sexual values. His descent into an ever-widening spiral of immorality and corruption, into which young society ladies like Lady Gwendolen are drawn, proposes radical formal 'alterations' to the conventional arc of late Victorian fiction, making a deeply political statement about the inadequacy of the romance to match the aesthetic requirements of literary art at the fin de siècle.[51]

With Wotton's claim that he is surrounded by 'men of some intellectual power',[52] Wilde also questions the nature of influence as the aristocrat unconsciously sympathises with 'the rage of English democracy against what they call the vices of the upper orders'. His ability to understand working-class indignation is limited by his own belief that aristocratic vice is an imitation of the excesses of the poor, and tantamount to 'poaching on their preserves'. Wilde's critique of indulgent Aestheticism indicates his dislike for 'persons with no principles',[53] while the novel's uniqueness (and lack of commercial success in 1891) stemmed from its expression of this cultural-political sensibility. By subverting the imperatives of the romance genre within an aesthetically conscious narrative, Wilde radically questioned the power and authority of bourgeois representation. By suggesting that anarchism and Aestheticism are inherently compatible, he assumed a revolutionary stance in regard to art, culture, society and selfhood. By questioning the legitimacy and authority of the bourgeoisie's judgement of art and, by extension, its political privilege, he drew careful attention to the structures and orientation of capitalist society in this exchange between the painter and the aristocrat. By testing the boundaries of morality in *The Picture of Dorian Gray*, Wilde synthesised revolutionary discourse with aesthetic doctrine in a manner that was at once covert but also, simultaneously, recognisable to informed contemporary readers, including even his literary and political opponents like 'H'. The result is a novel that is politically, formally and thematically unorthodox.

Wilde saw no tension between his desire to produce finer, more exquisite works and the needs of democracy. Basil Hallward raises this issue when he discusses his own wish to realise a 'new personality for art' that will create 'an entirely new manner' and mobilise his 'mode of style', allowing viewers of his paintings, like the readers of Wilde's novel, to 'think of' and 'see things differently'.[54] Hallward believes that his particularly subjective stress on the transformative nature of art will expose the vulgarity of realism alongside the contemporary preoccupation with 'ideality that is void'. His proposal for a new and radical art aimed at replacing emptiness with substance highlights the insubstantiality of capitalism and its contemporary valorisation through the literary medium of realism. Dorian, of course, embodies this new personality and his violence articulates the tension upon which it is founded. At once resistant to the artist's gaze and captured by it, he entrances Hallward who, while warning Lord Henry that '[y]ou might see nothing in him', also declares 'I see everything in him.' At once alluringly present and strangely absent, Dorian's flickering subjectivity, and its representation on Hallward's canvas, resists aesthetic convention:

> He is never more present in my work than when no image of him is there. He is a suggestion, as I have said, of a new manner. I find him in the curves of certain lines, in the loveliness and subtleties of certain colours.[55]

While Hallward makes what might appear to be a purely artistic comment about his newly discovered, perfect subject, he is also pointing to Dorian's subversive nature within the spheres of art and perception, both of which are deeply politicised.[56]

Hallward's new aesthetic ideal positions art creation as an act of refusal against the 'microscope'[57] gaze of the highly surveillant bourgeois society that he has begun to resist. By extending its influence into the field of representation, and by privileging what Wilde termed the 'brutality of plain realism'[58] as the dominant perceptive and conceptual modes rendering art as 'a form of autobiography', the capitalist optic threatens to render all culture static. Hallward counters this dynamic by stressing the need for detachment from it as well as the cultivation of an 'abstract sense of beauty', which explains his need to keep Dorian's portrait from the world. Hallward expresses his desire to withdraw from the real by suggesting that the key to any work is its autonomy: it is his opinion that art, like Wilde's soulful socialism, instils its subject with a unique aura. Wotton rejects this idea but the pair do agree that, without any capacity for abstraction, even the 'thoroughly well-informed man' becomes 'a dreadful thing' whose sterile imagination resembles the incoherent contents of 'a bric-á-brac shop, all monsters and dust, with everything priced above its proper value'.[59] Commercial, sordid, lifeless, unproductive and overvalued, his social type and their private imaginations are devoid of meaning.

Following this discussion, we also learn about the people who move in Wotton's privileged but 'tedious' aristocratic circles and for whom Wilde's concepts of the immediate and the real have no purchase:

> He pictured to himself with silent amusement the tedious luncheon that he had missed by staying so long with Basil Hallward. Had he gone to his aunt's, he would have been sure to have met Lord Goodbody there,

and the whole conversation would have been about the feeding of the poor and the necessity for model lodging-houses. Each class would have preached the importance of those virtues, for whose exercise there was no necessity in their own lives. The rich would have spoken on the value of thrift, and the idle grown eloquent over the dignity of labour. It was charming to have escaped all that![60]

By becoming aware of the counter-cultural dynamic of Dorian Gray's portrait, Wotton distances himself from these members of the static liberal scene that, to Wilde, seemed so immobile and hypocritical. Their values inform the capitalist ideology that he confronted so directly in 'The Soul of Man Under Socialism' and their irrationalism contrasts with the more substantial and exciting exchanges and challenges being generated by art. These fictional dialogues, along with the interpretation of art proposed by Aestheticism's programme for a more radical and culturally unorthodox subjectivity that might offer liberation for all, make the type of philanthropy advocated by Lord Goodbody appear like a poor imitation of radicalism.

Wotton recognises that he is being transformed by this new aesthetic consciousness and knows that he is becoming increasingly aware of his own aristocratic apostasy through his exposure to Hallward's ideas about art:

> To realize one's nature perfectly – that is what each of us is here for. People are afraid of themselves, nowadays. They have forgotten the highest of all duties, the duty that one owes to one's self. Of course, they are charitable. They feed the hungry and clothe the beggar. But their own souls starve, and are naked. Courage has gone out of our race. Perhaps we never really had it. The terror of society, which is the basis of morals, the terror of God, which is the secret of religion – these are the two things that govern us.[61]

Wilde argues here that capitalist modernity is governed through structural violence.

This form of official repression depends on the quieter, often unapparent but no less harmful forms of official forces and influences through which the modern subject is directed and controlled. Wilde suggests in the Preface that Aestheticism offers an alternative model of perception and consciousness by privileging the right to pleasure as key to the development of subjectivity. Individualism is the result of this self-realisation, which he regarded as the principal reason for existence and life's ultimate objective. Like Chuang Tsŭ, whose ancient but strikingly modern manifesto for a radicalised consciousness appealed to Wilde, Wotton aims to perfect and complete his identity by developing his own self-awareness. The alternative to this is acquiescence in the general atmosphere of social, political and cultural 'terror' – the state of fearful self-denial and intellectual collapse that forms the basis of moral and religious obedience and was, in Wilde's view, the foundation of modern government. The remedy for this dilemma is a fully developed and subversive consciousness that denies and resists these expressions of authority because:

> the bravest man amongst us is afraid of himself. The mutilation of the savage has its tragic survival in the self-denial that mars our lives. We are punished for our refusals. Every impulse that we strive to strangle broods in the mind and poisons us. The body sins once, and has done with its sin, for action is a mode of purification. Nothing remains then but the recollection of a pleasure, or the luxury of a regret. The only way to get rid of a temptation is to yield to it. Resist it, and your soul grows sick with longing for the things it has forbidden to itself, with desire for what its monstrous laws have made monstrous and unlawful. It has been said that the great events of the world take place in the brain. It is in the brain, and the brain only, that the great sins of the world take place also.[62]

By indulging in what the law has forbidden, the liberated individual can experience the kind of freedoms that are normally restricted to the imagination and are rarely materialised through the irreversible and cathartic practice of action. This counters the moral, cultural and political 'purification' demanded by late Victorian authority and it is at junctures like this, in which Wilde explores aesthetic ideas about gratification and pleasure, that the novel proposes a new subjectivity that can resist the interruption of desire by authority. The disruption that this imposes over the continuum between thought and deed frightens Dorian at first because his exposure to this revelation is overwhelming. As he warns Wotton: 'You bewilder me. I don't know what to say. There is some answer to you, but I cannot find it. Don't speak. Let me think. Or, rather, let me try not to think.' Dorian is troubled because he is stirred by the emergence of a strange and potentially radical imagination that is, as yet, as unformed as his own emotional response to music.

However, he acknowledges that its emotional charge can be conveyed through language:

> Music had stirred him like that. Music had troubled him many times. But music was not articulate. It was not a new world, but rather another chaos, that it created in us. Words! Mere words! How terrible they were! How clear, and vivid, and cruel! One could not escape from them. And yet what a subtle magic there was in them! They seemed to be able to give a plastic form to formless things, and to have a music of their own as sweet as that of viol or of lute. Mere words! Was there anything so real as words?[63]

Dorian's introspection conveys how reality is portrayed, mediated and even constructed through the musical language of Aestheticism. He compares his emergent and barely comprehended state of consciousness to the perilous and potentially self-destructive experience of 'walking in fire'[64] a practice that is as exciting as it is dangerous. The intensity of Walter Pater's 'gem-like flame' has a social and literary incandescence here that dissolves the boundary separating Aestheticism from contemporary political concerns.

Slavoj Žižek has interpreted the overlapping of the real and the symbolic within modernity's 'domain of appearing' as being dependent upon its imposition of an 'invisible order' over society. This order 'structures our experience of reality, the complex network of rules and meanings which makes us see what we see the way we see it (and what we don't see the way we don't see it)'.[65] For Wilde, the central challenge of art was the deconstruction of these structures and the boundaries, limitations and controls that they imposed. Rather than regarding anarchism's objectives as unrealisable, Wilde represented its relationship to art and life in *The Picture of Dorian Gray* as forming a complex synthesis of ideology and practice. The novel's fusion of politics with aesthetics and its radical philosophy of experience informs its strangely compelling dynamic, and explains much of the hostility that it provoked upon its initial publication. Like Wilde's 1887 parody of dynamite fiction, 'Lord Arthur Savile's Crime', *The Picture of Dorian Gray* challenges the narrative tendencies of late Victorian popular fiction. By rejecting the conventions against which it pushed, the novel introduces subversive political and aesthetic ideas and theories into another established genre, the gothic romance.[66] Rather than serving as a manifesto for a conflicted and divided selfhood, or expressing Wilde's capacity for 'living life at cross-purposes', as Jerusha McCormack has described his motivation for composing it, *The Picture of Dorian Gray* offers a complex yet consistent analysis of the relationship between Aestheticism and autonomy. Drawing on Wilde's very direct confrontations with bourgeois hypocrisy, McCormack describes him as a literary 'terrorist' and *'agent provocateur'* whose inclinations were, ultimately, self-destructive, but the revolutionary literary, political and aesthetic proposals for an alternative type of consciousness that he presented in this novel are culturally and socially constructive.[67]

Wilde believed that the achievement of self-realisation through art could subvert bourgeois ideology but his hope that the writer might translate 'into another manner or a new material his impression of beautiful things' is not realised through the character of Dorian Gray. His journey toward fulfilment takes a ruinous path that diverges from the ideal route proposed by Chuang Tsŭ, but Wilde's desire for aesthetic renovation assumes a political significance in *The Picture of Dorian Gray*, as the 'ethical sympathies' that he criticised in his 1891 Preface were those of late Victorian capitalism.[68] Politically progressive, aesthetically radical and formally experimental, the novel applies an anarchic sensibility to questions of art, taste and culture, none of which ought to be, in Wilde's opinion, subject to conservative values. Rebellion, disobedience and dissent constitute the artist's role in this novel. Wilde believed that it was only those artists who were at once anarchists and aesthetes who had the moral, political and cultural capacity to 'read the symbol [. . .] at their own peril' and then survive the experience, unlike the unfortunate Dorian Gray.

Notes

1. See Wilde's correspondence in *Complete Letters*: to the *St. James's Gazette*, 25–8 June 1890 (pp. 428–34); to the *Daily Chronicle*, 30 June 1890 (pp. 435–6); to the *Scots Observer*, 9 and 23 July and 13 August (pp. 428–34, 438–42, 446–9). The publications' initial reviews and Wilde's responses to them are reprinted in Christopher Millard (ed.) (as 'Stuart Mason'), *Oscar Wilde: Art and Morality* (London: Frank Palmer, 1907, reprinted 1912). Millard is hereafter cited as 'Mason'.
2. Gagnier, *Idylls of the Marketplace*, p. 66.
3. Kirsten MacLeod, *Fictions of British Decadence: High Art, Popular Writing, and the Fin de Siècle* (Basingstoke: Palgrave, 2006), p. 79.
4. Gagnier, *Idylls of the Marketplace*, pp. 34, 51, 85; Danson, *Wilde's Intentions: The Artist in his Criticism*, p. 17.
5. *Complete Works*, vol. 3: *The Picture of Dorian Gray: The 1890 and 1891 Texts*, ed. Joseph Bristow (Oxford: Oxford University Press, 2005), p. 357. Throughout this chapter I draw on the 1891 text.

6. Karl Marx, *Capital*, vol. 1(trans. from the German by Ben Fowkes, London: Penguin, 1990), p. 179.
7. John E. Barlas, 'Oscar Wilde: A Study', *The Novel Review*, 1.1, April 1892, pp. 42–6, pp. 42, 44–5.
8. Ibid. p. 42.
9. Ibid. pp. 42–3.
10. See Vincent Sherry, *Modernism and the Reinvention of Decadence* (Cambridge: Cambridge University Press, 2015), p. 24.
11. Barlas, 'Oscar Wilde: A Study', p. 45.
12. Ibid. pp. 45–6.
13. David Weir, *Anarchy and Culture: The Aesthetic Politics of Modernism* (Amherst: University of Massachusetts Press, 1992), p. 178.
14. Barlas, 'Oscar Wilde: A Study', p. 46.
15. Edward Carpenter, *Towards Democracy* (London: John Heywood, 1883), p. 12.
16. Ibid. p. 16.
17. Wilde, *The Picture of Dorian Gray*, p. 168.
18. Wilde, 'A Chinese Sage', in *Complete Works*, vol. 7, p. 146.
19. Wilde, *The Picture of Dorian Gray*, p. 168.
20. Joseph Bristow has explored the very diverse and complicated range of 'contextual conditions' that underline Wilde's literary and theoretical writing, including issues such as the repression of homosexuality during the 1890s, prison-writing, blackmail, philanthropy, journalism, feminism, Fenianism, masculinity, popular fiction and socialism. See Joseph Bristow, 'Introduction', in Bristow (ed.), *Wilde Writings: Contextual Conditions* (Toronto: University of Toronto Press, 2003), pp. 1–38.
21. Wilde, *The Picture of Dorian Gray*, p. 168.
22. Oscar Wilde, 'Common-Sense in Art', *Pall Mall Gazette*, 8 January 1887, in Robert Ross (ed.), *Collected Works*, vol. 12, *Reviews* 1 (Boston: John Luce & Co., 1908), pp. 119–23, p. 121.
23. Mason, *Oscar Wilde: Art and Morality*, p. 116.
24. Wilde, 'The Critic as Artist', in *Complete Works*, vol. 4, p. 165.
25. According to Millard, the first edition, consisting of about 1,000 copies, took five years to eventually sell out. Josephine M. Guy and Ian Small have pointed out that sales were probably undermined by the commercial success of the novel's earlier version, and that Wilde was fighting an uphill battle in trying to promote a text that had already been widely circulated and read in another format. However, the systematic opposition that it met with in such reviews certainly contributed to its lukewarm public reception. See Stuart Mason, 'Introduction', in *Oscar Wilde; Art and Morality*, p. 22. See also, Josephine M. Guy and Ian Small, *Oscar Wilde's Profession: Writing and the Culture Industry in the Late Nineteenth Century* (Oxford: Oxford University Press, 2000), especially chapter 3, 'Of Making Many Books'.

26. *Scots Observer*, 5 July 1890, reprinted in Mason, *Oscar Wilde; Art and Morality*, p. 76.
27. Wilde expressed his disdain for popular fiction prior to 1890. See Oscar Wilde, 'Mr. Morris's *Odyssey*', *Pall Mall Gazette*, 26 April 1887, reprinted in Robert Ross (ed.), *Collected Works*, vol. 12, *Reviews* 1(Boston: John Luce & Co., 1908), pp. 153–7. As well as describing the novel as decadent 'garbage' and condemning it as a celebration of 'paganism', a reviewer in the *St. James's Gazette* also attempted to isolate the text and its 'catchpenny revelations of the non-existent' by implying that it contained 'revelations only of the singularly unpleasant minds from which they emerge'. He attacked Wilde for expressing 'delight which outsiders cannot share or even understand'. Unsigned review, originally published in the *St. James's Gazette*, 24 June 1890, reprinted in Mason, *Oscar Wilde; Art and Morality*, pp. 27–34. Quotations from pp. 28, 34, 38.
28. Wilde responded to these criticisms by declaring:

> I am quite incapable of understanding how any work of art can be criticised from a moral standpoint. The sphere of art and the sphere of ethics are absolutely distinct and separate; and it is to the confusion between the two that we owe the appearance of Mrs. Grundy, that amusing old lady who represents the only original form of humour that the middle classes of this country have been able to produce. (Oscar Wilde, to the Editor of the *St. James's Gazette*, 26 June 1890, reprinted in Mason, *Oscar Wilde; Art and Morality*, pp. 35–7. Quotation from pp. 35–6)

29. Wilde to the *St. James's Gazette*, 26 June 1890, reprinted in Ibid. p. 43.
30. Oscar Wilde to the *St. James's Gazette*, 26 June 1890, reprinted in Ibid. p. 43.
31. *The Daily Chronicle*, 30 June 1890, reprinted in Ibid. p. 67.
32. Oscar Wilde to the *St. James's Gazette*, 26 and 28 June 1890, reprinted in Ibid. pp. 44, 48, 50–1.
33. *The Daily Chronicle*, reprinted in Ibid. p. 43.
34. J. Maclaren Cobban, to the Editor of the *Scots Observer*, undated, reprinted in Ibid. pp. 123–5, quotations from pp. 123–4.
35. *Christian Leader*, 3 July 1890, reprinted in Ibid. pp. 137–8, p. 138; *Daily Chronicle*, 30 June 1890, reprinted in Ibid. p. 68; Wilde to the *Daily Chronicle*, 26 June, reprinted in Ibid. p. 73.
36. Wilde to the *Scots Observer*, 9 July 1890, reprinted in Ibid. pp. 78–81, p. 80.
37. Quoted in Stuart Mason, *Oscar Wilde and the Aesthetic Movement* (Dublin: Townley Searle, 1920), p. 201.
38. T. E. Brown, to the editor of the *Scots Observer*, undated, reprinted in Mason, *Oscar Wilde; Art and Morality*, pp. 103–9, p. 104.

39. Merlin Holland and Rupert Hart-Davis, in *Complete Letters*, p. 438, n.2.
40. 'H' to the editor of the *Scots Observer*, 26 July 1890, reprinted in Mason, *Oscar Wilde; Art and Morality*, pp. 89–94, pp. 93–4.
41. 'H', to the editor of the *Scots Observer*, reprinted in Ibid. p. 91.
42. Ibid. p. 93.
43. Charles Whibley, to the editor of the *Scots Observer*, reprinted in Ibid. pp. 95–7, p. 96.
44. Wilde to the editor of the *Scots Observer*, 13 August 1890, reprinted in Ibid. pp. 113–22, pp. 120–1.
45. Linda Dryden, *The Modern Gothic and Literary Doubles: Stevenson, Wilde and Wells* (Basingstoke: Palgrave, 2003), p. 121.
46. Walter Pater, 'A Novel by Oscar Wilde', originally published in *The Bookman*, October 1891, reprinted in Mason, *Oscar Wilde; Art and Morality*, pp. 188–95, pp. 191, 194.
47. '[I]ts hero is a devil', complained the *Scots Observer*. 'Reviews and Magazines', *Scots Observer*, 5 July 1890, reprinted in Mason, *Oscar Wilde; Art and Morality*, p. 75.
48. Wilde to John Barlas, 19 January and 4 February 1892, in *Complete Letters*, pp. 510–11. Barlas' action was extreme, but an explanation for his opening fire lies in his own tragic history: he was so badly beaten by police during the 'Bloody Sunday' riot at Trafalgar Square in November 1887, that he suffered a permanent brain injury which rendered him mentally unstable. Wilde's surviving letters to him reveal genuine concern for his vulnerable friend. See *Complete Letters*, p. 511, fn. See also 'John Evelyn Barlas', in *Oxford Dictionary of National Biography* <http://www.oxforddnb.com/view/article/62130?docPos=1> accessed 19 October 2013.
49. Wilde, *The Picture of Dorian Gray*, p. 177.
50. Talia Shaffer, 'The Origins of the Aesthetic Novel: Ouida, Wilde and the Popular Romance', in Joseph Bristow (ed.), *Wilde Writings: Contextual Conditions* (Toronto: University of Toronto Press, 2013), pp. 212–29, pp. 213, 225–6.
51. Ibid. p. 225.
52. Wilde, *The Picture of Dorian Gray*, p. 175.
53. Ibid.
54. Ibid. pp. 176–7.
55. Ibid. p. 177.
56. For a discussion of the contemporary preoccupation with visual perception, see Jonathan Crary, *Techniques of the Observer: On Vision and Modernity in the Nineteenth Century* (Cambridge, MA: MIT Press, 1990) and *Suspensions of Perception: Attention, Spectacle and Modern Culture* (Cambridge, MA: MIT Press, 1999).
57. Wilde, *The Picture of Dorian Gray*, p. 177.

58. Oscar Wilde to the *Daily Chronicle*, 30 June, reprinted in Mason, *Oscar Wilde; Art and Morality*, pp. 71–4, p. 74.
59. Wilde, *The Picture of Dorian Gray*, p. 178.
60. Ibid. p. 179.
61. Ibid. p. 183.
62. Ibid.
63. Ibid. p. 184.
64. Ibid.
65. See Slavoj Žižek, *Event* (London: Penguin, 2014), p. 119.
66. See Philip K. Cohen, *The Moral Vision of Oscar Wilde* (Madison, WI: Fairleigh Dickinson University Press, 1978), p. 105.
67. Jerusha McCormack, 'The Wilde Irishman: Oscar as Aesthete and Anarchist', in McCormack (ed.), *Wilde the Irishman* (New Haven: Yale University Press, 1998), pp. 82–94, p. 83.
68. Wilde, *The Picture of Dorian Gray*, p. 167.

Chapter 6

Civil Disobedience and *The Importance of Being Earnest*

In his memoir, *Oscar Wilde: The Story of an Unhappy Friendship*, Robert Sherard recalled a moment during Wilde's extended visit to Paris in 1883 when the pair strolled through the ruined shell of the Tuileries Palace. Observing the extent of the destruction caused when the palace was mined and then burned by retreating Communards just over a decade earlier, Wilde told his friend that there was 'not [. . .] one little blackened stone' in the now derelict site 'which is not to me a chapter in the Bible of Democracy'.[1] The ruin symbolised for Wilde the recent history of urban insurgency, its ruin etching the story of political insurrection and its 'symbolic form'[2] into the very materiality of the city. The memory of insurrection, he believed, was a part of a radical imaginary that paralleled and defied late-nineteenth-century notions of capitalist progress. Indicating how the bloody suppression of the Paris Commune reinforced bourgeois domination in fin-de-siècle France, Wilde's comment also connected class violence to the wider spectacle of urban modernity. What he and Sherard encountered in the rubble (itself in the process of being removed from sight by the city authorities) was a lasting, subversive counter-image in the ruins that endured for over a decade after the destruction of the Paris Commune. Unlike the short-lived and brutally suppressed Commune, which was wiped out in a matter of days, this blackened trace of the rebellion stained the city's bourgeois surface until it was completely erased from sight with its demolition in 1883.[3]

In *The Importance of Being Earnest*, which premiered in a compressed three-Act version in 1895, Wilde explored how, within the late Victorian city, bourgeois normality was similarly imposed over the longer-term history of repression and insurrection in Britain. Drawing on the original four-Act draft, with its added and more explicit political content, this chapter argues that the play's most subversive claim is that any recollection of these revolutionary outbreaks is removed from public discussion by the middle classes, who cannot tolerate the memory of such events. This deletion of the history of revolt is an attempt to deny what Joshua Clover has identified as the urban insurrectionist's greatest strategy – the weaponisation of the city at capitalism's most vulnerable political, economic and symbolic points.[4] During outbreaks of popular revolt, the urban protester and rioter reverses urban capitalism's grandest spectacles (the market, the palace and the boulevard) by occupying and deploying them against the logic and practice of the state. Set firmly within the late Victorian, bourgeois society of the spectacle, *The Importance of Being Earnest* interrogates the establishment's political and historical denial of rebellion and revolt. The play attacks the system for refusing to acknowledge the influence of revolutionary past and present, and its key comedic turns hinge upon the need to contain the memory of revolutionary events that are staged beneath its own theatrical surface.

Regenia Gagnier has argued that Wilde's later plays explore the connections that bind society, politics and art through their psychological-realist critiques of the ideology of late Victorian spectacular society. These works are preoccupied with the relationship between ruling class affluence and the 'props and property' with which the bourgeoisie imposes and mediates its power.[5] As we have seen in *The Picture of Dorian Gray*, Wilde believed that the surface matter of capital and empire obscured as much as it revealed and in *The Importance of Being Earnest* this façade is exposed as a screen concealing the reality of class violence from the popular imagination. Bourgeois dissimulation is betrayed by Gwendolen Fairfax's politically significant claim, offered in Act 3 of the revised and performed text that '[i]n matters of grave importance, style, not sincerity is the vital thing'.[6] Her revealing nod toward the play's subversive content suggests how carefully Wilde inflected his drama with class tension, as a series of subtle revelations embed the spectre of contemporary radicalism into its characters' prosperous surroundings.

The play was attacked by critics for its lack of realism. The *World* criticised it as a 'barren and delusive' work that 'represents nothing, means nothing, is nothing', while George Bernard Shaw considered it mediocre, unoriginal and an 'essentially hateful' expression of Wilde's 'degeneracy'.[7] It was praised by admirers for what they perceived as its light comedic content,[8] but it is at once historically real and deeply political and as Sos Eltis has argued, Wilde's 'most subversive and satirical' play 'found a perfect dramatic form for his own uneasy relation to society' by concentrating on the theme of social revolution.[9] Through its carefully structured series of evasions, deceptions and false appearances it disrupts capitalist logic by drawing attention to the insincerity of capitalism and the illogicality of bourgeois identity. The uncertainty upon which Wilde's comedy is predicated is staged against the context of a revolutionary politics that might, as Lady Bracknell suggests, invade the urban spaces of ruling-class privilege at any time if left unchecked.

These hints at class warfare generate more than cheap laughs ridiculing the despair of the urban poor, as Wilde underlines with considerably anarchic and anticolonial intentions how the potential for a revolutionary outbreak simmers just below the surface of bourgeois normality. Gagnier has pointed to the relationship between Wilde's subversion of imperial and bourgeois language and his critique of the literary market. In this way Wilde turned the rhetoric and ideology of capital and empire against itself:

> The astonishing thing about his wit is not that he could always and so quickly find the right word to substitute the key term of the platitude, but rather that he knew the platitudes so well to begin with. His mind was stocked with commonplaces, and these seem to have been there for the sole purpose of their subversion. The situation is one in which an outsider has to a stunning degree taken upon himself the reflective apparatus of the dominant group and then used this apparatus to mock the group on, and with, its own terms. The use of such tactics endears the speaker to the group at the moment he mocks it. This is the technique of ironic reference: the use of popular symbology by its critics in order to be both commercially competitive and critical.[10]

Operating as a kind of infiltrater of the popular culture of the imperial and capitalist metropolis, Wilde introduced the theme of subversion into his later work with much more caution and strategic care than he had done in *Vera; or, The Nihilists*. In *The Importance of Being Earnest* the insertion of political and cultural confusion into the bourgeois sphere is embodied in the figure of Jack Worthing, a character who remains a member of the élite social club to which he has been abandoned by his birth parents. The play's resolution of his identity crisis (borrowed, brilliantly, from melodrama's preoccupation with foundlings and their uncertain origins) ultimately allows the violence of privilege to go unchecked. While Wilde's earlier society comedies also exploit the internal contradictions that characterised Victorian sentimentality, Gagnier has underlined how *The Importance of Being Earnest* functions on the consciously self-critical level of avant-gardism, as the performance merges with the audience, 'obliterating the disjunction of art from life'. Its positioning of 'theatre as collective and spectacular artefact' combines events on stage with the values of the bourgeois audience and in doing so 'reflects the conspicuous consumption that is the world of the play. Thus Wilde's theatre [. . .] was a version of modern spectacular society'.[11]

The Proximity of Class Violence

Violence and the spectacle are closely aligned in this play. Wilde warned readers of 'The Soul of Man Under Socialism' that bourgeois normality existed quite precariously on the edge of rebellion and in very dangerous proximity to the 'ungrateful, discontented, disobedient, and rebellious'.[12] This chapter will explore how *The Importance of Being Earnest* exposes the disruptive presence of civil disobedience within the marketised and spectacularised urban spaces of late Victorian capital that are staged in the play – the city flats, drawing rooms and gardens of the privileged. With the prospect of revolution seething below its carefully stylised plot, the play satirises the supposedly calm political, material and historical surfaces of the bourgeois sphere by alluding to the violence and despair that capital generates. As Gagnier has shown, the stasis of this socially disengaged world is conveyed through Wilde's rapid, epigrammatic dialogue which conveys the emptiness of capital and its vacant spectacle by articulating 'a closed system representing an exclusive society'.[13] What I propose here is that political and material reality exist, just off-stage, in the tumultuous, ungoverned space that heaves directly below the play's surface: the ungovernable world of the protesting working class – the world from which Lady Bracknell vigilantly protects her daughter. With these glimpses of rebellion the play offers an aestheticised theory of insurgency that highlights the vulnerabilities of capitalism and imperialism. The bourgeois sphere and its culture of conspicuous consumption are mirrored by the alternative spectacle and performance of the riot and by the possibility of an invasion of this staged world by the violent realism that is configured in the riot's destruction of property. The audience sees no outbreak of urban insurrection, of course, and the prospect of revolt is contained with the play's conclusion, but political anxieties focused on the revolutionary potential of the working class are articulated through Lady Bracknell's comments on the dangers of education. The potential for the dispossessed to infiltrate this hermetic world is also briefly manifested in Jack Worthing's very uncertain origin story. Despite the play's containment of these threats, Wilde presented audiences with a critique of the doctrine of counter-insurgency that underlined late Victorian property relations and, in doing so, drew attention to their vulnerability.

Wilde also addressed the close proximity of insurrectionary violence and the bourgeois sphere in his 1887 story, 'Lord Arthur Savile's Crime', first published in *The Court and Society Review* and collected in *Lord Arthur Savile's Crime and Other Stories* in 1891. This tale reflects on Wilde's representation of himself as an artist, 'dreamer',[14] cultural dissident and political subversive who, like the Shakespeare of 'The Truth of Masks', places 'the serge of the radical beside the silks of the lord' for the aesthetic benefits and 'stage effects' that can be drawn from their close association. This exposure of class tension challenges capitalism's simulation-effect, or what Wilde regarded as its cultivation of 'the illusion of actual life'.[15] The story reveals that economy is not a virtue of the rich, as the hierarchical capitalist system depicted in the story is portrayed as fraudulent and dependent on the projection of this self-perpetuating illusion. The tale's seemingly light parody of the popular genre of dynamite fiction and its exploitation of the violent political and historical event of the terrorist explosion also draws attention to the serious matter of the political contradictions at the core of bourgeois experience. Wilde describes this as the cultural and social 'discord' that exists 'between the shallow optimism of the day and the real facts of existence'.[16]

The story opens with an ironic depiction of the proximity of bourgeois and radical culture, as Lady Windermere entertains a mixture of conservative politicians, clergy, academics and aristocrats who mingle with dangerous revolutionaries at her parties:

> It was Lady Windermere's last reception before Easter, and Bentick House was even more crowded than usual. Six Cabinet Ministers had come on from the Speaker's Levée in their stars and ribands, all the pretty women wore their smartest dresses, and at the end of the picture-gallery stood the Princess Sophia of Carlsrühe, a heavy Tartar-looking lady, with tiny black eyes and wonderful emeralds, talking bad French

at the top of her voice and laughing immoderately at everything that was said to her. It was certainly a wonderful medley of people. Gorgeous peeresses chatted affably to violent Radicals, popular preachers brushed coat-tails with eminent sceptics, a perfect bevy of bishops kept following a stout prima-donna from room to room, on the staircase stood several Royal Academicians, disguised as artists, and it was said that at one time the supper-room was absolutely crammed with geniuses. In fact, it was one of Lady Windermere's best nights, and the Princess stayed till nearly half-past eleven.[17]

This vignette, with its 'wonderful medley' of authority figures and terrorists, reflects the British establishment's capacity for tolerating the political violence that it provokes. The soirée accommodates élite types along with revolutionaries who commit types of political disturbance that capitalism generates. The party's strange alignment of reactionaries and rebels suggests that the distance between the privileged and the marginalised, dispossessed, alienated, poor and colonised is not as distant as we might imagine. The roaring elephant in this room is the conspicuous presence of radicals and agitators within the spectacle of bourgeois pleasure. Like Lady Wilde's home in 1860s Dublin, Lady Windermere's drawing room and gallery are haunted by the spectre of revolution, as it is only the radicals who are described as violent (as already discussed, Wilde was exposed to a wide range of political, artistic and cultural influences, including Fenianism, during the salons held by his parents in Dublin). With this depiction we are presented with a key Wildean paradox – the fusion of resistance and coercion in a comedic dialectic that is emblematised within this scene featuring dangerous subversives openly circulating among those whom they would regard as their political enemies.

The severity of bourgeois violence is concealed beneath the polite surface of Lady Windermere's party and is not directly represented here. Instead, it is rendered invisible by spectacular decoys such as expensive outfits bearing state decorations and precious jewels, while the entire establishment is represented: hypocritical bishops, state-sanctioned artists, aristocrats and the political élite – bourgeois subjects who are themselves part of the distraction that facilitates power. By asking the reader to consider the reality that lies beneath the surface of the bourgeois-liberal imperial state, Wilde suggests that its structural violence harms more than those at whom it is directly aimed. As Jay Thomas Parker has shown, nineteenth-century liberalism was complicit in 'creating, perpetuating and widening gaps of power'.[18] This complicity is shown to have epidemic consequences in 'Lord Arthur Savile's Crime', contaminating the drawing-room circles of the privileged through a kind of political recoil that corrupts the architects and practitioners of coercion.

Melodrama and the Concealment of State Violence

Melodrama always ends in resolution, the solving of social problems and the restoration of hierarchical social order. Having its origins in late-sixteenth-century Italian opera, it was adapted for theatre by French dramatists who, at the end of the eighteenth century, popularised it by adding more elaborate dialogue and accelerating its spectacular content. Physical action, mortal danger, spiritual perils and violence were among its central tropes and its growing popularity in Victorian Britain saw its outlandish plots and highly affective scenarios being replicated and intensified across a range of media. Novels by Charles Dickens, Walter Scott, Mary Elizabeth Braddon, Mrs Henry Wood, Wilkie Collins and others were adapted for the stage, while these authors borrowed heavily from the melodramatic tradition itself. Its key features included sensationalism, emotional appeal and the excessive virtue of its protagonists which was presented in distinction to the pronounced villainy of their antagonists. It also featured elaborately staged visual thrills, unlikely coincidences, the uncovering of origin mysteries via the validation of the legitimacy of heroes or heroines with the establishment of their identities, the exposure of family secrets and guilty pasts, the discovery of hidden wills and, of course, plenty of romance against the odds. The genre always concludes with resolution and a necessary return to normality that recalibrates upset familial and social circumstances, usually with an accompanying restoration of wealth, the rebalancing and validation of class distinctions.[19]

All of these devices, along with what Ben Singer identifies as their ideological foundations and objectives,[20] are criticised and parodied by Wilde in *The Importance of Being Earnest*. The enormously popular genre is sent up in a comedy predicated on the threat posed by the possibility of the infiltration of the late Victorian bourgeois sphere by a potentially working-class pretender, Jack Worthing. The play's titular swipe at dishonesty establishes Wilde's critical stance on the imposition of social boundaries and the superficial proprieties that they represent. These are the economic and political borders that the masses threaten to transgress by means of the revolutionary action hinted at by Lady Bracknell in the first Act. The absent presence of the insurgent working classes and their potential for disturbance is also depicted in the insolence of Algernon Moncrieff's butler, Lane, who drinks his master's wine and counters his relentless consumption by reminding him that some things (in this case cucumbers) cannot be had 'even for ready money'.[21] While Lane's failure to acquire the fruit at the very beginning of the play signals the failure of capital, Lady Bracknell's arrival announces its coercive social presence.

The Importance of Being Earnest was not Wilde's first indication of his suspicion that revolutionary violence could invade the static bourgeois scene. Writing in the *Pall Mall Gazette* in April 1886, he warned that the West End Riots of the previous February were as much a consequence of the failure of poetry as an outcome of political crisis. Wilde proposed that democracy was failing because it did not aestheticise politics, or 'use poetry as a means for the expression of political opinion', and he claimed that the void between art and politics was now being filled by violence:

> The fact is that most modern poetry is so artificial in its form, so individual in its essence and so literary in its style, that the people as a body are little moved by it, and when they have grievances against the capitalist or the aristocrat they prefer strikes to sonnets and rioting to rondels.[22]

Socially disconnected and formally rigid, Wilde believed that poetry had now become the cultural expression of the bourgeoisie and he warned that it was antagonising the alienated victims of capitalism, not inspiring them. He believed that the circulation of this markedly private type of literary writing was actually contributing to popular despair as its staleness reflected the wider problem of social inequality. His play's radical proposal is that theatre (including, even, melodrama) can remedy this crisis: by staging hypocrisy, dramatic art could reveal the lies upon which Britain's simulation of democracy rested. This was how theatre constituted for Wilde the final 'meeting place of art and life',[23] as he now strategically protected his work from censorship by rendering its political message as comedic.

Violence and Origins

The secrecy with which Algernon pursues his pleasures, which he terms 'Bunburying', certainly has subversive sexual connotations, and the fulfilment of male homosexual desire has very political implications. His overlapping of identities and his doubling of behaviour is mirrored in the play's indirect paralleling of class, with the audience constantly being reminded of the bourgeoisie's invisible other – the working class – throughout the course of the comedy. The bourgeois mobility that is encoded as Bunburying is shown to be immoral, costly, based on false premises and ultimately quite dangerous. These qualities make it, in its dubiousness, 'perfectly invaluable' to Algernon in the original, four-Act draft of the play.[24] Ruling-class hegemony is disrupted by the prospect of a sudden appearance of revolutionary politics expressed through means of the riot, which after the Fenian dynamiting campaign of the 1880s was the most disruptive contemporary manifestation of urban violence. Insurrectionary outbreaks of revolutionary street violence occurred in London in 1886 and 1887, and took place repeatedly in Dublin during the same decade.[25]

In *The Importance of Being Earnest*, Wilde parodies and subverts the concept of private property which, he warned in 'The Soul of Man Under Socialism', was crushing the human spirit. While *Vera; or, The Nihilists* openly transgressed the boundaries that established politically acceptable dramatic themes and content, this (later) comedy criticises class and imperial structures more subtly by representing revolutionary politics as existing below a rather shallow surface of bourgeois normality. Wilde explores the crises provoked by colonialism, revolution and the instability of capitalism – issues that were first discussed in his Russia-bound melodrama, but here the theme of political crisis is registered in a more clandestine manner. Political issues are also more carefully thematised in plays such as *Salomé* and *An Ideal Husband*, and Wilde's critique of the anti-democratic tendencies of the late Victorian state is also carefully articulated in the original, longer draft of *The Importance of Being Earnest*. It confronts coercion and state terror through the medium of social comedy, while also criticising the culture of consumption that at once distracts popular attention from the problem of official violence and erases the memory of insurrection. As Sos Eltis has emphasised, Wilde's first play, with its clearly political subject matter, was not so ideologically distant from his later dramas as these also express his 'enduring beliefs in individual freedom, the corrupting influence of authority, and the importance of rebellion'.[26]

The disarticulation of political history is parodied in Act 2, when Algernon's habitual eating and drinking resonates with parodic hints at the bourgeois guilt that he represents:

Merriman: Luncheon is on the table, sir.
Algernon: Ah! That is good news. I am excessively hungry.
Cecily (interposing): But you have lunched already.
Jack: Lunched already?
Cecily: Yes, Uncle Jack. He had some pâté de foie gras sandwiches, and a small bottle of that champagne that your doctor ordered for you.
Jack: My '89 champagne!
Cecily: Yes. I thought you would like him to have the same one as yourself.
Jack: Oh! Well, if he has lunched once, he can't be expected to lunch twice. It would be absurd.
Miss Prism: To partake of two luncheons in one day would not be liberty. It would be licence.[27]

Algernon's destructive 'excess in eating'[28] occurs throughout the play and is here cast against the very suggestive date of ''89'. With his battening on foie gras sandwiches and its consequent imposition of licence over liberty, Algernon's compulsive eating assumes a decidedly political resonance that chimes with his taste for Gallic food. The vintage of ''89', of course, conveys the memory of the French Revolution of 1789 but the revolution's potential to liberate is subsumed on stage by the spectacle of Algernon's rapaciousness. This in itself is the end product of the Victorian weaponisation of food supply, as witnessed by Jane Francesca Wilde in Ireland, and which contributed to the ongoing Irish agrarian insurrections of the 1880s and 1890s.[29] As Felicia J. Ruff points out, food is central to Wilde's satire as cuisine here 'demonstrates class difference', and imperial supremacism is also implied in what she describes as the play's ideological arming of the treat.[30] Wilde, who believed that imperialist violence still had the ultimate objective of 'doing away with the Irish people' through mass starvation,[31] barely concealed his own radical, republican critique of capital and the social structures that support it by means of this minimally ciphered dialogue and his characters' politically-loaded use of props. The relationship between the culture of consumption and the politics of coercion are explored at a strategic remove here and Wilde's radical critique of ruling-class greed is rendered seemingly less serious for the censors who, he found, made the staging of republicanism 'unthinkable' in British theatre circles at the end of the nineteenth century.[32]

Wilde's translation of the formal aspects of Victorian melodrama into a vehicle for radical discourse and ideas is seen through the state's fear of the 'common mob'.[33] While this was criticised very openly in *Vera; or, The Nihilists*, the references to rioting that appear in *The Importance of Being Earnest* betray the crisis that hovers on the periphery of the play while also remaining central to it. The bourgeoisie's preoccupation with civil disobedience is illustrated by Lady Bracknell during her interrogation of Jack Worthing when, while trying to establish his economic status (which provides the young man with another source of identity trauma) she expresses her class position on the question of democracy. The dame's questioning of Jack is worth focusing on at length, as Wilde uses this scene, which features what is arguably the funniest exchange in the most polished society comedy of the fin de siècle, to highlight the threat posed by empire and class, and to expose the false legitimacy they confer upon the powerful:

> Lady Bracknell (pencil and note-book in hand): I feel bound to tell you that you are not down on my list of eligible young men, although I have the same list as the dear Duchess of Bolton has. We work together, in fact. However, I am quite ready to enter your name, should your answers be what a really affectionate mother requires. Do you smoke?
> Jack: Well, yes, I must admit I smoke.
> Lady Bracknell: I am glad to hear it. A man should always have an occupation of some kind. There are far too many idle men in London as it is. How old are you?
> Jack: Twenty-nine.
> Lady Bracknell: A very good age to be married at. I have always been of the opinion that a man who desires to get married should know either everything or nothing. Which do you know?
> Jack (after some hesitation): I know nothing, Lady Bracknell.[34]

Lady Bracknell's part in maintaining the conspiratorial and aristocratic power network secures privilege within a closed circuit of money and influence. The tight social, economic and political circle within which she operates reveals how power reproduces itself at the heart of the British Empire. Jack is suitably unproductive, which qualifies him for membership of this class, and his addiction to cigarettes (which symbolise, like Algy's sandwiches, the practice of pointless consumption) is taken as an acceptable indication of his suitability as a match for Lady Bracknell's daughter, Gwendolen. His admission to knowing 'nothing' when pressed on his intellectual capacity signals more than a lack of formal education; what Jack assures Lady Bracknell of at this point is his own willingness and ability to partake in the conspiracy of power, and to acquiesce in its circulation and performance. The spectacle of class power and the legitimacy that it confers and expresses sustains the structural violence that Wilde criticised in his reviews, essays and lectures and which he tackled so directly in *Vera; or, The Nihilists*, which was both politically explicit and a resounding commercial failure. In *The Importance of Being Earnest* Wilde exposes the political power of the ruling class much more carefully by satirising it. This strategic balance between concealment and exposure is apparent in Lady Bracknell's expression of her satisfaction with Jack's responses, and within it we find her acknowledgement of the real workings of class power:

> Lady Bracknell: I am pleased to hear it. I do not approve of anything that tampers with natural ignorance. Ignorance is like a delicate exotic fruit; touch it and the bloom is gone. The whole theory of modern education is radically unsound. Fortunately in England, at any rate, education produces no effect whatsoever. If it did, it would prove a serious danger to the upper classes, and probably lead to acts of violence in Grosvenor Square. What is your income?
> Jack: Between seven and eight thousand a year.
> Lady Bracknell (makes a note in her book): In land, or in investments?
> Jack: In investments, chiefly.
> Lady Bracknell: That is satisfactory. What between the duties expected of one during one's lifetime, and the duties exacted from one after one's death, land has ceased to be either a profit or a pleasure. It gives one position, and prevents one from keeping it up. That's all that can be said about land.
> Jack: I have a country house with some land, of course, attached to it, about fifteen hundred acres, I believe; but I don't depend on that for my real income. In fact, as far as I can make out, the poachers are the only people who make anything out of it.
> Lady Bracknell: A country house! How many bedrooms? Well, that point can be cleared up afterwards. You have a town house, I hope? A girl with a simple, unspoiled nature, like Gwendolen, could hardly be expected to reside in the country.
> Jack: Well, I own a house in Belgrave Square, but it is let by the year to Lady Bloxham. Of course, I can get it back whenever I like, at six months' notice.[35]

As Michael Pierse has shown, drama predicated on the absence of labour is an ideologically charged medium through which ruling class hegemony is communicated and preserved. While Pierse's study of Irish working-class literature focuses on texts written and published during the twentieth century, his identification of the longevity of the bourgeois dramatic techniques with which the realities of labour and class stratification are deliberately concealed from audiences is very relevant to our understanding of melodramatic representations of class in Victorian writing. For Pierse, the ideologically-motivated concealment of capital appears at its most glaring within the popular form of the soap opera and is achieved through its promotion of unlikely social relations and the construction of a misleading 'televisual reality'. This is most commonly manifested in the financial independence enjoyed by supposedly working-class characters, whose lifestyles (they are generally portrayed as business owners) provide updated versions of Jack Worthing's property speculation and his value as a prospective investment to Lady Bracknell. As Pierse argues, these distortions remain influential indices of the genuine 'aversion to the working class' that continues to permeate popular culture.[36] Wilde at once parodies this distorting feature of contemporary melodrama while also disclosing its origin in capitalist property relations, presenting Jack at once as a speculator, rural gentleman and urban landlord whose portfolio satisfies Lady Bracknell's ideological and economic requirements. With Lady Bracknell's austere formality the play's comedic dialogue reflects the brittle structure of the system supporting an élite that felt vulnerable to outbreaks of working-class resistance – a condition that is ironised in Act 2 with Reverend Chasuble's sermon to the Society for the Prevention of Discontent among the Upper Orders.

The potential for subversion is countered with the manipulation of perception and, as Lady Bracknell reassures her daughter's suitor, facts can always be distorted in order to secure privilege:

> Lady Bracknell: [. . .] What number in Belgrave Square?
> Jack: 149.
> Lady Bracknell (shaking her head): The unfashionable side. I thought there was something. However, that could easily be altered.
> Jack: Do you mean the fashion, or the side?
> Lady Bracknell (sternly): Both, if necessary, I presume.[37]

When necessary, urban geography can be subordinated to serve the needs of social privilege. This is followed by Lady Bracknell's most revealing question: 'What are your politics?' Jack's response aligns class privilege with loyalty to the British Empire but his social ranking is made tenuous by uncertainty over his family background. As well as hinting at his unusual geographical provenance, his contradictory name – a fusion of 'worth' with the end of the second syllable of 'foundling' – conveys the implicit bourgeois value that he carries as a man of means. It also suggests the profound social ambiguity associated with his abandonment, and his potentially democratic origins provoke Lady Bracknell's displeasure, while her odium for the poor also has colonial associations:

> Jack: Well, I am afraid I really have none. I am a Liberal Unionist.
> Lady Bracknell: Oh, they count as Tories. They dine with us. Or come in the evening, at any rate. Now to minor matters. Are your parents living?
> Jack: I have lost both my parents.
> Lady Bracknell: To lose one parent, Mr. Worthing, may be regarded as a misfortune; to lose both looks like carelessness. Who was your father? He was evidently a man of some wealth. Was he born in what the Radical papers call the purple of commerce, or did he rise from the ranks of the aristocracy?
> Jack: I am afraid I really don't know. The fact is, Lady Bracknell, I said I had lost my parents. It would be nearer the truth to say that my parents seem to have lost me . . . I don't actually know who I am by birth. I was . . . well, I was found.
> Lady Bracknell: Found!
> Jack: The late Mr. Thomas Cardew, an old gentleman of a very charitable and kindly disposition, found me, and gave me the name of Worthing, because he happened to have a first-class ticket for Worthing in his pocket at the time. Worthing is a place in Sussex. It is a seaside resort.
> Lady Bracknell: Where did the charitable gentleman who had a first-class ticket for this seaside resort find you?
> Jack (gravely): In a hand-bag.
> Lady Bracknell: A hand-bag?
> Jack (very seriously): Yes, Lady Bracknell. I was in a hand-bag—a somewhat large, black leather hand-bag, with handles to it—an ordinary hand-bag in fact.
> Lady Bracknell: In what locality did this Mr. James, or Thomas, Cardew come across this ordinary hand-bag?
> Jack: In the cloak-room at Victoria Station. It was given to him in mistake for his own.
> Lady Bracknell: The cloak-room at Victoria Station?
> Jack: Yes. The Brighton line.
> Lady Bracknell: The line is immaterial. Mr. Worthing, I confess I feel somewhat bewildered by what you have just told me. To be born, or at any rate bred, in a hand-bag, whether it had handles or not, seems to me to display a contempt for the ordinary decencies of family life that reminds one of the worst excesses of the French Revolution.

And I presume you know what that unfortunate movement led to? As for the particular locality in which the hand-bag was found, a cloak-room at a railway station might serve to conceal a social indiscretion—has probably, indeed, been used for that purpose before now—but it could hardly be regarded as an assured basis for a recognised position in good society.[38]

Lady Bracknell's reactionary attitude introduces the theme of coercion as the issues of democracy and anticolonialism are directly connected in this exchange. Her views on the links between rioting and education, unionism and personal legitimacy amplify Wilde's critique of imperialism. As Lady Bracknell insists, the location of one's origins is 'immaterial' in comparison to one's ability to appear as the legitimate product of a decent, conservative upbringing and this, in turn, is linked to her desire to contain insurgency. Wilde's second association of social anxiety with the outcome of the French Revolution again suggests British ruling class sensitivity to what it perceived as the existential threat posed by all things democratic. Despite having broken out a century before, the revolution's resonances, Lady Bracknell tells us, remain very immediate.

Rioting, Unionism and the Fenians

Lady Bracknell's disapproval of insurgency and of the threat posed to her class by the democratic crowd mirrors the views of late-nineteenth-century conservative thinking on the masses. In his influential study of crowd psychology, the conservative French sociologist, Gustave Le Bon, expressed his own anxiety over the vulnerability of the state to the 'startling suddenness' of political crowd mobilisation and the rapidity with which a minimum of 'active persuasion' could transform a pacific public gathering into a riot.[39] Closer to home, Irish Toryism expressed similar views on colonial politics and class violence, and Wilde's contemporary, the folklorist, Celtic revivalist and champion of coercion, Standish O'Grady, regarded Fenianism and democracy as posing a combined threat to the British Empire. He identified closely with the pro-British Loyal and Patriotic Union, which reprinted the *Times* allegations against Parnell, and feared that both communism and Irish republicanism had acquired significant purchase among 'the poor and unpropertied' to the extent that 'fretted and untaught people' were being radicalised by other 'intelligent, ambitious, and desperate minds'. These figures, he warned, were:

naturally formed to lead others at all times, and especially so in an age when revolutionary ideas are in the air, and when all traditional and customary conceptions as to the nature of property have been disturbed, and have lost their solidity and definiteness.

This was because revolutionary politics left 'all ideas [. . .] in a state of fusion' and subjected 'inherited notions [. . .] to the hottest fire'. Confronted with this ideological furnace, the traditional defence of property, founded upon Burkean pillars of '[t]radition and custom', would prove no match for a popular combination of socialism and republicanism. Threatened by 'the base desires of the base', unionism and its close ally, landlordism were, O'Grady warned, in immediate danger of being overrun by the Irish republican 'wolf of Democracy'. Its demand for 'absolute democratic power' announced an apocalypse for Toryism: coercion was the only suitable response to this 'day of reckoning and vengeance'. The slogan, 'Democracy subdued', would mobilise class interests in Ireland and defeat republicanism before the masses could have a chance to assert their 'filthy rights'.[40] As Wilde recognised, the Irish Land War had repercussions for domestic political culture in Britain, and the potential for revolutionary violence in Grosvenor Square that is feared by Lady Bracknell is an imagined transplantation of the Irish political crisis onto the very exclusive streets of the British metropolis. The dialectic that is so carefully exposed in *The Importance of Being Earnest*, in which the poor appear briefly but are very significantly represented as ungovernable, reflects the propinquity of colonial and class tensions.

The close relationship binding imperial and capitalist interests together is further unmasked by Jack's own self-identification as a unionist. Without a verifiable family, and therefore lacking any recognisable trace of authenticity, tradition or custom in Lady Bracknell's eyes, he aligns himself with the imperialist ideology of unionism – an association that he also, very significantly, proffers as evidence of his supposedly apolitical leanings. His ideological position is equivalent with Toryism (indeed, the Conservative and Unionist parties combined in 1912) and its explicit rejection of radicalism renders him a safe bet for her daughter.

At this point Wilde also exploits popular memory of the recent Fenian bombing campaign, which is indirectly but very obviously referred to here. In February 1884, the Fenian dynamiters bombed Victoria Station during a series of co-ordinated attacks on the London railway when a device concealed in luggage destroyed the station's cloakroom. These attacks were followed up a few months later by a far more spectacular coup in which Scotland Yard and the Conservative Party headquarters at the Carlton Club were also bombed.[41] Jack's anomalous status as a foundling is tied to his discovery in an 'ordinary' but suspiciously anonymous hand-bag which, as we learn at the end of the final Act, once even contained an explosive substance: Miss Prism's unstable temperance beverage. The play's key comedic crisis centres on the confusion surrounding this profound void in Jack's personal record, as the collision of private and political history that establishes his strangely dislocated self originates in the violent political disruption caused by the Fenian bombing campaign of the 1880s. Like the infant Jack, Fenian bombs were deposited in sites of public circulation in inconspicuous hand-bags and suitcases, and despite his profession of unionist sympathies he is unable to extricate himself from the 'worst excesses' of revolutionary republicanism.

Lady Bracknell's response suggests that Jack's lack of a verifiable identity points to the combination of militant Irish anticolonial activity with the kind of class violence alluded to in her warning about the folly of educating the poor. His indeterminacy is based not just on the coincidence of his discovery by a gentleman on his way to Worthing but also upon the contradictions that reside in his unionist self-identification with the British Empire. As Lady Bracknell complains, his strange origin story, like the issue of education, brings to the surface questions about civil disobedience and revolution. Jack's own feelings of being personally and politically adrift are problematic for his interrogator, who suspects his insurgent origins. If the railway line upon which he was discovered remains unimportant to her, his beginnings in the demographically uncertain space of Victoria station points to political as well as sexual indiscretion on the part of his parents.[42] His possible illegitimacy assumes a political significance that goes beyond the familial disgrace of having been born outside wedlock and abandoned. Unless he can prove that he was born into the bourgeoisie or aristocracy, where he really belongs, Jack will be suspected of membership of the community of the excluded. This social precarity explains his need to assume the provisional and very delicate identities of Ernest and unionist.

Jack, then, must validate himself by finding some relatives within the brief window offered by the annual round of economic networking that is 'the season':

> Jack: May I ask you then what you would advise me to do? I need hardly say I would do anything in the world to ensure Gwendolen's happiness.

> Lady Bracknell: I would strongly advise you, Mr. Worthing, to try and acquire some relations as soon as possible, and to make a definite effort to produce at any rate one parent, of either sex, before the season is quite over.
> Jack: Well, I don't see how I could possibly manage to do that. I can produce the hand-bag at any moment. It is in my dressing-room at home. I really think that should satisfy you, Lady Bracknell.
> Lady Bracknell: Me, sir! What has it to do with me? You can hardly imagine that I and Lord Bracknell would dream of allowing our only daughter—a girl brought up with the utmost care—to marry into a cloak-room, and form an alliance with a parcel? Good morning, Mr. Worthing![43]

Jack's true class status remains uncertain, erasing his potential as a suitor and reducing him to nothing in Lady Bracknell's opinion. This deletion of his real identity has potentially revolutionary political and class consequences that make his appearance within London's élite circles all the more disturbing. Now that he is anonymous and unidentifiable, except as a lost parcel, Jack must invest himself with history and meaning.

Empire and Starvation

As Terence Brown has pointed out, Wilde's plays offer powerful critiques of imperialism and capitalism, the twin pillars of late Victorian British identity. As Brown suggests, wealth is central to the class hierarchies that determine the social settings of these works and it ultimately depends on the possession of imperial power that is expressed and maintained through aggression and violence. Capital, as Brown argues, defines the 'wealth-dependent elegance' of the bourgeois experience captured by Wilde.[44] Unlike the fairy tales, in which starving, suffering but selfless characters often exist on the brink of annihilation, the characters in *The Importance of Being Earnest* prosper amid an abundance of champagne, cake, bread and butter, cigarettes, unpaid bills, second lunches and plenty of cucumber sandwiches. References to writs and the presence of the debt collector, Gribsby, who was written out of the final version of the play, are reminders of the limits of credit, but Wilde's characters exist in a permanent state of ignorance regarding the real social cost of their consumption. As polar opposites of the collectively-minded and self-sacrificing innocents of Wilde's fantasy tales, their corruption is made clear on stage through Algernon's relentless eating, Canon Chasuble's charitable efforts on behalf of the rich, Lady Bracknell's contempt for progress and, as we shall see, Jack Worthing's implication in the violence of empire. The trope of hunger was a central theme in Wilde's writing where it is consistently politicised and I have already argued that it was key to his radical imagination, where starvation was always perceived as the outcome of cruelty. The salver on which Algernon's sandwiches are presented symbolises the corruption of luxury while the cucumber sandwiches, with which the play opens, figuratively symbolise both the presence and absence of food commodities in late Victorian Britain, as Algernon's 'perfectly heartless' consumption occurs at a human cost. Romance, however, appears unbusinesslike, because its 'very essence [. . .] is uncertainty'. As he decides, 'there is nothing romantic about a definite proposal'.[45]

As atomised, drifting consumers, Algy and his kind do find some hope in one another's refusal to amount to anything: his sheer uselessness is the basis of Cecily's 'strange attraction' to him. Their failure to do good reveals their complicity in the political crises of the late Victorian bourgeois sphere, where generosity is perceived as foolishness and moral, political and economic responsibilities are avoided by just about everyone. Algernon's scrape with Jack's creditors is seen by Cecily as his 'tragic exposure', but the play reveals the deceptions, lies and concealments that allow the wealthy to serve, without conscience, as dedicated agents of capital and imperial power. The 'shallow mask of manners' that Cecily complains to Gwendolen about conceals more than the private, sexual deceptions practised by the bourgeois men and women who assume it. From behind it they can ignore the inherent class violence and colonial brutality that enables their consumption, performed as it is 'entirely for pleasure'.[46]

The precariousness of ruling class consumption is represented in Wilde's exploitation of credit anxiety. Lady Bracknell's steering of her daughter away from the democratic tendencies that, she suspects, may be genetically instilled in Jack is countered by Algernon's admission that 'No gentleman ever has any money.' We also find Algernon negotiating the fine line between excessive consumption and the potentially disastrous price to be paid for it. He narrowly avoids being imprisoned over debts racked up by Jack Worthing who, in the guise of his *faux* brother, Ernest, has failed to pay for over seven hundred pounds' worth of suppers. Having adopted the identity of Ernest Worthing in order to gain access to Jack's cousin and ward, Cecily, Algernon shares the fake brother's insatiability. The play interrogates the cost of the 'debts and extravagance' incurred and enjoyed by '[p]eople who live entirely for pleasure'. Identity is also tied to excess, as Algernon is told that he shares his 'aristocratic name' with '[h]alf of the chaps who get into the Bankruptcy Court'. Miss Prism, meanwhile, looks down on the poor, who 'don't seem to know what thrift is' while Jack's identities, position and relationship with Cecily are the result of his having inherited 'all the money' bequeathed by his adoptive father, Thomas Cardew. This kind of wealth makes Jack's and Algernon's mobility possible, and the ultra-clandestine practice that is 'advanced Bunburying' is particularly dependent on it; it is also a popular, even viral practice, with plenty of 'beastly competition' at large. It requires access to the kind of capital that leaves the pair vulnerable to the threat of financial ruin that hovers over them throughout the play. Writs and demands for repayment are not a source of embarrassment for them but are, instead, a potentially serious hindrance in that they promise to tie Jack and Algy to dead capital, preventing their assumption of newer, ever-mobile fake identities.[47]

Bunbury's near-death condition is also politically relevant as it mirrors the moribund state of capital. Responding to the crisis in bourgeois identity cultivated by the marketisation of selfhood, Algernon complains that 'it isn't easy to be anything nowadays' because identity is tied to the lifeless structures of capital. Despite Gwendolen's faith in the security provided by a name like Ernest, the dangerous game being played by Jack and Algernon keeps them on the very edge of crisis, failure and exposure. They pay no price for their risk-taking and the mild social embarrassment that they have to endure contrasts with the mortal dangers facing the characters in Wilde's melancholy fairy tales. The duo are driven by what they perceive as the importance of consumption, not by any desire to produce, as Bunburying simultaneously requires and makes possible kinds of mobility that are unavailable to the non-Bunburying working class. The violence of empire is made possible by such movement, as revealed by Cecily's study of economics and the depreciation of the imperial rupee (a currency, at this stage, which was imprinted with the image of Queen Victoria). Jack's own precarious social 'credit'[48] is also founded upon the application of force in the British colonies, but those who are about to inherit imperial wealth are shielded from the brutal reality of its origins – a theme that also appears in Wilde's 1892 comedy, *Lady Windermere's Fan*.

Imperial recoil is a key theme of the second Act during which, while studying with Miss Prism in the garden at Woolton, Cecily is warned to avoid the unpleasant subject of colonial violence:

> Miss Prism: [. . .] Cecily, you will read your Political Economy in my absence. The chapter on the fall of the Rupee you may omit. It is somewhat too sensational for a young girl. Even those metallic problems have their melodramatic style.
> Chasuble: Reading Political Economy, Cecily? It is wonderful how girls are educated nowadays. I suppose you know about the relations between Capital and Labour?
> Cecily: I am afraid I am not learned at all. All I know is about the relations between Capital and Idleness – and that is merely from observation. So I don't suppose it is true.
> Miss Prims: Cecily! That sounds like Socialism! And I suppose you know where Socialism leads to?
> Cecily: Oh yes! That leads to Rational Dress, Miss Prism. And I suppose that when a woman is dressed rationally, she is treated rationally. She certainly deserves to be.
> Chasuble: A wilful lamb! Dear child!
> Miss Prism (smiling): A sad trouble sometimes.[49]

Capital, as Cecily points out, facilitates unproductive consumption by idle imperialists through means of the economic destruction of colonised economies, as was inflicted with Britain's deliberate deflation of the Indian currency, itself an economic shock consequent upon the direct military violence of empire. Warfare, mass starvation and displacement, all of which are historical, political and material realities not to be disclosed to imperial students of economics – are the secret consequences of the violence of imperial capital and what Alex Tickell terms its 'wreckage of colonial history'.[50] Miss Prism's anxiety about the possible exposure of this violence reveals that the destruction wrought by the British Empire forms the basis of the economically buoyant metropolis within which Wilde's characters circulate. It also provides the permanently famished Algy with the 'ready' capital required to pay off his debts and fund the pleasures that he enjoys as an advanced Bunburyist. At home, the type of moral economy recommended by Canon Chasuble, whose charitable efforts to prevent ruling class discontent, facilitate the kind of activity being indulged in by Algy.

At the play's conclusion we learn that the domestic class crisis triggered by the mystery surrounding Jack's identity also has distinctly colonial origins and that he is closely tied to violence in India. Like the economy being studied by Cecily, the bag in which he was found as an infant carries its own history, including the 'incident' caused by the detonation of Miss Prism's beverage, implicating him in the much wider practice of global imperialism. The final revelation of his true identity connects him directly to the British occupation of India with the discovery that his father is General Moncrieff, whom Lady Bracknell remembers as having a 'violent' personality,[51] reminding her why she dislikes the name Ernest. His role in India receives a passing but significant mention that exposes the complicity of the liberal unionist, Jack, along with the class to which he has always belonged, in the global theatre of imperial repression. Gwendolen's declaration, 'Ernest! My own Ernest! I felt from the first that you could have no other name!' is followed by Jack's realisation of the 'terrible' fact of his identity. This is conveyed through the shock that it is 'for a man to find out suddenly that all his life he has been speaking nothing but the truth'. Expunged of any possible association with the revolutionary Left by the discovery of his identity, now finally proven by the location of his father in the British Army Lists, Jack appears at last to be as legitimate as he would have been had he hailed 'from the ranks of the aristocracy'. This validation is the only other positive resolution of the riddle surrounding his identity that Lady Bracknell is capable of imagining. His pedigree as the lost son of a colonial hard man now includes him among the beneficiaries of imperial power and when the comedy is read backwards, we learn that these imperial associations, strangely present despite being offstage, provide the basis for the 'romantic origin' that triggers Gwendolen's 'incomprehensible' attraction to him.[52]

Closure and Conscience

In 'The Soul of Man Under Socialism' Wilde discussed civil disobedience as an expression of social despair and the tremendously 'unhealthy' circumstances that produced it.[53] In *The Importance of Being Earnest*, he parodied the concealment of this anguish beneath the veil of consumption; and, as Eltis has argued, his drama was consistently radical and expressive of his social conscience. Through its exposure of the false exteriors of bourgeois society this play deconstructs the conceptual boundaries separating politics from art.[54] The immediate crises of capitalism and colonialism pervade *The Importance of Being Earnest* and the ambiguity of its closure, whereby tension between the seemingly earnest face of liberal imperialism and the 'violent [. . .] manner'[55] of its agents is exposed as hypocritical. Having been lost, left adrift and rejected until this point, the affable unionist, Jack, finally has his identity renewed and legitimised as that of Ernest, whose validity originates in the kind of colonial violence portrayed by Wilde in his story, 'The Young King'. The play closes with Ernest experiencing acceptance and enjoying his now-legitimate romance with Gwendolen, thanks to the incontrovertible proof of military data. This evidence binds his personal, political and economic identities to the experimental laboratories of imperialist violence that were Ireland and India, and to the domestic application of this violence against working-class people on the streets of London.

Notes

1. Sherard, *Oscar Wilde: The Story of an Unhappy Friendship*, p. 35. For an account of the ferocity with which the Commune was suppressed by the Versailles government, see John Merriman, *Massacre: The Life and Death of the Paris Commune of 1871* (New Haven: Yale University Press, 2014).
2. Eric Hazan, *A History of the Barricade* (trans. by David Fernbach from *La Barricade: Histoire d'un objet révolutionnaire*, Éditions Autrement, 2013; London: Verso, 2015), p. 77.
3. Describing the site where the Tuileries once stood as a *'lieu d'oubli* rather than a *de mémoire'*, Louis J. Iandoli describes its demolition by the Third Republic in 1882–3 as a deliberate act of political and historical erasure. See Louis J. Iandoli, 'The Palace of the Tuileries and its Demolition', *The French Review*, 79.5, April 2006, pp. 998–1008, p. 1003.
4. See Joshua Clover, *Riot, Strike. Riot: The Era of New Uprisings* (London: Verso, 2016), especially chapter 1: 'What is a Riot?'
5. Gagnier, *Idylls of the Marketplace*, p. 106.
6. Oscar Wilde, *The Importance of Being Earnest*, in *The Importance of Being Earnest and Other Plays* (Oxford: Oxford University Press, 2008), Act 3, p. 295.
7. George Bernard Shaw, 'My Memories of Oscar Wilde', in Frank Harris, *Oscar Wilde: His Life and Confessions* (Ware: Wordsworth, 2007), pp. 355–68, p. 358.
8. William Archer, *The World*, 20 February 1895, reprinted in Beckson, *Oscar Wilde: The Critical Heritage*, pp. 217–18, p. 218; George Bernard Shaw, *Saturday Review*, 79, 23 February 1895, pp. 249–50, in Beckson, *Oscar Wilde: The Critical Heritage*, pp. 221–2.
9. See Eltis, *Revising Wilde*, chapter 6: *'The Importance of being Earnest'*. Quotations from p. 171.

10. Gagnier, *Idylls of the Marketplace*, pp. 7–8.
11. Ibid. p. 8.
12. Wilde, 'The Soul of Man', in *Complete Works*, vol. 4, pp. 229–68, p. 234.
13. Gagnier, *Idylls of the Marketplace*, p. 113.
14. Oscar Wilde, 'Lord Arthur Savile's Crime', in *The Complete Short Stories*, p. 15.
15. Oscar Wilde, 'The Truth of Masks', in *Complete Works*, vol. 4, pp. 207–28, pp. 214, 217.
16. Wilde, 'Lord Arthur Savile's Crime', in *The Complete Short Stories*, p. 12.
17. Ibid. p. 3.
18. Jay Thomas Parker, '"He was one of us": Rortyian Liberal Ethnocentrism and Ironic Narrative Voice in Joseph Conrad's *Lord Jim*', *Textual Practice*, 31.4, 2017, pp. 823–38.
19. Ben Singer argues that the melodrama's intensity and rapidity conveys the 'extraordinary discontinuity' of nineteenth-century life. See Ben, Singer, *Melodrama and Modernity: Early Sensational Cinema and its Contexts* (New York: Columbia University Press, 2001), pp. 1–22. Quotation on p. 19.
20. Ibid. p. 2.
21. Wilde, *The Importance of Being Earnest*, in *The Complete Works of Oscar Wilde* (London: HarperCollins, 2003), Act 1, p. 365. Quotations hereafter are drawn from this text of the original four-Act text of the play.
22. Oscar Wilde, 'Béranger in England', from the *Pall Mall Gazette*, 21 April 1886. Reprinted in Robert Ross (ed.), *Collected Works*, vol. 12, *Reviews* 1, pp. 60–2, p. 61.
23. Oscar Wilde to Clarisse Moore, March–April 1883, in *Complete Letters*, pp. 204–5, p. 205.
24. Wilde, *The Importance of Being Earnest*, Act 1, p. 362.
25. Studies of rioting during the late Victorian period are comparatively rare. The relationship between literary writing and crowd politics during the first half of the nineteenth century is discussed by Matthew Plotz in his *The Crowd: British Literature and Public Politics* (Berkeley: University of California Press, 2000). For an account of rioting at the end of the nineteenth century, see Clive Bloom, *Violent London: 2,000 Years of Riots, Rebels and Revolts* (London: Pan, 2004), chapter 11: 'Persecuting Pigeons: Trafalgar Square and Bloody Sunday'.
26. Eltis, *Revising Wilde*, p. 26.
27. Wilde, *The Importance of Being Earnest*, Act 2, p. 388.
28. Ibid.
29. Jessica Martell has discussed the long-term, popular memory of the Great Hunger, which endured well into the revolutionary period of the early twentieth century. See Jessica Martell, 'Food Sovereignty, the

Irish Homestead, and the First World War', *Modernist Cultures* 13.3, August 2018, pp. 399–416.
30. Felicia J. Ruff, 'Transgressive Props: Or Oscar Wilde's E(a)rnest Signifier', in Joseph Bristow (ed.), *Wilde Discoveries*, pp. 315–35, p. 328.
31. Oscar Wilde, 'Mr Froude's Blue-Book', originally published in the *Pall Mall Gazette*, 13 April 1889, p. 3. Reprinted in *Complete Works*, vol. 7, pp. 203–6. Quotation on p. 206.
32. Oscar Wilde to an unidentified correspondent, circa September 1880, in *Collected Letters*, p. 97.
33. Wilde, *Vera; or, The Nihilists*, Act 3, p. 707.
34. Wilde, *The Importance of Being Earnest*, Act 1, p. 368.
35. Ibid.
36. See Michael Pierse, *Writing Ireland's Working Class: Dublin after O'Casey* (Basingstoke: Palgrave, 2011), p. 250.
37. Wilde, *The Importance of Being Earnest*, Act 1, pp. 368–9.
38. Ibid. Act 1, pp. 369–70.
39. Gustave Le Bon, *The Crowd: A Study of the Popular Mind* (trans. from *La Psychologie des foules*, London: T. Fisher Unwin, 1909), p. 90.
40. Standish O'Grady, *The Crisis in Ireland* (Dublin: E. Ponsonby, 1882), pp. 24–6, 29–31, 51.
41. See Niall Whelehan, *The Dynamiters*. For accounts of how the Fenians' 'dynamite war' saturated the popular imagination at the fin de siècle, see my *Blasted Literature*. See also Gillian O'Brien, 'Methodology and Martyrs: Irish American Republicanism in the Late Nineteenth Century', in Peter S. Herman (ed.), *Terrorism and Literature* (Cambridge: Cambridge University Press, 2018), pp. 70–89; and Barbara Arnett Melchiori, *Terrorism in the Late Victorian Novel* (London: Croom Helm, 1985).
42. As Nicholas Daly argues, the transnational and characteristically urban 'demographic imagination' that is showcased in much nineteenth-century literary writing (along with swathes of painting, advertising and the opera) was consistently preoccupied with the advance of democracy. These works range from the early Victorian volcano narratives that responded to the passage of the 1832 Reform Bill to the essentially privatised fantasies of the fin-de-siècle ghost story. See Nicholas Daly, *The Demographic Imagination and the Nineteenth-Century City: Paris, London, New York* (Cambridge: Cambridge University Press, 2015).
43. Wilde, *The Importance of Being Earnest*, Act 1, p. 370.
44. Terence Brown, 'The Plays', in *The Complete Works of Oscar Wilde* (2003), pp. 351–6, pp. 351, 352, 354.
45. Wilde, *The Importance of Being Earnest*, Act 3, p. 403; Act 2, p. 389.
46. Ibid. Act 3, p. 391; Act 2, pp. 388, 384.
47. Ibid. Act 2, pp. 385, 380, 381; Act 3, p. 396; Act 1, pp. 361, 363.
48. Ibid. Act 1, p. 370.

49. Ibid. Act 2, p. 377.
50. Alex Tickell, *Terrorism, Insurgency and Indian-English Literature, 1830–1947* (New York: Routledge, 2012), p. 13.
51. Wilde, *The Importance of Being Earnest*, Act 4, p. 417.
52. Wilde, *The Importance of Being Earnest*, Act 4, pp. 417–8; Act 1, pp. 369, 373.
53. Wilde, 'The Soul of Man', in *Complete Works*, vol. 4, pp. 229–68, p. 267.
54. See Eltis, *Revising* Wilde, pp. 12–15.
55. Wilde, *The Importance of Being Earnest*, Act 4, p. 417.

Chapter 7

'De Profundis', 'The Ballad of Reading Gaol' and the Politics of Imprisonment

With their critiques of bourgeois values, Wilde's plays and fictions offered radical, socially-engaged analyses of late Victorian society. His stories, 'The Happy Prince' and 'The Star-Child', propose mutualism as a constructive alternative to existing social relations and practices. 'The Selfish Giant' attacks the concept of property, while 'The Young King' exposes imperialist violence; these issues are also central to *The Picture of Dorian Gray*, discussion of which, according to Wilde's barrister, Edward Clarke, constituted 'the literary part' of his trial.[1] Like 'The Soul of Man Under Socialism', all of these works invited readers and audiences to think critically about capital and empire. Focusing on 'De Profundis', which was written in prison, edited and then published after Wilde's death by Robert Ross, and 'The Ballad of Reading Gaol', composed shortly after Wilde's release, this chapter explores how Wilde's key writings about his experience of imprisonment were equally political and form part of this longer continuum of radical literary writing and practice. David Lloyd has read 'The Ballad of Reading Gaol' in relation to the historical tradition of republican writing beginning with Shelley's 'The Masque of Anarchy' and which continued with Speranza's poetry during the mid-nineteenth century. Lloyd emphasises how Wilde's own work, in turn, inspired the prison writings of the IRA hunger striker, Bobby Sands, and directly influenced his H-Block protest poem, 'The Crime of Castlereagh'.[2] As Lloyd explains, the political, legal, military and penal experiments conducted in British-occupied Ireland from the early nineteenth century onward inform the later practices of neoliberalism. When Wilde's works are considered against these historically persistent models of colonial state violence, we can better understand the connection between his conviction for 'gross indecency', which

Jerusha McCormack has described as of 'an act of concentrated social revenge', and homophobia's colonial origins.[3]

Through strategies involving long-term, scientifically developed and professionally applied methods of physical, psychological, legal, economic and surveillance forms of control, the colonial state apparatus has policed Irish speech, identity, expression, movement, space and even thought according to practices that remain important models for present-day techniques of statecraft and corporate control.[4] These forms of political, physical and psychological regulation are interrogated in Wilde's prison writings.

Politics and the Criminalisation of Homosexuality

As Joseph Bristow has argued, the political context that underlined Oscar Wilde's persecution and imprisonment has not been investigated against the longer-term history of the politicisation of sexual scandal and homophobia.[5] This was clear to the contemporary anarchists who criticised Wilde's incarceration, which they claimed was his punishment for his own subversive sexual practice, literary genius and radical opposition to the British state.[6] They recognised the political nature of his imprisonment and described him as a political prisoner immediately after his conviction, placing his radicalism and literary work within the long historical context of Irish rebellion and insurgency. Like Charlotte Wilson and the other *Commonweal* anarchists, John Barlas also regarded Wilde's prosecution as political and highlighted the riskiness of his friend's expression of radical beliefs:

> [T]here is no doubt in my mind that his troubles were more due to his attack on the Capitalist System in the *Fortnightly Review* than to anything else. He said what he pleased about God and man until, in an evil hour for him, he punched the British public very hard on the well-filled waistcoat pocket, and found out by too bitter experience where its real deity resided.[7]

Robert Harborough Sherard also cited Wilde's prosecution as an example of the state's repressive dealings with subversive authors and their work, and believed that literary writing had now come so completely under close political observation that 'any man can be hanged on two lines of his writing'.[8]

Other friends and supporters, including Alfred Douglas and More Adey, also claimed that his prosecution was political,[9] while Arthur

Lee Humphreys published 'The Soul of Man Under Socialism' just days after Wilde was convicted. Ford Madox Ford also recalled how the trial generated considerable social anxiety as it exposed Wilde's connections among 'the immense, frightening quicksand of the Lower Classes and the underworld'.[10] With class transgression firmly woven into the prosecution's narrative, Edward Carson pointed out that Wilde's crime was his possession of a 'democratic soul', which ensured that 'no social distinctions' were maintained in his relationships: 'it is exactly the same pleasure to him to have a sweeping-boy from the street [. . .] to lunch with him or to dine with him, as the best educated artist or *littérateur* in the whole kingdom'.[11]

Wilde's co-accused, Alfred Taylor, was also condemned for having transgressed these boundaries. Having inherited wealth, he was accused of using it to access forbidden sexual pleasures, but the defence claimed that this was impossible for a man of his standing:

> No doubt Taylor had been a very unwise young man, but it did not follow that he had been a criminal. He was the son of a man of property and of high commercial position, whose business was still being carried on successfully as a limited company. Educated at Marlborough and by private tutors, he had tried his best to get a commission in the Army through the Militia. Unfortunately for him, he succeeded too early in the uncontrolled possession of a large fortune left him by his father and his uncle. Being thus led into the habits of idleness and extravagance, and into what [. . .] [was] a more or less vicious mode of life, the result was the common one – he soon spent the whole of his money and a great deal more, so that in the course of the previous year he had found himself in the Bankruptcy Court. But Mr. Grain found it incredible that a man beginning life under such favourable circumstances should be guilty of those unmentionable acts.[12]

Homosexuality, in Taylor's case, was the result of profound class slippage and this tale of social transgression was used by the establishment to warn the public about the absorption of wealthy but vulnerable young men by the homosexual underground.

During Taylor's cross-examination he was interrogated about cross-dressing ('fancy attire') and his involvement in the 'burlesque' performance of a mock wedding as queerness and conspicuous consumption became key features of the prosecution's case.[13] Capital might have maintained social boundaries but its circulation among homosexual men – people who were also portrayed as being given to undisciplined consumption – is contrasted in this account with the promise of reassuring sexual and economic regulation provided by the military service that might have saved Taylor. Class and imperial interests collided here: the kind of spending that Taylor indulged in along with Wilde was projected by the prosecution as having broader social consequences, and his failure to perform a productive role in the British Army became the context for his 'vicious' life as a homosexual bankrupt. When asked by the prosecution to define a gentleman, to which he replied someone of 'private means',[14] Taylor was then accused of betraying his class: 'You are an old Public School Boy. Was it not repugnant to your Public School ideas, this habit of sleeping with men?' Taylor replied: 'Not to me. Where there is no harm done I can see nothing repugnant in it.'[15]

This cautionary tale, which was still being circulated in a pamphlet a decade after Wilde's death, underlined how the model of a violently masculinised, heteronormative imperial and bourgeois identity was central to the British state. In contrast to its construction of homosexuality as a form of social treason, the poet and humanitarian, James H. Wilson, writing under the pseudonym 'I. Playfair', argued that the Criminal Law Amendment Act of 1885 was designed to reinforce the class system and to police what John Sloan has termed the 'interaction between sexual conduct and class attutudes'.[16] His pamphlet, *Gentle Criticisms on British Justice*, argued that the Act was designed to protect the political establishment, and that it regularly concealed 'hushed-up offences' from the public through its very selective deployment (indeed, five of those cited in Wilde's trial remained anonymous and were described only as 'persons unknown'). Wilson claimed that this was why anti-homosexual legislation would never be applied in public schools or generally within ruling class circles, and demanded: 'Let offenders of every rank be equally punished, from Prince to Peasant.'[17]

Wilde's Prison Letters as Expressions of Resistance

When he was imprisoned in 1895 for committing the crime of 'gross indecency with men', Wilde encountered a spectrum of total penal violence. Writing to Michael Davitt shortly after his release, he compared their common experience of 'terrible life in an English prison' and asked the former Fenian and MP to help him with publicising the abuse of child prisoners in Wandsworth Prison and Reading Gaol, which he blamed on 'the stupidity of officialism, and the immobile ignorance of centralisation'. Wilde also stressed to Davitt how his own treatment by the state as a gay man corresponded with the experiences of incarcerated children and Fenian prisoners.[18] Written at the same time, Wilde's letter to the editor of the *Daily Chronicle* publicly criticised the routinised forms of physical and psychological violence that he had witnessed being inflicted on child prisoners. Published just over a month after his own release, it reiterated the critique of authority expressed in 'The Soul of Man Under Socialism', warning: 'What is inhuman in modern life is officialism. Authority is as destructive to those who exercise it as it is to those on whom it is exercised.' Writing in response to the dismissal of the Reading Gaol warder, Thomas Martin, who was sacked for giving biscuits to a frightened and hungry child under his custody, Wilde pointed out that Martin's offence was to have fed the smallest boy he had seen during the two years of his own imprisonment. Repeating his mother's view that individuals and institutions bore responsibility for structural violence, Wilde argued that the weaponisation of hunger in prison was made possible by the doctrinal assumption that 'because a thing is the rule it is right'. He condemned the Prison Board for its role as 'the primary source' of this cruelty and its only outcome, he warned, was simple terror.[19] In this letter, Wilde again connected the state and its apparatus to the circulation of fear and violence just as directly as he had confronted colonial power in his book reviews and speeches of the 1880s. By associating the authority of the state and its institutions to the official exercise of force, he emphasised the relationship that bound the Victorian managerial classes to the force they dispensed on behalf of the state.

As Nicholas Frankel has shown, Wilde's imprisonment is best understood in relation to the application of coercion in Ireland. As an Irish republican he was very familiar with British statecraft and with the prison system's magnification of the dialectics of official violence. He was aware of its historical deployment against what he termed the 'noble cause' of Irish political prisoners[20] and his strategy, as Gagnier has described it, was to resist and 'refuse to meet authority on its own ground'. The act of writing these texts, first in prison and then after his release, maintained his identity against the brutalising 'system' described in 'De Profundis' and, as Gagnier argues, he raised in these texts an 'imaginative world against the frozen time and alien space of imprisonment'.[21] This total system extended the power of the violent, coercive state by deploying violence against the body and the very subjectivity of the prisoner, with its saturating presence designed to isolate, erode, anonymise and dehumanise every one of its inmates, including children. It was against this monolithic structure that Wilde refined the thoughts on suffering and identity that he had already expressed in his short stories and in 'The Soul of Man Under Socialism'.

Autonomy and Incarceration

Gagnier has emphasised how, under these conditions, Wilde interpreted Christ as a 'fully aestheticized and autonomous' figure who embodied rebellion and resistance, and that he regarded prison as the symbol of the social basis of debt, and the latter as a disciplinary phenomenon: 'For every single thing that is done someone has to pay.'[22] In prison he experienced the physical, psychological and material cost of his resistance to late Victorian authority and, as Frankel points out, this did not diminish after his release. 'De Profundis' and 'The Ballad of Reading Gaol' are anarchic texts centred on Wilde's rejection of social and penal authority. Both draw upon the assertion of radical individualism and should be interpreted in relation to Wilde's final years, during which he lived among political and sexual dissidents, particularly in Paris.[23] Initially composed as a letter to Alfred Douglas, then revised and enlarged, 'De Profundis' was ultimately intended by Wilde to be published as a literary work.[24] It conveyed the material reality of imprisonment to Alfred Douglas while also documenting it for the much broader public readership by whom Wilde really intended the piece to be read.

His opposition to carceral violence was also conveyed after his release in his other letters defending Thomas Martin. In these, Wilde testified to the totality and the violent nature of prison authority that was being concealed from society. While the original text of 'De Profundis' was written within the prison and in defiance of its penal régime and the political authority of the state, it was a carefully edited, composite document.[25] Originally written within what Gagnier has described as Reading Gaol's 'material matrix of prison, space and time', it resists the compression of space and the elastication of time that form the basis of the prisoner's experience. As Gagnier argues, by resisting these violent and traumatic distortions of time, space and selfhood through the act of writing, Wilde preserved his own life and sanity.[26]

In his 1889 review of Wilfred Scawen Blunt's collection of poems *In Vinculis*, which includes the titular piece about his imprisonment in Galway and Kilmainham gaols, Wilde praised the anticolonial poet's depiction of A. J. Balfour's coercion régime in Ireland. He admired Blunt's efforts against imperial policy in Ireland and Egypt and condemned his incarceration as unjust. It was, Wilde believed, part of the wider, global practice of imperial violence: 'Balfour may enforce "plain living" by his prison regulations', he complained, but 'he cannot prevent "high thinking", or in any way limit or constrain the freedom of a man's soul'.[27] The relationship between socialism and anticolonialism that Wilde raised in his expression of solidarity with Blunt is also apparent in 'The Soul of Man Under Socialism', where he repeated this sentiment by declaring that 'even in prison, a man can be quite free. His soul can be free [. . .] Personality is a very mysterious thing'.[28] Wilde believed that personality, or identity, originated in the self's autonomy and agency and that it could overcome the aggressive authority of the prison – ideas that were drawn from the broader atmosphere of coercion and inspired by people like Scawen Blunt who resisted it. Combined with his Kropotkinian theory of the individual, Wilde's model of the subversive and resistant personality was tested during his own imprisonment and then developed through his belief – expressed in his letter to Douglas – that prisoners underwent an experience of purification. A key measure of his enduring radicalism, 'De Profundis' distils the ideas about suffering, selfhood and identity expressed throughout his writings, and particularly in his stories.

Wilde's sympathy for the colonised and dispossessed intensified during his imprisonment in Reading Gaol, where he spoke to a visitor about the famous speech delivered from the dock by the Irish republican leader, Robert Emmet, who was executed by the British in 1803. Sherard spoke to this unnamed source, who recalled that Wilde described Emmet as the ideal imaginative, romantic and republican type. This ideal had been crystallised through his combination of idealism and suffering:

> We had been talking of Robert Emmet, when I incidentally remarked that it was curious that he an atheist should have made so many allusions to the Supreme Being and a future state in the course of his speech from the dock. 'That was no doubt due to his Celtic temperament,' said Oscar Wilde. 'Those who are governed by their emotions are more given to hero-worship and the worship of the gods than practical people who believe in logic and are governed by what they choose to term their reason. Imaginative people will invariably be religious people for the simple reason that religion has sprung from the imagination.'[29]

Wilde believed that imagination in its purest form and unadulterated by authority represented the epitome of human perfectibility and his statement conveyed his continuing interest in what he regarded as the innocence and divinity of the oppressed. The disobedient Celtic temperament that Matthew Arnold identified also countered the 'governed' consciousness cultivated by the state. In this exchange Wilde used Arnold's model of the Celt to place himself within the context of a century-long pattern of insurgency that linked Emmet and his rebellion of 1803 to the late romanticism of the Young Ireland movement, in which his mother participated, and to his own anarchism and the radical socialism of the fin de siècle. Whereas Arnold depicted the Celt as a docile, dreamy type, Wilde believed that the rebelliousness of the Irish expressed their active and liberated imaginations.

Anarchic Divinity

The exploration of radical divinity that Wilde proposed in his short stories emerges again in 'The Ballad of Reading Gaol', in which he also insisted on the need for autonomy and self-awareness. Here Wilde explained that the treatment of the themes of dispossession and suffering by writers and artists such as Victor Hugo, Charles Baudelaire, Paul Verlaine, Michelangelo, Edward Burne-Jones and William Morris formed, for him, 'the very keynote of romantic art'.[30] He explained to Douglas that '[w]here there is Sorrow there is holy ground',[31] and argued that the harsh consequences of bourgeois disgrace contrasted with the behaviour of poor people who displayed to one another 'the perfect wisdom of Love'.[32] With its assertion that '[t]hose who have little always share', *De Profundis* echoes Peter Kropotkin's stress on the co-operative solidarity of the poor.[33] Wilde explained that his understanding of suffering was underlined by his experience of imprisonment, during which his understanding of the potential of his own agency actually intensified under the disciplinary régime of the prison. Wilde described how this experience revealed to him the historical tensions that determined the relationship between the subject and the state. Rather than forcing him to forget the person he had been before imprisonment, his time in prison magnified his understanding of the meaning of art and selfhood by illustrating with greater refinement the social purpose and political function of culture. This revealed to him with greater clarity his own, personal relationship with and responsibility to culture and history.

As Ian Small argues, the published versions of *De Profundis* were drawn from five drafts of an original letter that was not ultimately intended for private circulation.[34] The circumstances of its composition and extensive revision point to Wilde's intention for it to serve as a public text that after its publication would be widely circulated and read. This was was not the private apology that it was traditionally interpreted as having been, as it articulated Wilde's intensifying radicalism and again conveyed his belief that the trauma of colonisation originated in the violent expansion of markets. Prison, then, provided him with a practical, political and dialectical application of Paterian theory:

> Clergymen and people who use phrases without wisdom sometimes talk of suffering as a mystery. It is really a revelation. One discerns things one never discerned before. One approaches the whole of history from a different standpoint. What one had felt dimly, through instinct, about art, is intellectually and emotionally realised with perfect clearness of vision and absolute intensity of apprehension.
>
> I now see that sorrow, being the supreme emotion of which man is capable, is at once the type and test of all great art. What the artist is always looking for is the mode of existence in which soul and body are one and indivisible: in which the outward is expressive of the inward: in which form reveals.[35]

Prison rendered suffering all the more visible to Wilde, who was already deeply sensitive to the existence of hardship, deprivation and the marginalisation of the poor. By aligning his artistic consciousness more closely to the needs of the outcast and excluded populations of prisons and to those more generally dismissed by society, Wilde's perspective was clarified by his now intensified consciousness of suffering. He believed that his own experience of official violence would liberate his aesthetic imagination by drawing it more closely to the actual, fusing more intensively the intellectual and ideological positions that characterised his pre-imprisonment writings.

Despite the isolation imposed by the cellular organisation of the prison and its violent disruption of the human being's social existence, Wilde found himself evolving and resisting. The letter conveys his growing realisation that his encounters in prison with totalising formations of state power could focus his art's mediation of experience by providing him with what he had always sought – the full realisation of the self as a socially-involved being. The key theoretical point to which he continually returns in *De Profundis* is that, once visible, the antagonism between the state and the dispossessed can be demystified through art, and that the process of its elaboration is in itself an important dialectical experience both for the artist and for those who experience his now more aesthetically refined work. For Wilde, imprisonment was the platform for this next stage of socially-committed aesthetic attainment:

> Behind joy and laughter there may be a temperament, coarse, hard and callous. But behind sorrow there is always sorrow. Pain, unlike pleasure, wears no mask. Truth in art is not any correspondence between the essential idea and the accidental existence; it is not the resemblance of shape to shadow, or of the form mirrored in the crystal to the form itself; it is no echo coming from a hollow hill, any more than it is a silver well of water in the valley that shows the moon to the moon and Narcissus to Narcissus.[36]

The truth found in art reflected the material conditions of life, the principal of these being the experience of suffering. In prison, art demonstrated the real to Wilde, and it did so with even greater focus than before and underlined Walter Pater's theory of the intensity of art. Its capacity to reveal truth provided the basis of its form which in turn expressed the reality of experience through its exploration of matter and spirit:

> Truth in art is the unity of a thing with itself: the outward rendered expressive of the inward: the soul made incarnate: the body instinct with spirit. For this reason there is no truth comparable to sorrow. There are times when sorrow seems to me to be the only truth. Other things may be illusions of the eye or the appetite, made to blind the one and cloy the other, but out of sorrow have the worlds been built, and at the birth of a child or a star there is pain.[37]

This is the reason for sorrow's 'intense [. . .] extraordinary reality'. Wilde's own social and aesthetic position in society, which, as he famously declared, was occupied 'in symbolic relations to the art and culture of my age', is related in *De Profundis* to the subaltern status of the other inmates held in Reading Gaol: 'There is not a single wretched man in this wretched place along with me who does not stand in symbolic relation to the very secret of life. For the secret of life is suffering. It is what is hidden behind everything.' Through the lens of his prison experience, Wilde learned that all impressions were composed and constituted through the reality of pain inflicted by the state.

While his earlier works elaborate on the relationship between authority and suffering by illustrating the imposition of power over the dispossessed, Wilde found in Reading that the cruelty of the surveillant capitalist and imperialist state was total. He believed that this was concealed behind the state's simulation of democracy and its relentless 'starving [of] the soul'. Recalling his own enjoyment of financial success, Wilde noted that the false consciousness that it sustained was maintained by a psychic screen that masked reality from those who did not observe it. This generated 'Pleasure for the beautiful body, but Pain for the beautiful soul'.[38] His realisation of this truth was the basis of his survival, or 'the continuance, by means of development, and evolution, of my former life'. Wilde's anarchic self did not wither in prison, then, but was consolidated further there. Misery and social exclusion brought him beyond the experience of spectatorship that, he believed, characterised much of cultural life but here, in prison, he encountered 'the ultimate realisation of the artistic life'.

Wilde reminded Douglas that all of this was prefigured in his writings, where he explained that 'Art is a symbol, because man is a symbol.' Repeating the comparison made in 'The Soul of Man Under Socialism' between 'the true life of Christ and the true life of the artist', Wilde insisted that Christianity could be translated directly into art because Christ shared the artist's purity and 'flamelike imagination'. These qualities of the fully realised subject, or 'deeper man' and his relationship to 'the Christ who is not in Churches', resulted from the artist's political solidarity and 'imaginative sympathy' with the marginalised and dispossessed. The Kropotkinian, mutualistic consciousness of the aesthetically minded placed the creative alongside the Christian because 'Christ's place is with the poets. His whole conception of Humanity sprang right out of the imagination and can only be realised by it.' With this, Wilde repeated Pater's insistence upon 'intensity' as 'the true aim of modern Art' and applied it to his own progressive political practice.[39]

Like Kropotkin, Wilde regarded mutualism as the driving force behind human progress, describing it as 'the mysticism of sympathy'. He argued that co-operation motivated the true artist who, like Christ, found beauty in the masses, amid 'the sufferings of those whose name is Legion'. These were the poor, the dispossessed and the colonised and Wilde maintained that beauty was a democratising phenomenon, discernible among those 'whose dwelling is in the tombs, oppressed nationalities, factory children, thieves, people in prison, outcasts, those who are dumb under oppression and whose silence is heard only of God'. The artist, like Christ, revealed his sympathy with the oppressed through his work's articulation of 'the voice of Love'. Through its expression of sympathy, art revealed 'the lost secret of the world' and the humility of the artist allowed society to discover the meaning of this enigma. Wilde's Christianity was firmly located in contemporary politics, and he claimed that Christ was the original and 'most supreme of Individualists' whose divinity lay in making 'the history of each separate individual [. . .] the history of the world'. Christ, like the artist and the anarchist, countered alienation by establishing the agency and 'self-perfection' of the individual. This subjective fulfilment was now possible again through modern culture's intensification of consciousness, which Wilde believed would lead to the discovery of the human soul 'in its ultimate essence'. All of this countered the modern problem of alienation, which Wilde described as the outcome of society's imposition of 'dull lifeless mechanical systems that treat people as if they were things'.[40]

'The Ballad of Reading Gaol'

Wilde returned to his critique of authority and alienation in 'The Ballad of Reading Gaol'. While his short stories often propose that redemption can be achieved through self-sacrifice, this poem explores the deliberate destruction of human life by the state. Its subject is the execution of Charles Thomas Wooldridge, a trooper in the Royal Horse Guards who murdered his wife and was hanged at HMP Reading in July 1896. Rather than exploring the kind of suffering, agency and liberation in the fantastic register that is key to many of Wilde's stories, the poem depicts and condemns the harsh reality of institutionalised power in a very direct and more immediately recognisable discourse. Originally published under the pseudonym, C. 3. 3, which was Wilde's cell number in Reading, the poem addresses the immediate problem of violent authority through the medium of the popular ballad form. Although it deals with the fatal outcome of a notorious murder case, Wilde's identification with the murderer's isolation and eventual death at the hands of the disciplinary state explains how '[s]uffering [. . .] is the only means by which we become conscious of existing'. The poem underlines how the remembrance of suffering becomes what he described to Alfred Douglas in *De Profundis* as 'the warrant, the evidence of our continued identity'.[41]

Wilde pointed to the conscious subject's creativity by describing imaginative people as 'individuals who can claim individuality' and who are subsequently endowed with divinity. Christ, like the Irish revolutionary, Robert Emmet, was a master of speech and language, and his command of words made him an artist of the highest order:

> Christ, to me, is the one supreme Artist, and not one of the brush, or the pen, but, what is more rare, he was an Artist in words. It was by the voice he found expression – that's what the voice is for, but few can find it by that medium, and none in the manner born of Christ.[42]

As the expression of subjectivity, human voice is invested with radical potential. The word that gives expression is the weapon of the artist and the revolutionary, both of whom are visionaries at odds with the state. This explanation of the connection between language and radical practice revealed to Sherard that Wilde did not accept 'the divinity of Christ [. . .] in its generally accepted sense [. . .] as [. . .] an angel sitting on the clouds'.[43] Wilde's radical Christianity presented Christ as a historically-formed and politically-conscious subject whose message was subversive and continued to pose a challenge to capitalism and the state.[44]

Wilde proposed in 'The Soul of Man Under Socialism' that the removal of the compulsive authority of the state would immediately lead to the abandonment of punishment and change the course of history which, he believed, was characterised 'not by the crimes that the wicked have committed, but by the punishments that the good have inflicted'.[45] 'The Ballad of Reading Gaol' returns to themes raised in the essay, such as Wilde's identification with the marginalised and outcast, violence against labour, repressive authority and the immorality of punishment. The political consequences of these problems are amplified by the poem's prison setting, in which the rigours of imprisonment and its denial of voluntary association intensify the coercive reach of the state. Its political content was read by the Scottish anarchist, Thomas Hastie Bell, as a literary protest against the violence of 'governmentalism' as well as that of the Victorian prison system. Bell concluded that its significance as an anarchist text equalled Peter Kropotkin's account of his own political imprisonment in his *Memoirs of a Revolutionist* and Alexander Berkman's *Prison Memoirs of an Anarchist*.[46]

Violence is portrayed as the result of romantic infatuation and capital:

> Some kill their love when they are young,
> And some when they are old;
> Some strangle with the hands of Lust,
> Some with the hands of Gold:
> The kindest use a knife, because
> The dead so soon grow cold. (ll.43–8)[47]

Wilde's association of debt, which he regarded as the most disciplinary arm of capital, with execution, identifies capitalism very clearly with the violence of capital punishment. For all of its horror, the direct and personalised violence of the individualised murder committed with the knife is portrayed as having more humane consequences than the violence committed with 'the hands of Gold'. The poem exposes the rhetorical and ideological slippage between the coercive state and the brutalising economies of capitalism:

> And strange it was to see him pass
> With a step so light and gay,
> And strange it was to see him look
> So wistfully at the day,
> And strange it was to think that he
> Had such a debt to pay. (ll.127–32)

Debt and alienation are combined in the isolation of the prisoner from the rest of the outcast community of the prison. Capital and the state are mirrored here through their disciplinary practices, as shame and punishment circulate together in the Debtor's Yard, where the prisoner's life, up until the point of execution, is protected by prison authority as if it were a valuable commodity:

> In Debtor's Yard the stones are hard
> And the dripping wall is high,
> So it was there he took the air
> Beneath the leaden sky,
> And by each side a Warder walked,
> For fear the man might die. (ll.175–80)

The state's ironic preservation of the prisoner for the purpose of his destruction requires his accompaniment by warders whose role is to prevent him from taking his own life in the Debtors' Yard. His mortality is measured in terms of the value attached to the disciplinary ritualisation of his execution, while the poet's ability to convey his own sympathy to the condemned man is prevented by the warders' surveillance. The strange ritual that renders the condemned man invisible and preserves him by preventing any possibility of his committing suicide continues with the state's provision of tobacco and beer, as a routine of quiet consumption that marks the prisoner's last days of existence:

> And twice a day he smoked his pipe,
> And drank his quart of beer:
> His soul was resolute, and held
> No hiding-place for fear;
> He often said that he was glad
> The hangman's hands were near.

The threat now posed to the state is that of the prisoner's auto-destruction through suicide. Through the warders' close surveillance the prison denies him any chance of asserting his own agency by killing himself – an action that would prevent the state's performance of its ultimate sanction against the individual and, by extension, against society at large. The harm caused by authority is made explicit by Wilde, who highlights its contagion as the warders are themselves shown to have been silenced:

> But why he said so strange a thing
> No Warder dared to ask:
> For he to whom a watcher's doom
> Is given as his task,
> Must set a lock upon his lips,
> And make his face a mask.
>
> Or else he might be moved, and try
> To comfort or console:
> And what should Human Pity do
> Pent up in Murderers' Hole?
> What word of grace in such a place
> Could help a brother's soul? (ll.193–210)

Grace, pity, sympathy and solidarity are forbidden by the state in the moral void that constitutes its 'Murderers' Hole'. The prevention of sympathy being expressed by agents of power toward a 'brother' provides the reader with a microscopic view of the internalisation of the violent dynamics of authority by the complicit subject. Something of the warders' personalities and souls also die as they have been conditioned to conform by the rule of silence, which imposes the discipline of isolation upon them. For Wilde, isolation was the most traumatic aspect of his own imprisonment, and here it is presented as contaminating the warders through their own assumption of this particularly destructive form of prison discipline. The expression of sympathy and solidarity is impossible without the use of words and gestures, and the other prisoners who have been watching and listening for the condemned man reverse the violent dialectics of surveillance, as the 'watchers' come to realise when they check their cells on the eve of the execution:

> He lay as one who lies and dreams
> In a pleasant meadow-land,
> The watchers watched him as he slept,
> And could not understand
> How one could keep so sweet a sleep
> With a hangman close at hand.
>
> But there is no sleep when men must weep
> Who never yet have wept:
> So we – the fool, the fraud, the knave –
> That endless vigil kept,
> And through each brain on hands of pain
> Another's terror crept.
>
> Alas! It is a fearful thing
> To feel another's guilt!
> For, right within, the sword of Sin
> Pierced to its poisoned hilt,
> And as molten lead were the tears we shed
> For the blood we had not spilt.
>
> The warders with their shoes of felt
> Crept by each padlocked door,
> And peeped and saw, with eyes of awe,
> Gray figures on the floor,
> And wondered why men knelt to pray
> Who never prayed before. (ll.253–76)

Here the structural formation of official violence and its seeming permanence within the prison régime's elastication of time is countered by the inmates' quiet but not entirely subdued collective expression of sympathy with the condemned man. Through their expression of pity for him – voiced through the medium of prayer – they share in his fear and in doing so attempt to share in his 'terror'. Although they are unable to prevent the course of his execution their solidarity with the condemned man resists and refuses the dynamic of prison authority. As fear saturates the prison wing, their common appeal to divinity becomes a shared rejection of the atomisation that prison imposes upon them and the condemned man. Although physically separated from one another by the prison's cellular division, the inmates reveal that society's most marginalised subjects can exhibit a profound capacity for collective sympathy. The prison's materialisation of state power occurs within the dimensional planes of space (the cell) and the chronological movement of time (the sentence), but its authority falters within the subjective space of the sympathetic imagination. The prison stands for the control of physical space and time, but its control of the mind is broken through the prisoners' radical collective action.

The violence with which the state functions and performs its own authority is manifested in the hangman's noose, or 'rope of shame' (l.353):

> For Man's grim Justice goes its way,
> And will not swerve aside:
> It slays the weak, it slays the strong,
> It has a deadly stride:
> With iron heel it slays the strong,
> The monstrous parricide! (ll.361–6)

The indiscriminate violence of authority harms everyone who is subjected to it and justice is portrayed as inflexible, irrational and qualified by the final sanction of force, as Wilde's depiction of its lethal momentum, or 'deadly stride' conveys its immoveable and unreasonable dynamic. This violent energy is met with the poet's reflection on the state's denial of freedom to prisoners, as liberation is imagined by the inmates to be like the free mobility of clouds drifting above the prison yard:

> I never saw sad men who looked
> With such a wistful eye
> Upon that little tent of blue
> We prisoners called the sky,
> And at every careless cloud that passed
> In happy freedom by. (ll.415–20)

Another kind of circulation then assumes control of the prisoners who, as they continue to walk around the yard, begin to internalise further the trauma of state-deployed violence. Their imaginations are seized by terror, which is itself amplified by the guilt that has been pronounced on all of them by the judicial system:

> Silently we went round and round,
> And through each hollow mind
> The Memory of dreadful things
> Rushed like a dreadful wind,
> And Horror stalked before each man,
> And Terror crept behind. (ll.439–44)

The inmates' pacing of the yard mirrors the repetitive flickering of memory and the processing of their own guilt by their confined imaginations. Having emptied their minds of all stimulation, the prison régime condemns each man to a pure experience of fear which, when internalised, assumes this circular motion. The prisoners' hollow psyches are mental voids mirroring the moral and political emptiness of the wider prison environment and the system that maintains it, while their feelings of pain, fear and guilt are intensified by the monotony of their routine. Circulating within the vacuum of the prison, their trauma amplifies the terror-effect of incarceration that Wilde described in his 1897 correspondence to the *Daily Chronicle*.

The rapid erosion of the condemned man's remains with quicklime that, as well as dissolving the body, 'eats the heart always', is a reminder of the psychic and social anaesthetisation that violence causes. Applied with official sanction, this final act of physical destruction and erasure consumes the heart or conscience of the prisoner, and by 'disappearing' his physical remains it also erases the moral culpability of the state that has condemned him. Just as prison discipline wipes the individual's imagination to the extent that any self-awareness of its insidious and invasive operation is lost, this operation is repeated on a much broader social level with the prison's erasure of the condemned man's corpse. Wilde observes that this act of sterilisation continues to manifest itself in the yard where the prisoner is buried long after his execution:

> For three long years they will not sow
> Or root or seedling there:
> For three long years the unblessed spot
> Will sterile be and bare,
> And look upon the wondering sky
> With unreproachful stare. (ll.469–74)

Despite this act of total erasure, strong traces of Wooldridge's presence remain in Wilde's memory and imagination, where exploring the fact of his existence becomes an act of profound resistance. Regenia Gagnier has interpreted Wilde's reflection upon the destruction of Wooldridge's corpse as an act of reclamation that salvages the prisoners' bodies and minds from the destructive sphere of state power. The inmates, she argues, are returned to humanity as the condemned man's remains function as 'a sort of habeas corpus' served on the authorities at Reading Gaol, educating the reader as to the 'humanizing' counter-practices of its community of prisoners. The broken heart, through which the radical example of Christ enters the poet's imagination, must be fractured by pain in order to unite his suffering consciousness and body. As Gagnier points out, this continues Wilde's preoccupation with the motif of the divided self. This broken subjectivity is torn between serving the interests of individual purpose and serving society – a theme that Wilde had already made central to his stories, 'The Fisherman and His Soul', 'The Happy Prince' and 'The Nightingale and the Rose'.[48]

The broken-hearted poet-narrator continues to narrate this radical Christian theme:

> They think a murderer's heart would taint
> Each simple seed they sow.
> It is not true! God's kindly earth
> Is kindlier than men know,
> And the red rose would but blow more red,
> The white rose whiter blow.
>
> Out of his mouth, a red, red rose!
> Out of his heart a white!
> For who can say by what strange way,
> Christ brings his staff to light,
> Since the barren staff the pilgrim bore
> Bloomed in the great Pope's sight? (ll.475–86)

Although beauty is forbidden in the midst of the disciplinary space of prison, kindness can still find some space for expression there, where it can take hold and develop. Humanity's potential and possibility is depicted in the symbolism of the miraculous growth of flowers from the corpse's heart and mouth – from those parts of the body associated with passion and expression. Cleansed of actual and symbolic beauty, however, the sterile environment of the prison yard is not a site where hope can flourish:

> But neither milk-white rose nor red
> May bloom the prison air;
> The shard, the pebble, and the flint,
> Are what they give us there:
> For flowers have been known to heal
> A common man's despair.
>
> So never will wine-red rose or white,
> Petal by petal, fall
> On that stretch of mud and sand that lies
> By the hideous prison-wall,
> To tell the men who tramp the yard
> That God's son died for all. (ll.475–98)

Established, organised and maintained in contradiction to the democratic imperative of the deity who 'died for all', the prison itself is condemned as constituting an 'unholy ground' that wounds all of its occupants, warders and prisoners alike (l.504). Gagnier has pointed out how Wilde here draws on Ernest Renan's image of Christ as an exile and outsider,[49] which contrasts with the poem's condemnation of clerical complicity in the execution:

> The Chaplain would not kneel to pray
> By his dishonoured grave:
> Nor mark it with that blessed Cross
> That Christ for sinners gave,
> Because the man was one of those
> Whom Christ came down to save.
>
> Yet all is well; he has but passed
> To Life's appointed bourne:
> And alien tears will fill for him
> Pity's long-broken urn,
> For his mourners will be outcast men,
> And outcasts always mourn. (ll.523–34)

The victim is rejected and further marginalised in death by the cleric because, like the Wildean Christ, he is one of the excluded and despite his isolation from the other inmates is accepted and sympathised with by the community of the incarcerated. This critique of the allegiance of church and state along with their combined servicing and perpetuation of authority echoes the political arguments that Wilde presented in 'The Soul of Man Under Socialism' and in his short stories. He condemns their shared, violent authority and its articulation through law and government:

> But this I know, that every Law
> That men have made for Man,
> Since first Man took his brother's life,
> And the sad world began,
> But straws the wheat and saves the chaff
> With a most evil fan.
>
> This too I know – and wise it were
> If each could know the same –
> That every prison that men build
> Is built with bricks of shame,
> And bound with bars lest Christ should see
> How men their brothers maim.
>
> With bars they blur the gracious moon,
> And blind the goodly sun:
> And they do well to hide their Hell,
> For in it things are done
> That Son of God nor son of Man
> Ever should look upon. (ll.547–58)

Built upon the shameful actions and ideology of the disciplinary state, the prison system is condemned for the affront that it presents to human dignity and even divinity. It is exposed as brutalising its administrators as much as it harms the prisoners they incarcerate, and Wilde's radical indictment includes the entire political system that has constructed and maintained it. His anarchic critique of capital punishment, with its exposure of the régime's violence against inmates, equates the severity of more explicit forms of violence committed against prisoners with the harm caused by the isolation that is imposed upon them. This cycle is internalised by the inmates and amplified in their imaginations as 'every stone one lifts by day / Becomes one's heart by night' (ll.587–8):

> And never a human voice comes near
> To speak a gentle word:
> And the eye that watches through the door
> Is pitiless and hard:

And all forgot, we rot and rot,
With soul and body marred. (ll.595–600)

The violence of confinement is countered by the redemptive power of 'God's eternal laws' and their power to 'break' the penal system's 'heart of stone'. (ll.605–6). These laws are recognised by the poet during this experience of suffering but, as Wilde explained in 'The Soul of Man Under Socialism', he did not believe that misery in itself was redemptive as it did not lead to self-fulfilment. The poem acknowledges the structural, institutional and political causes behind imprisonment and the suffering that incarceration inflicts. The broken bodies of its tortured subjects are revealed to be the vessels of a pared-down and exposed subjectivity and hope is shown to reside in their capacity to endure and quietly resist this violence during prolonged moments such as the execution ritual. Their solidarity with the condemned man conveys the sanctity that Christ represented to Wilde, and which the violence of prison is designed to erode:

And every human heart that breaks,
In prison-cell or yard,
Is as that broken box that gave
Its treasure to the Lord,
And filled the unclean leper's house
With the scent of costliest nard. (ll.607–12)

Although the prisoners' bodies are degraded almost to the point of physical destruction in their cells and in the prison yard, or violated and mortally injured by the hangman's noose, Wilde maintains that the 'broken heart', or damaged subjectivity of the imprisoned subject possesses a grander divinity that will ensure their salvation:

And he of the swollen purple throat,
And the stark and staring eyes,
Waits for the holy hands that took
The Thief to Paradise;
And a broken and a contrite heart
The Lord will not despise. (ll.619–24)

In this obvious comparison the execution of the prisoner is equated to the crucifixion of Christ, and in particular to the redemption of the Penitent Thief. Mirroring the modern practice of corporal punishment, the violence of the crucifixion ensures that 'the crimson stain that was of Cain / Became Christ's snow-white seal' (ll.635–6). The institutionalised destruction of life – the beloved 'thing' that all men do violence to – renders the state complicit in murder:

> And all men kill the thing they love,
> By all let this be heard,
> Some do it with a bitter look,
> Some with a flattering word,
> The coward does it with a kiss,
> The brave man with a sword! (ll.649–54)

For Wilde, the controlling tendencies of 'officialism' had as their objective the degradation of everyone who came into contact with the prison system. Whether exercised directly or indirectly, these applications of state violence are shown to have the same objective: the destruction of the prisoner on the most subjective level possible. Aggression, betrayal and hypocrisy are represented by him in 'The Ballad of Reading Gaol' as a set of dehumanising phenomena practised and cultivated by the state.

Toward the end of his life, when he complained that 'it is difficult to teach the English either pity or humanity', Wilde's anticolonial perspective continued to influence his efforts when campaigning for prison reform.[50] Upon his own release his correspondence with the press described the prison system as a key structural and political element of state terrorism but this was not a novel concept for him. In *Vera; or, The Nihilists*, he had already drawn on this when the President of the revolutionaries declares, 'I know more about the inside of prisons than of palaces,' echoing the experiences of Fenian prisoners such as Michael Davitt, Jeremiah O'Donovan Rossa and Christopher O'Keeffe. Wilde's own imprisonment should be seen as a form of political persecution that followed the incarceration of other Irish political prisoners – dissidents and literary writers whose prison memoirs mobilised Irish opposition to British imperialism during the twentieth century.[51] When viewed in this way, we can better understand the criminalisation of homosexuality as a part of a wider *suite* of state violence that dehumanises its practitioners as much as it harms those whom it targets. As well as testifying to the historical and ongoing persecution of homosexual people, *De Profundis* and 'The Ballad of Reading Gaol' were also significant contributions to contemporary anarchist and anti-imperialist discourse that were aimed at accelerating resistance on all of these fronts. Wilde's concluding point in *De Profundis*, in which he claimed that '[t]here is no prison in any world into which Love cannot force an entrance',[52] articulates the need to disrupt the power of the imperial state, and the necessity of resisting the coercive authority that imprisoned him.

Notes

1. Stuart Mason, *Oscar Wilde: Three Times Tried* (London: Ferrestone Press, 1912), p. 216.
2. The hunger strike on which Sands died in 1981 drew directly upon the strategies of refusal and endurance practised and developed by Jeremiah O'Donovan Rossa and other Fenian prisoners over the course of three decades from the 1860s until the 1890s. See David Lloyd, *Irish Culture and Colonial Modernity, 1800–2000: The Transformation of Oral Space* (Cambridge: Cambridge University Press, 2011), pp. 170–1.
3. Jerusha McCormack, 'Introduction: The Irish Wilde', in McCormack (ed.), *Wilde the Irishman*, p. 2.
4. See Lloyd, *Ireland after History*.
5. In his keynote paper, 'Ireland, Modernity, and the Male Homosexual Margin: Dublin Castle, Oscar Wilde, and Roger Casement', delivered at Liverpool John Moores University in September 2016, Bristow pointed out that the fusion of sexual scandal with political coercion was central to imperial repression during the decades leading up to the partition of Ireland. The British state's conflation of sexual and political fear influenced the outcome not only of Wilde's trial, but also the fates of the Irish nationalist leader, Charles Stewart Parnell, and Roger Casement, the humanitarian campaigner and organiser of the 1916 Easter Rising.
6. See Alexander Cohen, untitled, *The Torch*, 2.1, 18 June 1895, p. 6; and 'News at Home and Abroad', *The Torch*, 2.2, July 1895, p. 17. For a discussion of Cohen's articles in *The Torch*, see my *Blasted Literature*, especially chapter 4, 'The Doctrine of Dynamite: Anarchist Literature and Terrorist Violence'.
7. John Barlas to Henry Salt, 10 May 1909, quoted in Philip K. Cohen, *John Evelyn Barlas: A Critical Biography* (High Wycombe: Rivendale Press, 2012), pp. 151–2.
8. Sherard, *Oscar Wilde: The Story of an Unhappy Friendship*, p. 82.
9. See Gagnier, *Idylls of the Marketplace*, p. 184.
10. Ford Madox Ford, 'Memories of Oscar Wilde: On the Collapse of a Famous Writer and his Final Attempts to Shock the Bourgeoisie', in *The Saturday Review Cavalcade: A 25-Year Anthology* (Saturday Review Associates, Inc. [no place of publication, no original date of publication], 1950), pp. 22–31, p. 22.

11. Merlin Holland (ed.), *Irish Peacock and Scarlet Marquess: The Real Trial of Oscar Wilde* (London: Fourth Estate, 2004), p. 254.
12. Anon, Oscar Wilde: *Three Times Tried* (Paris: privately published, nd. [1912?]), p. 323.
13. Ibid. p. 327.
14. Ibid. p. 334.
15. Ibid. p. 336.
16. John Sloan, *Oscar Wilde: Myths, Miracles and Imitations* (Cambridge: Cambridge University Press, 1996), p. 54.
17. I. Playfair, *Gentle Criticisms on British Justice* (privately published, 1895), pp. 1–2. UCLA Clark Library Wilde W749M3 G338 [1895].
18. Wilde to Michael Davitt, late May or early June 1897, in *Complete Letters*, pp. 870–1.
19. Wilde, to the editor of the *Daily Chronicle*, 27 May 1897, in *Complete Letters*, pp. 847–55, p. 848.
20. As Frankel points out, Wilde was familiar with the history of Irish prisoner struggle and told Robert Sherard of his admiration for Irish political prisoners. See Frankel, *Oscar Wilde: The Unrepentant Years*, p. 36.
21. Gagnier, *Idylls of the Marketplace*, pp. 186–7. David Lloyd's interpretation of Bobby Sands' prison writings draws similar conclusions regarding Sands' deployment of the written word as a form of cultural resistance to the carceral violence of the colonial state. See Lloyd, *Irish Culture and Colonial Modernity, 1800–2000,* chapter 5, 'The Breaker's Yard: From Forensic to Interrogation Modernity'.
22. Gagnier, *Idylls of the Marketplace*, pp. 190, 192.
23. Ibid. p. 180. See also Frankel, *Oscar Wilde: The Unrepentant Years*.
24. Ian Small, 'Introduction', in *Complete Works*, vol. 2: *De Profundis; Epistola: In Carcare et Vinculus* (Oxford: Oxford University Press, 2005), pp. 1–3.
25. Ibid.
26. Gagnier, *Idylls of the Marketplace*, p. 179.
27. Oscar Wilde, 'Poetry and Prison', *Pall Mall Gazette*, 3 January 1889, p. 3. Reprinted in Robert Ross (ed.), *Collected Works*, vol. 7, Journalism 2, pp. 149–51, pp. 149, 151.
28. Wilde, 'The Soul of Man', in *Complete Works*, vol. 4, pp. 229–68, p. 242.
29. Sherard, *The Life of Oscar Wilde*, pp. 377–8.
30. Wilde to Lord Alfred Douglas, in *Complete Letters*, January–March 1897, pp. 683–780, p. 751.
31. Wilde to Lord Alfred Douglas, in *Complete Letters*, January–March 1897, p. 722.
32. Ibid. p. 728.
33. Ibid. p. 731. See Peter Kropotkin, *Mutual Aid* and *The Conquest of Bread*.

34. Small, 'Introduction', in *Complete Works*, vol. 2, p. 25.
35. Wilde to Lord Alfred Douglas, in *Complete Letters*, January–March 1897, pp. 683–780, p. 737.
36. Ibid.
37. Ibid.
38. Ibid. pp. 737–8.
39. Ibid. pp. 740–2, 755.
40. Ibid. pp. 742–5, 750.
41. Ibid. p. 696.
42. Sherard, *The Life of Oscar Wilde*, p. 379.
43. Ibid. p. 380.
44. Similar arguments were presented by Leo Tolstoy in his 1894 book, *The Kingdom of God is Within You*. Tolstoy's book offers a comprehensive study of the relationship between violence, authority and the state. See Leo Tolstoy, *The Kingdom of God is Within You and Peace Essays* (trans. by Aylmer Maude, 1894, reprinted New Delhi: Rupa, 2001).
45. Wilde, 'The Soul of Man', in *Complete Works*, vol. 4, pp. 229–68, p. 245.
46. Bell, *Oscar Wilde without Whitewash*, p. 103.
47. Subsequent quotations from the poem are from the text published in Oscar Wilde, *Complete Poetry* (Oxford: Oxford University Press, 2009). Citations are hereafter provided as line numbers from the text.
48. Gagnier, *Idylls of the Marketplace*, pp. 175–6.
49. Ibid. p. 156.
50. Wilde to Georgina Weldon, 31 May 1898, in *Complete Letters*, pp. 1080–1, p. 1080.
51. *Vera; or, The Nihilists*, Act 1, p. 687. See Lloyd, *Irish Culture and Colonial Modernity*, p. 14 and chapter 6, 'The Breaker's Yard: from Forensic to Interrogation Modernity'.
52. Wilde to Alfred Douglas, January–March 1897, in *Complete Letters*, p. 779.

Conclusion: Oscar Wilde – The Lost Revolutionary?

In a letter written to his mother in June 1875, Wilde recorded his first impressions of Venice. Impressed by the city's architecture and its historical beauty, he described its 'long line of crowded churches and palaces' crowded with white and gilded domes. A gondola ride through its 'gorgeous' and 'splendid' canals brought him to the Church of San Marco, a building 'covered with gilding and mosaics, inside and out', where a great floor of coloured marble struck him as being 'indescribable'. His overall impression was of 'everything glorious'. Later, in the Doge's Palace, he marvelled at Renaissance frescoes that were so magnificent as to be 'beyond praise'. Everywhere in the city he found gold: 'the ceiling crossed by gilded beams and rich in gilded carving; rooms fit for the noble-looking grave senators whose pictures are on the walls by Titian or Tintoretto'. However, he was also mindful that, having been created for the wealthy and powerful élites of Venice, these aesthetically pleasing sights were visible products and symbols of a deeper violence that lay beneath the gilded surface of the city:

> Council Room of the celebrated 'Three', black marble and gold. Two dismal passages lead from it across the Ponte dei Sospiri. In size and colour and dignity the rooms are beyond description, and the view from the windows across the sea wonderful. Beneath all this greatness are the most dismal dungeons and torture-rooms – most terrible.[1]

Despite his opinion that the city's grandeur was incomparable, the fact that the 'extreme' beauty of medieval and renaissance Italy[2] rested upon the concealed historical sediment of human misery and aristocratic tyranny troubled the young aesthete. The young Wilde's radicalism is apparent in these observation, as they contextualise the claim made in his first play, *Vera; or, The Nihilists*, that '[h]eroics are out of place in a palace'.[3]

A year after this trip, Wilde also complained about the power of untruthful, or 'unauthenticated histories'[4] – the official narratives that erased the experiences of the defeated and dispossessed. His awareness of these historical formations of violence influenced his aesthetic consciousness by combining it with his very pronounced political awareness. From the earliest stages of his career he recognised the need to restore this history and felt a responsibility to inscribe the possibility of resistance into the literary and cultural narratives that he wanted to establish as a critic and author. As the twenty-year-old aesthete discovered in Italy, the histories of power and resistance that were masked by beauty and distorted by violence could be made visible and discernible by art. He emphasised this point in *Vera; or, The Nihilists* by exposing the reality of coercive power and suffering. When he replies to his father, the Czar, that victims of oppression are an 'instrument of God',[5] much as the community of prisoners is in 'The Ballad of Reading Gaol', the Czarevitch expresses Wilde's compassion for the dispossessed and the politically subjugated, along with his belief in the divinity of the oppressed. These ideas were repeated throughout his career and their articulation within the broad spectrum of his literary writing underlines the consistency of his radicalism.

Ian Small has stressed the continuities that link Wilde's poetic practice to his later writings. Emphasising how his literary strategy was far more consistent than has generally been acknowledged, Small calls for a reimagining of the relationship between Wilde's journalism and his art.[6] For Small, the key tension in Wilde's early work centred on his equating his public status with his publications:

> Wilde wanted the best of two increasingly incompatible ambitions: to achieve the status which poetry, as the highest form of literary art, had traditionally bestowed, but without forgoing the social and commercial opportunities made possible by new forms of mass culture.[7]

This was why Wilde felt that modern authors found validation 'not in Prince, or Pope, or patron', but in the 'high indifference' with which they pitted their work against authority.[8]

Capital, Conscience and *Lady Windermere's Fan*

The destruction of innocence is a key theme in Wilde's 1893 play, *Lady Windermere's Fan*, in which Lord Darlington admits that masculinity has been warped by capitalism. Responding to Cecil

Graham's claim that 'The world is perfectly packed with good women' and that '[t]o know them is a middle-class education', Darlington claims that the mysterious Mrs Erlynne's 'purity and innocence' should serve men as a reminder of 'everything we [. . .] have lost'. Graham's retort is revealing: 'My dear fellow, what on earth should we men do going about with purity and innocence? A carefully thought-out buttonhole is much more effective.' Late Victorian masculinity is presented here as a fellowship involving a wilful but emasculating participation in commodity culture, as the middle classes have chosen to conform. The bourgeois dandification against which Wilde set Aestheticism appears in the play as the product of surrendered agency, which leads to the paradoxical experience of consumption. This is summarised by Dumby, who tells his friends: 'In this world there are two tragedies. One is not getting what one wants, and the other is getting it. The last is much the worst; the last is a real tragedy!' By distancing themselves from women, ruling-class men surrender to the deadening imperatives of consumption and, in doing so, erode their own potential to exercise social, political and personal agency. To some extent this is realised by Dumby, whose expression of his desire 'to forget all I have learned' draws an accusation of cynicism from Lord Darlington. When asked to qualify his charge, Darlington explains that a cynic is a 'man who knows the price of everything and the value of nothing', to which Cecil Graham responds: 'And a sentimentalist, my dear Darlington, is a man who sees an absurd value in everything, and doesn't know the market price of any single thing.' The sentimentalist, aesthete or dreamer culturally and politically defies the 'market' definition of value by asserting that experience cannot be commodified. 'Experience,' Graham stresses, 'is a question of instinct about life,' but Dumby retorts that it is also 'the name every one gives to their mistakes'.[9]

Dumby's opinion of experience as a dangerous phenomenon reflects Wilde's preoccupation with his own liminality and his consciousness of his precarious situation as a writer, aesthete, public wit, social commentator and political subversive. The play's focus on the theme of public disgrace is also reflected in Lady Windermere's comments, which express views on the uncertainty of life that closely mirror Wilde's: 'How securely one thinks one lives – out of reach of temptation, sin, folly. And then suddenly – Oh! Life is terrible. It rules us, we do not rule it.'[10] To be bourgeois and conscionable, Wilde warned his audiences, was to exist on the edge of a very uncertain abyss.

The key theoretical point to which Wilde continually returned is that, once rendered visible, the tension between the state and those it has dispossessed can be demystified through the medium of art. The very process of its explanation, he believed, was in itself an important dialectical experience, both for the artist and for those who experienced his work. Wilde's treatment of this dialectic also exposes how the interests of capitalism corresponded very directly with the practices of colonialism. As discussed earlier in this monograph, his internationalism included expressions of solidarity with migrant workers in the United States and his anti-authoritarianism appealed very directly to the anarchists of the fin de siècle. Wilde's literary exposures of the violent dynamics of class and empire are the measure of his radical consciousness. By asking his readers and audiences to consider the human and moral cost of imperial and capitalist modernity, he urged them to confront the actual violence and 'real tragedy' that Dumby warns of. This is the reality of suffering that is described throughout his writings as the ultimate consequence of empire and capital.

Intellectual Criticism and the Analysis of Culture

In his 1891 essay, 'The Critic as Artist', Wilde also argued that neither emotional need nor 'greed for gain' would improve modern subjectivity. Instead of satisfying these needs, 'intellectual criticism' and the structured analysis of culture would allow for the creative development of a truly cosmopolitan society. Citing the example of the Enlightenment poet, Johann Wolfgang von Goethe, Wilde argued that such criticism would counter racism by pitting culture against barbarism; that Goethe's loyalty to culture and its cultivation of a shared humanity superseded his attachment to the nation state. His universalism countered jingoism and warfare by proposing solidarity between peoples and across the borders imposed by empires and nation states, bringing 'the peace that springs from understanding'.

For Wilde, 'the unity of the human mind' proved that the consciousness of the Other always reflected 'an element of our own culture, and possibly its most important element'.[11] Wilde believed that culture elevated humanity by bringing readers and their imaginations together across the political divisions fostered by authority. The cultural terrain of human intellect was of greater significance to human development than the physical territory of the modern nation state, and literature, in Wilde's view, was key to the formation of this common legacy. This literary internationalism was another means of subverting bourgeois culture from within. Wilde's criticism of the vulgarisation of art through the 'exercise of popular authority' had ambitious scope. He believed that authority threatened to neutralise culture by restricting the author's ability to work structurally on plot; it also inhibited the development of expressive style and restricted authors from providing a complex exploration of psychology. These are the very formal and stylistic issues that distinguish *The Picture of Dorian Gray* as an aesthetically experimental and theoretically innovative novel. These matters, along with the author's self-reflective treatment of the relationship between life and literature were diminished when art was subjected to the authority of 'the very meanest capacity and the most uncultivated mind'.[12]

Contrary to hostile depictions of him as a *poseur*, faddist and class traitor, many of Wilde's contemporaries believed that his writings were politically charged, with one remembering that his work 'challenged the world of the upper ten'.[13] These ideas were pursued in his verse play of 1883, *The Duchess of Padua*, in which contemporary class tensions are discussed through the medium of Renaissance melodrama, where desire for personal revenge is tempered by the collective experience of social conflict. As well as writing these politically-charged works, Wilde enjoyed reading socially-conscious literature such as Elizabeth Barrett Browning's verse novel, *Aurora Leigh*, because it reminded him of the dangers of a purely 'aesthetic training'.[14] Likewise Victor Hugo's *Les Misérables* captured the Christ-like innocence of the poor, while he believed that Charles Baudelaire's *Les Fleurs du mal* also conveyed the reality of their suffering.[15]

Wilde was concerned that Aestheticism's sophistication was being endangered by the prescriptive cultural 'violence' of the middle classes, to the extent that 'the artist [. . .] would have to suppress his individualism, forget his culture, annihilate his style, and surrender everything that is valuable in him'.[16] He was convinced that Goethe's dilemma was also his as modernity was an extended period of crisis, and Wilde was convinced that the tensions confronted in his own work were complicated by the internal class dynamics of the late Victorian imperial state. The base, controlling and 'popular forms' that it promoted at the expense of genuine art were expressions of its destructively violent bourgeois culture. These were aimed at eradicating the necessarily theoretical sensibility of the self-conscious artist:

> Any attempt to extend the subject-matter of art is extremely distasteful to the public; and yet the vitality and progress of art depend in a large measure on the continual extension of subject-matter. The public dislike

novelty because they are afraid of it. It represents to them a mode of Individualism, an assertion on the part of the artist that he selects his own subject, and treats it as he chooses.[17]

As this essay and the experimental form and content of *The Picture of Dorian Gray* illustrate, Wilde's concept of literature was of an art form that could never remain static and which would always be in development. Aligning Wilde with the key Marxist literary theorists of the twentieth century, Mikhail Bakhtin and Bertolt Brecht, Terry Eagleton has shown how his exploration of the relationship between art, cultural theory and political reality was expressed through his fusion and expression of a radical style that elaborates advanced and progressive ideas about commitment and identity.[18] These questions came to the fore as Wilde was accused by his critics of being politically suspect, insincere, lazy or downright mad (one even suggested that he was a victim of demonic possession).[19] Wilde's engagement with this criticism emphasised the connections that bound art to subjective and social liberation by connecting the personal to the political. His radical Aestheticism was committed, as one contemporary reviewer put it, 'to the development of a taste for all that is beautiful on earth'.[20]

Notes

1. Oscar Wilde to Lady Wilde, 24 June 1875, in *Complete Letters*, pp. 9–10.
2. Oscar Wilde to William Ward, 30 December 1876, in *Complete Letters*, p. 36.
3. Wilde, *Vera; or, The Nihilists*, Act 2, p. 705.
4. Wilde to William Ward, 26 July 1876, in *Complete Letters*, p. 26.
5. Wilde, *Vera; or, The Nihilists*, Act 2, p. 705.
6. Ian Small, 'Introduction', in *Complete Works*, vol. 1: *Poems and Poems in Prose*, p. x. For example, lines from 'Humanitad' appear in *Ravenna*, others appear in *The Duchess of Padua* and in 'The Critic as Artist' and 'The Young King'. For Small, this is not plagiarism but strategic repetition.
7. Ibid. p. xii.
8. Oscar Wilde to the editor of the *Daily Telegraph*, 19 February 1892, in *Complete Letters*, pp. 518–20, p. 520.
9. Oscar Wilde, *Lady Windermere's Fan*, in *The Importance of Being Earnest and Other Plays*, Act 3, pp. 44–5.
10. Ibid. p. 45.
11. Wilde, 'The Critic as Artist', in *Complete Works*, vol. 4, pp. 124–206, p. 203.

12. Wilde, 'The Soul of Man', in *Complete Works*, vol. 4, p. 250.
13. Baroness Franzisca von Hedemann, 'A Reminiscence of Lovely Days between the Sun God and Pan', p. 1, from 'Two Articles on Oscar Wilde', UCLA Clark Library, Wilde H452M3 T974.
14. Wilde to William Ward, 26 July 1876, in *Complete Letters*, p. 26. Wilde wrote of Barrett Browning's work: 'It is one of those books that, written straight from the heart – and from such a large heart too – never weary one: because they are sincere. We tire of art but not of nature after all our aesthetic training.'
15. Wilde to Lord Alfred Douglas, in *Complete Letters*, January-March 1897, pp. 683–780, p. 747.
16. Wilde, 'The Soul of Man', in *Complete Works*, vol. 4, p. 250.
17. Wilde, 'The Soul of Man', in *Complete Works*, vol. 4, pp. 229–68, p. 250.
18. See Eagleton, 'Foreword', in *Saint Oscar*, pp. ix–x.
19. Coulson Kernahan believed that Wilde's vanity, along with the 'devils' doctrines' espoused by Henry Wotton in *The Picture of Dorian Gray*, were proof of his having been a victim of demonic possession. See Coulson Kernahan, *In Good Company* (London: John Lane, 1917), pp. 228–35. Quotation on p. 228.
20. *New York Mirror*, 25 August 1883, quoted in Mason, *Bibliography of Oscar Wilde*, p. 273.

Bibliography

Anon., *Oscar Wilde: Three Times Tried* (Paris: privately published, nd. [1912?]).

Arata, Steven, 'Oscar Wilde and Jesus Christ', in Joseph Bristow (ed.), *Wilde Writings: Contextual Conditions* (Toronto: University of Toronto Press, 2013), pp. 254–72.

Arnold, Matthew, *The Study of Celtic Literature and Other Essays* (London: Dent, 1919).

— *Culture and Anarchy* (Cambridge: Cambridge University Press, 1994).

Backus, Margot Gayle, *The Gothic Family Romance: Heterosexuality, Child Sacrifice and the Anglo-Irish Colonial Order* (Durham, NC: Duke University Press, 1999).

Barlas, John E., 'Oscar Wilde: A Study', *The Novel Review*, 1.1, April 1892, pp. 42–6.

Beaumont, Matthew, *Utopia Ltd.: Ideologies of Social Dreaming in England, 1870–1900* (Chicago: Haymarket Books, 2009).

Beckson, Karl, *Oscar Wilde: The Critical Heritage* (London: Routledge [1970], 2005).

Bevir, Mark, *The Making of British Socialism* (Princeton: Princeton University Press, 2011).

Bloom, Clive, *Violent London: 2,000 Years of Riots, Rebels and Revolts* (London: Pan, 2004).

Bristow, Joseph, 'Introduction', in Joseph Bristow (ed.), *Wilde Writings: Contextual Conditions* (Toronto: University of Toronto Press, 2003), pp. 1–38.

Bristow, Joseph (ed.), *Wilde Discoveries: Traditions, Histories, Archives* (Toronto: University of Toronto Press, 2013).

Butterworth, Alex, *The World That Never Was: Dreamers, Schemers and Secret Agents* (London: Bodley Head, 2010).

Campbell, James, 'Sexual Gnosticism: The Procreative Code of "The Portrait of Mr. W.H."', in Joseph Bristow (ed.), *Wilde Discoveries: Traditions, Histories, Archives* (Toronto: University of Toronto Press, 2013), pp. 169–89.

Carlyle, Thomas, *The French Revolution: A History* (originally published, 1837; Oxford: Oxford University Press, 2019), p. 559.

Carpenter, Edward, *Towards Democracy* (London: John Heywood, 1883–1902, reprinted London: GMP, 1985).

Castle, Gregory, *Modernism and the Celtic Revival* (Cambridge: Cambridge University Press, 2001).

— 'Misrecognising Wilde: Media and Performance on the American Tour of 1882', in Joseph Bristow (ed.), *Wilde Discoveries: Traditions, Histories, Archives* (Toronto: University of Toronto Press, 2013), pp. 85–117.

Cleary, Joe, *Outrageous Fortune: Capital and Culture in Modern Ireland* (Dublin: Field Day Publications, 2007).

— 'Republicanism and Aristocracy in Modern Ireland', *Field Day Review*, 10 (2014), pp. 4–39.

Clover, Joshua, *Riot, Strike. Riot: The Era of New Uprisings* (London: Verso, 2016).

Cohen, Philip K., *The Moral Vision of Oscar Wilde* (Madison: Fairleigh Dickinson University Press, 1978).

— *John Evelyn Barlas: A Critical Biography* (High Wycombe: Rivendale Press, 2012).

Cole, Sarah, *At the Violet Hour: Modernism and Violence in England and Ireland* (Oxford: Oxford University Press, 2012).

Crary, Jonathan, *Techniques of the Observer: On Vision and Modernity in the Nineteenth Century* (Cambridge, MA: MIT Press, 1990)

— *Suspensions of Perception: Attention, Spectacle and Modern Culture* (Cambridge, MA: MIT Press, 1999).

Curtis, Liz, *Nothing But the Same Old Story: The Roots of Anti-Irish Racism* (London: Information on Ireland, 1983).

Curtis, L. Perry, *Apes and Angels: The Irishman in Victorian Caricature* (Washington, DC: Smithsonian Institution Press, 1997).

Daly, Nicholas, *Modernism, Romance and the Fin de Siècle: Popular Fiction and British Culture, 1880–1914* (Cambridge: Cambridge University Press, 1999).

—*The Demographic Imagination and the Nineteenth-Century City: Paris, London, New York* (Cambridge: Cambridge University Press, 2015).

Danson, Lawrence, *Wilde's Intentions: The Artist in his Criticism* (Oxford: Oxford University Press, 1987).

Davitt, Michael, *Leaves from a Prison Diary; Or, Lectures to a 'Solitary' Audience*, vol. 2 (London: Chapman and Hall, 1885).

— *The Fall of Feudalism in Ireland, or The Story of the Land League Revolution* (London: Harper & Brothers, 1904).

Deane, Seamus, *Strange Country: Modernity and Nationhood in Irish Writing since 1790* (Oxford: Oxford University Press, 1997).

De Bouhélier, Saint-Georges, 'The Soul of Man Under Socialism', *Liberty*, 16.4, October 1907, pp. 45–9.

Dryden, Linda, *The Modern Gothic and Literary Doubles: Stevenson, Wilde and Wells* (Basingstoke: Palgrave, 2003).

Eagleton, Terry, 'Foreword', in *Saint Oscar* (Derry: Field Day, 1989).

— *Heathcliff and the Great Hunger: Studies in Irish Culture* (London: Verso, 1995).

Edwards, Owen Dudley, 'Impressions of an Irish Sphinx', in Jerusha McCormack (ed.), *Wilde the Irishman* (New Haven: Yale University Press, 1998), pp. 55–6.

Ellmann, Richard, *Oscar Wilde* (New York: Knopf, 1988).

Eltis, Sos, *Revising Wilde: Society and Subversion in the Plays of Oscar Wilde* (Oxford: Clarendon Press, 1996).

Farrell, Michael, *Emergency Legislation: The Apparatus of Repression* (Derry: Field Day, 1986), p. 5.

Foldy, Michael, *The Trials of Oscar Wilde* (New Haven: Yale University Press, 2007).

Ford, Ford Madox, 'Memories of Oscar Wilde: On the Collapse of a Famous Writer and his Final Attempts to Shock the Bourgeoisie', in *The Saturday Review Cavalcade: A 25-Year Anthology* (Saturday Review Associates, Inc. [no place of publication, no original date of publication], 1950), pp. 22–31, p. 22.

Frankel, Nicholas, *Oscar Wilde: The Unrepentant Years* (Cambridge, MA: Harvard University Press, 2017).

Freeman, Nicholas, *1895: Drama, Disaster and Disgrace in Late Victorian Britain* (Edinburgh: Edinburgh University Press, 2011).

Friedman, David M., *Wilde in America: Oscar Wilde and the Invention of Modern Celebrity* (New York: Norton, 2014)

Froude, James Anthony, 'A Fortnight in Kerry. Part 1', in *Short Studies on Great Subjects* (New York: Charles Scribner and Company, 1872), pp. 178–210.

Gagnier, Regenia, *Idylls of the Marketplace: Oscar Wilde and the Victorian Public* (Stanford: Stanford University Press, 1986).

Gandhi, Leela, *Affective Communities: Anticolonial Thought, Fin-de-Siècle Radicalism, and the Politics of Friendship* (Durham, NC: Duke University Press, 2006).

Gerald of Wales, *The History and Topography of Ireland* (trans. from the Latin by John J. O'Meara, London: Penguin, 1982).

Goldman, Emma, *Anarchism and Other Essays* (originally published 1911, reprinted New York: Dover, 1969).

Goodway, David, *Anarchist Seeds Beneath the Snow: Left-Libertarian Thought and British Writers* (Liverpool: Liverpool University Press, 2006).

Grave, Jean, *Moribund Society and Anarchy*, trans. from *Société mourante et l'anarchie* by Voltairine de Cleyre (San Francisco: Free Society Library, 1899).

Guy, Josephine M., '"The Soul of Man Under Socialism": A (Con)Textual History, in Joseph Bristow (ed.), *Wilde Writings: Contextual Conditions* (Toronto: University of Toronto Press, 2003), pp. 59–85.

Guy, Josephine M. and Ian Small, *Oscar Wilde's Profession: Writing and the Culture Industry in the Late Nineteenth Century* (Oxford: Oxford University Press, 2000).

Harris, Frank, *Oscar Wilde: His Life and Confessions* (Ware: Wordsworth, 2007).

Halperin, Joan Ungersma, *Félix Fénéon: Aesthete and Anarchist in Fin-de Siècle Paris* (New Haven: Yale University Press, 1989).

Hazan, Eric, *A History of the Barricade* (trans. by David Fernbach from *La Barricade: Histoire d'un objet révolutionnaire*, Éditions Autrement, 2013; London: Verso, 2015).

Henderson, Archibald, 'The Dramas of Oscar Wilde', *Arena*, 38, August 1907, pp. 134–9, reprinted in Karl Beckson (ed.), *Oscar Wilde: The Critical Heritage* (London and New York: Routledge, 1970), pp. 270–7.

Hext, Kate, *Walter Pater: Individualism and Aesthetic Philosophy* (Edinburgh: Edinburgh University Press, 2013).

Hichens, Robert, *The Green Carnation* (London: Robin Clark, 1992).

Holland, Merlin (ed.), *Irish Peacock and Scarlet Marquess: The Real Trial of Oscar Wilde* (London: Fourth Estate, 2004).

Holland, Vyvyan, *The Son of Oscar Wilde* (Oxford: Oxford University Press, 1987).

Hugo, Victor, *Les Misérables* (Paris: Gallimard, 2017).

Huysmans, Joris Karl, *À Rebours* (Paris: Gallimard, 1983).

Iandoli, Louis J., 'The Palace of the Tuileries and its Demolition', *The French Review*, 79.5, April 2006, pp. 998–1008.

Kenneally, Ian, *From the Earth, a Cry: The Story of John Boyle O'Reilly* (Dublin: Collins Press, 2011).

Kernahan, Coulson, *In Good Company* (London: John Lane, 1917).

Killeen, Jarlath, *The Fairy Tales of Oscar Wilde* (Aldershot: Ashgate, 2007).

Kinealy, Christine, *This Great Calamity: The Irish Famine, 1845–52* (Dublin: Gill and Macmillan, 1994).

Klein, Naomi, *The Shock Doctrine: The Rise of Disaster Capitalism* (London: Penguin, 2007).

Kohl, Norbert, *Oscar Wilde: The Works of a Conformist Rebel* (Cambridge: Cambridge University Press, 1989), originally published as *Oscar Wilde: Das literarische Werk zwischen Provokation und Anpassung* (Heidelberg: Carl Winter Universitätsverlag, 1980).

Kropotkin, Peter (as 'Prince Kropotkin), *Ideals and Realities in Russian Literature* (New York: Knopf, 1915).
— *Anarchism: A Collection of Revolutionary Writings* (New York: Dover, 1970).
— *Mutual Aid: A Factor of Evolution* (Mineola, NY: Dover, 2006).
— *The Conquest of Bread* (London: Penguin, 2015).
Laird, Heather, 'Decentring the Irish Land War: Women, Politics and the Private Sphere', in Fergus Campbell and Tony Varley (eds), *Land Questions in Modern Ireland* (Manchester: Manchester University Press, 2013), pp. 175–93.
Le Bon, Gustave, *The Crowd: A Study of the Popular Mind* (trans. from *La Psychologie des foules*, London: T. Fisher Unwin, 1909).
Leersseen, Joep, *Remembrance and Imagination: Patterns in the Historical and Literary Representation of Ireland in the Nineteenth Century* (Cork: Cork University Press, 1996).
Lewis, Lloyd and Henry Justin Smith, *Oscar Wilde Discovers America, 1882* (New York: Harcourt, Brace and Company, 1936).
Linton, William James., *Ireland for the Irish: Rhymes and Reasons Against Landlordism* (New York: The American News Company, 1867).
Livesey, Ruth, *Socialism, Sex and the Culture of Aestheticism in Britain, 1880–1914* (Oxford: Oxford University Press, 2007).
Lloyd, David, *Nationalism and Minor Literature: James Clarence Mangan and the Emergence of Irish Cultural Nationalism* (Berkeley: University of California Press, 1987).
— *Ireland after History* (Cork: Cork University Press, 1999).
— *Irish Culture and Colonial Modernity: The Transformation of Oral Space, 1800–2000* (Cambridge: Cambridge University Press, 2011).
Lloyd, David and Paul Thomas, *Culture and the State* (New York: Routledge, 1998).
Lyons, Francis Stewart Leland, *Charles Stewart Parnell* (London: Fontana, 1978).
MacLeod, Kirsten, *Fictions of British Decadence: High Art, Popular Writing, and the Fin de Siècle* (Basingstoke: Palgrave, 2006).
Malthus, Thomas, *An Essay on the Principle of Population* (originally published 1798; reprinted London: Penguin, 1985).
Maltz, Diana, *British Aestheticism and the Urban Working Classes, 1870–1900: Beauty for the People* (Basingstoke: Palgrave, 2006).
Marez, Curtis, 'The Other Addict: Reflections on Colonialism and Oscar Wilde's Opium Smoke Screen', *ELH*, 64.1 (Spring 1997), pp. 257–87.
Markey, Ann, *Oscar Wilde's Fairy Tales: Origins and Contexts* (Dublin: Irish Academic Press, 2015).
Marlow, Louis, 'The Gorgon's Head', *Adam International Review*, 241–3 (1954), p. 15.

Martell, Jessica, 'Food Sovereignty, the *Irish Homestead*, and the First World War', *Modernist Cultures* 13.3, August 2018, pp. 399–416.

Martin, Amy E., *Alter-Nations: Nationalisms, Terror, and the State in Nineteenth-Century Britain and Ireland* (Columbus: Ohio State University Press, 2012).

— 'Victorian Ireland: Race and the Category of the Human', *Victorian Review*, 40.1, Spring 2014, pp. 52–7.

Marx, Jenny (as J. Williams), 'Agrarian Outrages in Ireland', *La Marseillaise*, 2 April 1870, reprinted in Marx and Engels, *Ireland and the Irish Question*, pp. 396–9, pp. 396–7.

Marx, Karl, *Grundrisse: Foundations of the Critique of Political Economy (Rough Draft)*, trans. from *Grundrisse der Kritik der Politischen Ökonomie (Rohentwurf)* by Martin Nicolaus (London: Penguin, 1973).

— *Capital*, vol. 1 (trans. from the German by Ben Fowkes, London: Penguin, 1990).

Marx, Karl and Frederick Engels, *Ireland and the Irish Question* (London: Lawrence and Wishart, 1971).

Mason, Stuart, *Oscar Wilde: Art and Morality* (London: Frank Palmer, 1907, reprinted 1912).

— *Oscar Wilde: Three Times Tried* (London: Ferrestone Press, 1912).

— *Bibliography of Oscar Wilde* (London: T. Werner Laurie, 1914).

— *Oscar Wilde and the Aesthetic Movement* (Dublin: Townley Searle, 1920).

McCormack, Jerusha, 'The Wilde Irishman: Oscar as Aesthete and Anarchist', in Jerusha McCormack (ed.), *Wilde the Irishman* (New Haven: Yale University Press, 1998), pp. 82–94, p. 83.

— 'Oscar Wilde: As Daoist Sage', in Michael Y. Bennett (ed.), *Philosophy and Oscar Wilde* (Basingstoke: Palgrave, 2017), pp. 73–104.

McFeeley, Deirdre, *Dion Boucicault: Irish Identity on Stage* (Cambridge: Cambridge University Press, 2012).

Melchiori, Barbara Arnett, *Terrorism in the Late Victorian Novel* (London: Croom Helm, 1985).

Melville, Herman, *Moby-Dick or, The Whale* (London: Penguin, 2003).

Melville, Joy, *Mother of Oscar Wilde: The Life of Jane Francesca Wilde* (London: Allison and Busby, 1999).

Mendelsohn, Michèlle, *Making Oscar Wilde* (Oxford: Oxford University Press, 2018).

Meredith, Isabel, *A Girl Among the Anarchists* (Lincoln: University of Nebraska Press, 1992).

Merriman, John, *Massacre: The Life and Death of the Paris Commune of 1871* (New Haven: Yale University Press, 2014).

Miller, Elizabeth Carolyn, 'Reconsidering Wilde's *Vera; or, The Nihilists*', in Joseph Bristow (ed.), *Wilde Discoveries: Traditions, Histories, Archives* (Toronto: University of Toronto Press, 2013), pp. 65–84.

— *Slow Print: Literary Radicalism and Late Victorian Print Culture* (Stanford: Stanford University Press, 2013).

Morley, John, *The Life of William Ewart Gladstone* (London: MacMillan, 1903), vol. 2.

Mulry, David, *Joseph Conrad Among the Anarchists: Nineteenth-Century Terrorism and The Secret Agent* (London: Palgrave, 2016).

Nordau, Max, *Degeneration* (New York: D. Appleton and Company, 1895).

Nunokawa, Jeff, *The Tame Passions of Oscar Wilde: The Styles of Manageable Desire* (Princeton: Princeton University Press, 2003).

O'Brien, Gillian, *Blood Runs Green: The Murder that Transfixed Gilded Age Chicago* (Chicago: University of Chicago Press, 2015).

— 'Methodology and Martyrs: Irish American Republicanism in the Late Nineteenth Century', in Peter S. Herman (ed.), *Terrorism and Literature* (Cambridge: Cambridge University Press, 2018), pp. 70–89.

Ó Donghaile, Deaglán, *Blasted Literature: Victorian Political Fiction and the Shock of Modernism* (Edinburgh: Edinburgh University Press, 2011).

O'Grady, Standish, *The Crisis in Ireland* (Dublin: E. Ponsonby, 1882).

Parker, Jay Thomas, '"He was one of us": Rortyian Liberal Ethnocentrism and Ironic Narrative Voice in Joseph Conrad's *Lord Jim*', *Textual Practice*, 31.4, 2017, pp. 823–38.

Parnell, Anna, *The Tale of a Great Sham* (Dublin: Arlen House, 1986).

Parry, Jonathan, 'Cavendish, Spencer Compton, Marquess of Hartington and Eighth Duke of Devonshire (1833–1908)', *Oxford Dictionary of National Biography*, Oxford University Press, 2004; online edition, 2008 <http://www.oxforddnb.com/view/article/32331>, accessed 13 January 2017.

Pater, Walter, *Marius the Epicurean* (London: Penguin, 1985).

— *The Renaissance: Studies in Art and Poetry* (Oxford: Oxford University Press, 1998).

Pierse, Michael, *Writing Ireland's Working Class: Dublin after O'Casey* (Basingstoke: Palgrave, 2011).

Playfair, I., *Gentle Criticisms on British Justice* (privately published, 1895). UCLA Clark Library Wilde W749M3 G338 [1895].

Plotz, Matthew, *The Crowd: British Literature and Public Politics* (Berkeley: University of California Press, 2000).

Powys, John Cowper, 'Oscar Wilde', in *Essays on Joseph Conrad and Oscar Wilde* (Girard, KS: Haldeman-Julius, 1916), pp. 29–49.

Reich, Emile, 'Art and the People', *Free Society* (San Francisco), New Series No. 22, Whole No. 158, Sunday, 10 April 1890, pp. 5–6.

Rose, David, 'Oscar Wilde: Socialite or Socialist', in Ewe Boker, Richard Corballis and Julie Hibbard (eds), *The Importance of Reinventing Oscar: Versions of Wilde during the Last 100 Years* (Amsterdam: Rodopi, 2002), pp. 35–56.

Rogers, William Warren, 'In Defense of Oscar Wilde: Mary E. Bulloch on his Savannah Appearance in 1882', *The Georgia Historical Quarterly* 84.3, Fall 1990.

Ross, Margery (ed.), *Robert Ross, Friend of Friends: Letters to Robert Ross, Art Critic and Writer* (London: Jonathan Cape, 1952).

Ruff, Felicia J., 'Transgressive Props: Or Oscar Wilde's E(a)rnest Signifier', in Joseph Bristow (ed.), *Wilde Discoveries: Traditions, Histories, Archives* (Toronto: University of Toronto Press, 2013), pp. 315–35.

Ruskin, John, 'Idolatry', in *Aratra Pentelici* (London: George Allen, 1907), pp. 35–68.

— *Unto This Last and Other Essays on Art and Political Economy* (London: Dent, 1913).

Said, Edward, *Orientalism* (London: Penguin, 1995).

Sanders, Mike, *The Poetry of Chartism: Aesthetics, Politics, History* (Cambridge: Cambridge University Press, 2012).

Shaffer, Talia, 'The Origins of the Aesthetic Novel: Ouida, Wilde and the Popular Romance', in Joseph Bristow (ed.), *Wilde Writings: Contextual Conditions* (Toronto: University of Toronto Press, 2013), pp. 212–29.

Shaw, George Bernard, *The Impossibilities of Anarchism* (London: The Fabian Society, 1895).

Sherard, Robert Harborough, *Oscar Wilde: The Story of an Unhappy Friendship* (London: Greening & Co., 1909).

— *The Life of Oscar Wilde* (London: T. Werner Laurie, 1906, reprinted 1911).

Sherry, Vincent, *Modernism and the Reinvention of Decadence* (Cambridge: Cambridge University Press, 2015).

Singer, Ben, *Melodrama and Modernity: Early Sensational Cinema and its Contexts* (New York: Columbia University Press, 2001).

Sloan, John, *Oscar Wilde: Myths, Miracles and Imitations* (Cambridge: Cambridge University Press, 1996), p. 54.

Sonn, Richard D., *Anarchism and Cultural Politics in Fin de Siècle France* (Lincoln: University of Nebraska Press, 1989).

Stepniak, Sergius, *The Russian Storm-Cloud or, Russia in Her Relations to Neighbouring Countries* (London: Swan Sonnenschein, 1886).

Stevenson, Robert Louis, 'Confessions of a Unionist: An Unpublished "talk on things current"' (Cambridge, MA: Privately Published, 1921).

Stokes, John and Turner, Mark W., 'Introduction', in *The Complete Works of Oscar Wilde*, vol. 6: *Journalism* 1 (Oxford: Oxford University Press, 2013), pp. xi-li.

Sturgis, Matthew, *Oscar: A Life* (London: Head of Zeus, 2018).

Sumpter, Caroline, *The Victorian Press and the Fairy Tale* (Basingstoke: Palgrave, 2008).

Symons, Arthur, *A Study of Oscar Wilde* (London: Charles J. Sawyer, 1930).

Thompson, Edward Palmer, *The Making of the English Working Class* (London: Penguin, 1968).

Tickell, Alex, *Terrorism, Insurgency and Indian-English Literature, 1830–1947* (New York: Routledge, 2012), p. 13.

Tolstoy, Leo, *The Kingdom of God is Within You and Peace Essays* (trans. by Aylmer Maude, 1894, reprinted New Delhi: Rupa, 2001).

Tracy, Robert, 'Introduction', in Joseph Sheridan Le Fanu, *In a Glass Darkly* (Oxford: Oxford University Press, 2008), pp. vii–xviii.

Turgenev, Ivan, *Fathers and Sons* (trans. from the Russian by Richard Freeborn, Oxford: Oxford University Press, 1991).

Valente, Joseph, *Dracula's Crypt: Bram Stoker, Irishness and the Question of Blood* (Urbana and Chicago: University of Illinois Press, 2002).

Ward, Margaret, *Unmanageable Revolutionaries: Women and Irish Nationalism* (London: Pluto, 1995).

Watson, Mary, *People I Have Met: Short Sketches of Many Prominent Persons* (San Francisco: Francis, Valentine and Company, 1890).

Weir, David, *Anarchy and Culture: The Aesthetic Politics of Modernism* (Amherst: University of Massachusetts Press, 1992).

Whelan, Kevin, 'The Memories of "The Dead"', *The Yale Journal of Criticism*, 15.1 (2002), pp. 59–97.

Whelehan, Niall, *The Dynamiters: Irish Nationalism and Political Violence in the Wider World, 1867–1900* (Cambridge: Cambridge University Press, 2012).

Wilde, Jane Francesca, 'The American Irish' (Dublin: William McGee, 1882, originally published New York, 1879).

— (as Lady Wilde), *Poems by Speranza* (Dublin: James Duffy, 1864).

— (as Lady Wilde), *Poems by Speranza* (Glasgow: Cameron and Ferguson, 1871).

Wilde, Oscar, 'Béranger in England', *Pall Mall Gazette*, 21 April 1886, in Robert Ross (ed.), *Collected Works*, vol. 12: *Reviews* 1 (Boston: John Luce & Co., 1908), pp. 60–2, p. 61.

— 'Common-Sense in Art', *Pall Mall Gazette*, 8 January 1887, in Robert Ross (ed.), *Collected Works*, vol. 12, *Reviews* 1 (Boston: John Luce & Co., 1908), pp. 119–23, p. 121.

— *Miscellanies* (London: Methuen, 1908).
— 'Mr. Morris's *Odyssey*', *Pall Mall Gazette*, 26 April 1887, in Robert Ross (ed.), *Collected Works*, vol. 12, *Reviews* 1 (Boston: John Luce & Co., 1908), pp. 153–7.
— 'The American Invasion', in Robert Ross (ed.), *Collected Works*, vol. 14, *Miscellanies* (Boston: John Luce & Co., 1908), pp. 77–82.
— 'Irish Poets and Poetry of the Nineteenth Century' (San Francisco: The Book Club of California, 1972).
— 'Impressions of America' (privately published by Mildred Sherrod Bissinger, Kentfield, CA, 1975).
— *The Complete Works of Oscar Wilde* (London: HarperCollins, 2003).
— *The Complete Letters of Oscar Wilde* (London: Fourth Estate, 2000).
— *The Complete Works of Oscar Wilde*, vol. 1: *Poems and Poems in Prose*, ed. Bobby Fong and Karl Beckson (Oxford: Oxford University Press, 2000).
— *The Complete Works of Oscar Wilde*, vol. 2: *De Profundis; Epistola: In Carcere et Vinculis*, ed. Ian Small (Oxford: Oxford University Press, 2005).
— *The Complete Works of Oscar Wilde*, vol. 3: *The Picture of Dorian Gray: The 1890 and 1891 Texts*, ed. Joseph Bristow (Oxford: Oxford University Press, 2005).
— *The Complete Works of Oscar Wilde*, vol. 4: *Criticism*, ed. Josephine M. Guy (Oxford: Oxford University Press, 2007).
— *The Importance of Being Earnest and Other Plays* (Oxford: Oxford University Press, 2008).
— *Complete Poetry* (Oxford: Oxford University Press, 2009).
— *The Complete Short Stories* (Oxford: Oxford University Press, 2010).
— *The Complete Works of Oscar Wilde*, vol. 6: *Journalism* 1, ed. John Stokes and Mark W. Turner (Oxford: Oxford University Press, 2013).
— *The Complete Works of Oscar Wilde*, vol. 7: *Journalism* 2, ed. John Stokes and Mark W. Turner (Oxford: Oxford University Press, 2013).
Wilde, William, *Lough Corrib, its Shores and Islands* (Dublin: McGlashan and Gill, 1867).
Wilson, Charlotte (as 'An English Anarchist'), 'Justice', *The Anarchist*, 1.5, July 1885, reprinted in Charlotte Wilson, *Anarchist Essays* (London: Freedom Press, 2000), pp. 29–30.
Woodcock, George, *The Paradox of Oscar Wilde* (London and New York: Boardman & Co., 1949).
Žižek, Slavoj, *Violence: Six Sideways Reflections* (London: Profile, 2008).
— *Event* (London: Penguin, 2014).

Archives

Correspondence

Carte, Richard D'Oyly, to Howard Paul, 25 December 1881. UCLA Clark Library Wilde C322L P324 1881 Dec. 25, Box 10, Folder 43.

Forbes, Archibald, to Oscar Wilde, 26 January 1882. UCLA Clark Library Wilde F692L W6721 1882 Jan. 26.

Marbury, Elizabeth, to Oscar Wilde, 10 November 1894. UCLA Clark Library Wilde M312L W6721 [1894?] Nov. 10.

O'Keeffe, C. M., to William Wilde, 20 September 1862. UCLA Clark Library Wilde 04122L W6723 1862 Sep. 20.

O'Keeffe, C. M., to Lady Wilde, 23 June 186–?. UCLA Clark Library Wilde 04122L W6712 [186]? Jun. 23.

Sauls, Charles G., to Oscar Wilde, 2 October 1882. UCLA Clark Library, Wilde S256L W672 1882 Oct. 2.

Wilde, Jane Francesca, to Oscar Wilde, 8 May 1882. UCLA Clark Library Wilde W6712L W6721 [1882?] May 8.

Manuscripts, Press Cuttings and Miscellaneous Material

UCLA Clark Library

Bell, Thomas Hastie, *Oscar Wilde without Whitewash*, MS. Wilde B435M3 0814 [19–]?

Carte, Richard D'Oyly, 'Oscar Wilde's Visit to America', 4 February 1882. Uncat. Wilde MSS, pp. 1–2.

'Editorial', *Denver Daily Times*, 13 April 1882, in Glaenzer, *Wildeana*, Folder 11.

'E. M. N.' to the *Philadelphia Times*, undated (early 1882), in Glaenzer, *Wildeana*, Folder 6, p. 20. Wilde G54M3 081.

'Exit Oscar', *Truth*, 19 July 1883 (no page no.), *Wildeana*, Box 10: 'Wilde in America', 10.19.

Glaenzer, Richard Butler, *Oscar Wilde in America*, unpublished MSS, Folder 5. Wilde G543M3 081 [1900–20].

'Impressions of an Impressionist', *Punch*, 21 July 1883 (no page no.), *Wildeana*, Box 10: *Wilde in America*, 10.16.

'Mr. Oscar Wilde's "Impressions"', *The Daily Telegraph*, 12 July 1883 (no page no.), *Wildeana*, Box 10: *Wilde in America*, 10.17B.

'Mr. Oscar Wilde on America', cutting from *Freeman's Journal*, 11 July 1883 (no page no.), Box 10: *Wilde in America*, 10.18 A.

'Mr. Oscar Wilde on America', cutting from *Freeman's Journal*, 11 July 1883 (no page no.), *Wildeana*, Box 10: *Wilde in America*, 10.18 A.

'Mr. Oscar Wilde on America', *The West Midlands Advertiser and Chelsea and Pimlico Chronicle*, 14 July 1883 (no page no.), *Wildeana*, Box 10: *Wilde in America*, 10.17 A.

'Oscar Wilde's Lecture', *Denver Daily Times*, 13 April 1882, recorded in Richard Butler Glaenzer, *Oscar Wilde in America* (unpublished MS. and notes), *Wildeana*, Folder 11.

Pall Mall Gazette, 7 July 1883. (untitled, no page no.), Glaenzer, *Wildeana*, Box 10: *Wilde in America* 10.15A.

Untitled, *Denver Daily Times*, 11 April 1882, Glaenzer, *Oscar Wilde in America*, Folder 11.

Von Hedemann, Baroness Franzisca, 'A Reminiscence of Lovely Days between the Sun God and Pan', p. 1, from 'Two Articles on Oscar Wilde', UCLA Clark Library, Wilde H452M3 T974.

Huntington Library

Wilde, Oscar, 'The Soul of Man Under Socialism' (New York: The Humboldt Publishing Company, n.d.), Huntington Library's Jack London Collection (Ephemera: Pamphlets, W-Z, JLE 2208).

Contemporary Newspapers and Periodicals

'Art and Aesthetics', *The Tribune* (Denver), 13 April 1882, p. 8.
'Asinine Oblations', *The Wasp*, 9.333, 16 December 1882, pp. 791–2.
Cohen, Alexander, untitled, *The Torch*, 2.1, 18 June 1895, p. 6.
'Funeral of Lord F. Cavendish at Chatsworth', *Illustrated London News*, 20 May 1882, p. 501.
'Funeral of Mr. Burke at Dublin', *Illustrated London News*, 20 May 1882, p. 501.
'Home Rule', *Punch*, 4 April 1885, p. 162.
'Irish Secret Societies', *The Wasp*, 10.357, 2 June 1883, p. 12.
'Lady Cavendish on the Evil in Ireland', *Evening News*, 13 May 1882, p. 3.
'Land League: Proclamation of the President of the American Branch', *Philadelphia Enquirer*, 8 May 1882, p. 1.
'Murder Made Easy: A Ballad à la Mode. By "Brother Jonathan"' Wilde', *Punch*, 14 January 1882, p. 18.
'Mr Oscar Wilde's Play', *Derby Daily Telegraph*, 22 August 1883, p. 4
'News at Home and Abroad', *The Torch*, 2.2, July 1895, p. 17.
'Oscar Wilde – Very Wild', *Moonshine*, 18 March 1882, p. 129.

'Oscar Wilde's Lecture', *The Evening Light* (San Antonio), 22 June 1882.
'Reign of Murder in Ireland', *Manchester Courier*, 9 May 1882, p. 5.
'Serious Affray at Ballina', *Daily News*, 8 May 1882, p. 3.
'Swinburne and Water', *Punch*, 23 July 1881, p. 26.
'The Affray in Ballina', *The Freeman's Journal*, 8 May 1882, p. 2.
'The Assassinations in Dublin', *The Times*, 9 May 1882, p. 6.
'The Assassinations in Dublin', *The Times*, 12 May 1882, p. 10.
'The Ballina Tragedy', *Freeman's Journal*, 25 May 1882, p. 3.
'The Ballina Tragedy', *Freeman's Journal*, 24 May 1882, p. 5.
'The Fenian Murders in Dublin', *Illustrated London News*, 20 May 1882, p. 489.
'The Play's Not the Thing', *Punch*, 1 September 1883, p. 99.
'The Poet's Corner', *Pall Mall Gazette*, 24 June 1889, p. 3.
'To an Æsethtic Poet', *Punch*, 14 January 1882, p. 18.
Untitled, *Sporting Times*, 8 February 1896, p. 7.
Untitled, *The Wasp*, 9.333, 16 December 1882, p. 797.

Index

Adey, More, 201
aestheticism, 1–4, 7–9, 14, 17, 19–21, 36, 51, 60, 88–92, 96, 100–1, 113, 127–8, 141–2, 144, 151–2, 154–68, 228, 230
Afghan War of 1878–80, 58, 140
anarchism, 9, 15–16, 25n, 26n, 93, 103, 106, 110–12, 122, 158, 164, 168, 207
Anglo-Egyptian War, 140
Arnold, Matthew
   Culture and Anarchy, 9, 33, 52n
   'On the Study of Celtic Literature', 30–6, 38–40, 42, 49, 207

Bakhtin, Mikhail, 231
Balfour, Arthur, 61, 95, 97, 205–6
Barlas, John, 15–16, 88, 151–7, 163, 172n, 201
Baudelaire, Charles, 100, 207, 230
Bell, Thomas Hastie, 13, 15, 25n, 99, 212
Bierce, Ambrose, 27, 37
Blunt, Wilfred Scawen, 6, 9, 205–6
Bonaparte, Napoleon, 50

Boston Pilot, 13
Boucicault, Dion, 59–60
Brecht, Bertolt, 231
Bristow, Joseph, 170n, 201, 223n
Brown, Terence, 191
Burke, Edmund, 2
Burke, Thomas, 58, 62–6
Burne-Jones, Edward, 207
Byron, George Gordon, 50, 100

Carlyle, Thomas, *The French Revolution: A History*, 104
Carpenter, Edward, 9, 13
   Towards Democracy, 155
Carson, Edward, 202
Carte, Richard D'Oyly, 37–8
Catalpa Rescue, 30
Cavendish, Frederick, 58, 62–5, 83–4n
Chicago Morning News, 36
Christ, Jesus, 10, 41, 110, 122, 124, 129–34, 142–3, 205, 210–12, 218–22, 230
Christian Leader, The, 159, 162
Cleary, Joe, 15, 134–5, 148n
Coercion Acts, The, 4–6, 52n, 77
Cohen, Alexander, 12
Commonweal, 201
Criminal Law Amendment Act, 203

Daily Chronicle, 204, 159, 217
Daly, Nicolas, 143, 148n, 198n
Davitt, Michael, 6, 48, 53n, 62, 64–5, 73, 132–3, 203–4, 222
De Bouhélier, Saint-Georges, 13
Democratic Federation, The, 95
Douglas, Alfred, 201, 205–7, 210, 212
Dryden, Linda, 161–2
Dublin University Magazine, 17

Eagleton, Terry, 9–10, 86n, 133–4, 231
Eltis, Sos, 58, 60, 69, 83n, 175–6, 182, 195
Emmet, Robert, 38, 206–7, 212
Engels, Frederick, 39–40, 54n, 67, 121, 145–6n

Fénéon, Félix, 16
Fenians, The, 3–4, 6, 12–13, 30–1, 36, 39, 52n, 53n, 59, 61–8, 77, 145–6n, 160–1, 182, 189–90, 203–4, 223n
Ford, Ford Madox, 202
Fortnightly Review, The, 98, 201
Frankel, Nicholas, 204–5, 224n
Froude, James Anthony, 18, 98

Gagnier, Regenia, 150–1, 158, 175–7, 204–5, 218–19
Gandhi, Leela, 9, 11
Gautier, Théophile, 153
Giraldus Cambrensis, 18, 27n
Gladstone, William Ewart, 79, 86n, 95–6
Goethe, Johann Wolfgang von, 50, 229–30
Goldman, Emma, 15, 26n
Grave, Jean, 26n, 112

Great Hunger, The, 40, 61, 69, 75–7, 81, 115, 132–41, 183, 191–4, 197–8n
Guiteau, Charles J., 65

Habeas Corpus, suspension of, 30, 61, 84, 218
Henley, W. E., 160–3
Hichens, Robert, *The Green Carnation*, 14
Home Rule, 161
homosexuality, 98, 181–2
  criminalisation of, 201–3, 222–3
  politicisation of, 170n
Hugo, Victor, 99, 100, 207
  Les Misérables, 128
Huysmans, Joris-Karl, *À Rebours*, 141
Hyndman, Henry Mayers, 88, 95

India, 34, 135, 140, 194–6

Joyce, James, 12
  A Portrait of the Artist as a Young Man, 50
  'The Dead', 11
  Ulysses, 11

Keats, John, 50
Kelly, Mary, 50, 55n
Kilmainham Treaty, The, 62
Kingsley, Charles, 123, 146n
Kravchinsky, Sergius (Stepniak), 16, 67
Kropotkin, Peter, 15–16, 26n, 41, 88, 103, 110–15, 117n, 120–4, 210

Ladies Land League, The, 73–4
Laird, Heather, 73–4

Land League, The, 6, 37, 48, 62, 65, 67, 73–4, 77, 146n
Le Bon, Gustave, *The Crowd: A Study of the Popular Mind*, 188
Linton, W. J., 67, 84n
Lloyd, David, 23n, 29–30, 200–1
Lomasney, William Mackey, 59
London, Jack, 99

McCormack, Jerusha, 168–9, 200–1
MacLeod, Kirsten, 150–1
Mahaffy, John Pentland, 13, 98
Malthus, Thomas, 76, 86n, 121
Mangan, James Clarence, 11
Marlow, Louis, 125, 129
Martin, Thomas, 204–5
Marx, Eleanor, 88
Marx, Jenny, 63, 69
Marx, Karl, 67, 69, 77, 78, 99, 117n, 151
Mason, Stuart, 169n; *see also* Millard, Christopher
melodrama, 58–60, 67–9, 77, 80–1, 81–2n, 82n, 163, 176, 180–3, 186, 197n, 230
Melville, Herman, *Moby-Dick*, 67
Michel, Louise, 88
Michelangelo, 207
Millard, Christopher, 157, 170n; *see also* Mason, Stuart
Mitchel, John, 48
Moore, Thomas, 11, 43, 50
Morris, William, 1, 16, 207

Nation, The, 12, 22n, 29–30, 50, 55n, 123, 133
Nechaev, Sergei, 69
New York Tribune, 36–7, 83n
Nineteenth Century, The, 8
Nordau, Max, 1

O'Brien, Fitz-James, 'What Was it? A Mystery', 133
O'Donovan Rossa, Jeremiah, 3, 12, 53n, 59, 66, 222, 223n
O'Grady, Standish, 188–9
O'Keeffe, Christopher Manus, 12, 43, 66, 222
Omaha Bee, 47
O'Neill, Henry, 17–18
O'Reilly, John Boyle, 13, 30, 65
Orientalism, 32, 127

Pall Mall Gazette, 13, 91–2, 98, 181
Paris Commune, 146n, 174, 196n
Parnell, Anna, 65, 84n
Parnell, Charles Stewart, 65, 105–6, 188, 223n
Parnell Commission, 105–6
Pater, Walter, 162–3, 168, 208–10
  Marius the Epicurian, 25n
  The Renaissance: Studies in Art and Poetry, 14, 25n, 42, 93
Philadelphia Enquirer, 64
Phoenix Park Killings, 62–5, 105
Powys, John Cowper, 13–14
Prescott, Marie, 80
Punch, 3–4, 18, 36–7, 60, 160

Renan, Ernest, 219
Retté, Adolphe, 16
Ross, Robert, 36, 111, 157, 160, 200

Royal Irish Constabulary, 30, 62, 83–4n
Ruff, Felicia J., 183
Ruskin, John, 18, 30, 34–6, 38, 39, 45–6, 89, 111, 123–4

Said Edward, 32
St James's Gazette, 150, 159, 171n
San Francisco Chronicle, 49
Sands, Bobby, 200, 223n, 224n
Scots Observer, 150, 160–1
Shaffer, Talia, 163
Shakespeare, William, 101–2
Shaw, George Bernard, 15, 16, 24n, 88, 92, 175
Shelley, Percy Bysshe, 52, 100, 153, 200
Sherard, Robert Harborough, 22n, 99, 117n, 145, 174, 196n, 201, 206, 212, 224n
Sloan, John, 203
Smyth-Pigott, Edward, 60
socialism, 88–119, 120–49, 150, 165–6, 170n, 182, 189, 194–5, 206–7, 212
Speranza *see* Wilde, Jane Francesca
Stevenson, Robert Louis, 123, 146n
Sullivan, T. D., 160–1
Swinburne, Algernon Charles, 4
Symbolism, 16, 141, 151, 153–4
Symons, Arthur, 13, 58

Taylor, Alfred, 202–3
Times, 63, 105, 160, 188
Tolstoy, Leo, 121, 225n
Torch, The, 12, 16
Transcript, 36
Truth, 1–3
Tsŭ, Chuang, 15, 92–100, 106, 155–6, 160, 167, 169

Tucker, Benjamin, 13
Turgenev, Ivan, 70, 121
Fathers and Sons, 70

utopianism, 15, 101, 120, 122, 145n, 155

Verlaine, Paul, 207

Washington Post, 37
Wasp, The, 27n, 37, 53n
Weir, David, 154
Whelan, Kevin, 11–12
Whistler, James Abbot McNeill, 14–15
Wilde, Jane Francesca, 6, 29–30, 48–9, 65, 66, 82n, 200
 'Jacta Alea Est', 22n
 'The American Irish', 39–45, 133–4
 'The Stricken Land', 76, 133
Wilde, Oscar
 'A Chinese Sage', 92–100, 103, 116n
 An Ideal Husband, 37, 182
 De Profundis, 5, 42, 57, 122, 127, 200–26
 Lady Windermere's Fan, 37, 193, 227–31
 'Lord Arthur Savile's Crime', 122, 168, 178–80
 Salomé, 16, 182
 'The Ballad of Reading Gaol', 5, 200–25, 227
 'The Canterville Ghost', 122, 124, 132
 'The Critic as Artist', 7–8, 10, 57, 98–9, 103, 105, 107, 109, 116n, 158, 229–30, 231n
 'The Fisherman and His Soul', 145, 218

Wilde, Oscar (*cont.*)
  'The Happy Prince', 10, 122, 124, 125–9, 131–2, 136, 145, 200, 218
  'The Model Millionaire', 149n
  'The Nightingale and the Rose', 129, 218
  The Picture of Dorian Gray, 5, 10, 16, 17, 141, 150–73, 175, 200, 230–1, 232n
  'The Portrait of Mr W.H.', 10, 125, 147n
  'The Selfish Giant', 122, 124, 129–44, 200
  'The Soul of Man Under Socialism', 5, 6, 13, 26n, 41, 52, 57, 76, 88–119, 122, 129, 132, 145, 150, 158, 166, 177, 182, 195, 200, 202, 204–6, 210, 212, 220–1
  'The Sphinx Without a Secret: An Etching', 9
  'The Star-Child', 122, 144–5
  'The Truth of Masks', 178
  'The Young King', 122, 132–44, 196, 200, 231n
Wilde, Sir William, 12, 37–8, 39, 45
Wilde, Willie, 60, 105, 133
Wilson, Charlotte, 88, 201
Wilson, James H., 203
Woman's World, The, 123

Yeats, William Butler, *The Wanderings of Oisin and Other Poems*, 123
Young Ireland Movement, 12, 17, 22n, 29–30, 38–9, 42, 45–6, 48, 50, 123, 207

Zassoulich, Vera, 70
Žižek, Slavoj, 168
Zola, Émile, 13

EU representative:
Easy Access System Europe
Mustamäe tee 50, 10621 Tallinn, Estonia
Gpsr.requests@easproject.com

www.ingramcontent.com/pod-product-compliance
Lightning Source LLC
Chambersburg PA
CBHW051608230426
43668CB00013B/2033